Related Books of Interest

Related Books of Interest

The New Language of Marketing 2.0
How to Use ANGELS to Energize Your Market

by Sandy Carter
ISBN: 0-13-714249-8

Use ANGELS and Web 2.0 Marketing to Drive Powerful, Quantifiable Results

Today, marketers have an array of radically new Web 2.0-based techniques at their disposal: viral marketing, social networking, virtual worlds, widgets, Web communities, blogs, podcasts, and next-generation search, to name just a few. Now, leading IBM marketing innovator Sandy Carter introduces ANGELS, a start-to-finish framework for choosing the right Web 2.0 marketing tools—and using them to maximize revenue and profitability.

Carter demonstrates winning Web 2.0 marketing at work through 54 brand-new case studies: organizations ranging from Staples to Harley Davidson, Coca-Cola to Mentos, Nortel to IBM itself. You'll discover powerful new ways to market brands and products in both B2B and B2C markets...integrate Web 2.0, experiential, and conventional marketing... maximize synergies between global and local marketing...gain more value from influencers, and more.

Listen to the author's podcast at:
ibmpressbooks.com/podcasts

Search Engine Marketing
Driving Search Traffic to Your Company's Web Site

by Mike Moran and Bill Hunt
ISBN: 0-13-606868-5

The #1 Step-by-Step Guide to Search Marketing Success...Now Completely Updated with New Techniques, Tools, Best Practices, and Value-Packed Bonus DVD!

Thoroughly updated to fully reflect today's latest search engine marketing opportunities, this book guides you through profiting from social media marketing, site search, advanced keyword tools, hybrid paid search auctions, and much more. You'll walk step-by-step through every facet of creating an effective program: projecting business value, selling stakeholders and executives, building teams, choosing strategy, implementing metrics, and above all, execution.

IBM Press

Visit ibmpressbooks.com
for all product information

Related Books of Interest

The Greening of IT
How Companies Can Make a Difference for the Environment
by John Lamb
ISBN: 0-13-715083-0

Drawing on leading-edge experience, John Lamb helps you realistically assess the business case for green IT, set priorities, and overcome internal and external challenges to make it work. He offers proven solutions for issues ranging from organizational obstacles to executive motivation and discusses crucial issues ranging from utility rate incentives to metrics. Along the way, you'll discover energy-saving opportunities—from virtualization and consolidation to cloud and grid computing—and solutions that will improve business flexibility as they reduce environmental impact.

Lamb presents case studies, checklists, and more—all the practical guidance you need to drive maximum bottom-line value from your green IT initiative.

Can Two Rights Make a Wrong?
Reger
ISBN: 0-13-173294-3

RFID Sourcebook
Lahiri
ISBN: 0-13-185137-3

Mining the Talk
Spangler, Kreulen
ISBN: 0-13-233953-6

The New Language of Business
Carter
ISBN: 0-13-195654-X

SOA Governance
Brown, Laird, Gee, Mitra
ISBN: 0-13-714746-5

Service-Oriented Architecture (SOA) Compass
Bieberstein, Bose, Fiammante, Jones, Shah
ISBN: 0-13-187002-5

Reaching the Goal
Ricketts
ISBN: 0-13-233312-0

Eating the IT Elephant
Hopkins and Jenkins
ISBN: 0-13-7130120

Web 2.0 and Social Networking for the Enterprise

Web 2.0 and Social Networking for the Enterprise

Guidelines and Examples for Implementation and
Management Within Your Organization

Joey Bernal

IBM Press
Pearson plc

Upper Saddle River, NJ • Boston • Indianapolis • San Francisco
New York • Toronto • Montreal • London • Munich • Paris • Madrid
Cape Town • Sydney • Tokyo • Singapore • Mexico City

ibmpressbooks.com

IBM Press Program Managers: Steven M. Stansel, Ellice Uffer

Cover design: IBM Corporation

Associate Publisher: Greg Wiegand

Marketing Manager: Kourtnaye Sturgeon

Acquisitions Editor: Katherine Bull

Development Editor: Ginny Bess Munroe

Publicist: Heather Fox

Managing Editor: Kristy Hart

Designer: Alan Clements

Project Editors: Julie Anderson and Jovana San Nicolas-Shirley

Copy Editor: Keith Cline

Indexer: Cheryl Lenser

Compositor: Jake McFarland

Proofreader: Water Crest Publishing

Manufacturing Buyer: Dan Uhrig

Published by Pearson plc

Publishing as IBM Press

The following terms are trademarks or registered trademarks of International Business Machines Corporation in the United States, other countries, or both: IBM, the IBM logo, IBM Press, CloudBurst, DB2, developerWorks, Domino, FileNet, Informix, InfoSphere, iNotes, Lotus, Notes, OmniFind, QuickPlace, Quickr, Rational, Sametime, Symphony, Unyte, WebSphere, z/OS. Adobe, Flex, Macromedia, and Flash are either registered trademarks or trademarks of Adobe Systems Incorporated in the United States, and/or other countries. Microsoft, Windows, Outlook, Excel, SQL Server, and SharePoint are trademarks of Microsoft Corporation in the United States, other countries, or both. Java, JavaScript, JavaServer, J2EE, and all Java-based trademarks are trademarks of Sun Microsystems, Inc. in the United States, other countries, or both. UNIX is a registered trademark of The Open Group in the United States and other countries. Linux is a registered trademark of Linus Torvalds in the United States, other countries, or both. Other company, product, or service names may be trademarks or service marks of others.

Library of Congress Cataloging-in-Publication Data

Bernal, Joey.

Web 2.0 and social networking for the enterprise : guidelines and examples for implementation and management within your organization / Joey Bernal.

p. cm.

Includes bibliographical references and index.

ISBN 978-0-13-700489-8 (pbk. : alk. paper) 1. Web 2.0. 2. Online social networks. 3. Business—Data processing. I. Title.

TK5105.88817.B47 2009

0 6.7'54—dc20

2009029324

Pearson Education, Inc.
Rights and Contracts Department
501 Boylston Street, Suite 900
Boston, MA 02116
Fax (617) 671-3447

ISBN-13: 978-0-13-700489-8

ISBN-10: 0-13-700489-3

Text printed in the United States on recycled paper at R.R. Donnelley in Crawfordsville, Indiana.

First printing October 2009

Dedicated to all my family and friends who were only slightly annoyed that I was writing yet another book. I promise to stop, for awhile.

To my children, whom I constantly threaten to leave out of my dedications if they don't leave me alone when I am writing. They never do, and yet I never follow through on my threats. Daniel, Christopher, Julia, and Oliver: Enjoy every day no matter how hard it seems. Find your passion and don't let yourself get distracted.

A shout out to my brother Chuck, who as of this writing is about to earn his MBA after several years of hard work. Well done!

Last but definitely not least to Christiane, my confidant, best friend, and soul mate of over 24 years, who is enjoying her first summer off in quite a few years. Here's to many more relaxing and fun-filled summers "together" to come.

Contents

Foreword

Humans are creatures of collaboration. Since the beginning of time, we have sought each other out and wanted to communicate and share. Language finds its very purpose in this. As social beings, and aided by all manner of advancement, our ability to interact has evolved.

Centuries ago, man stood on hilltops separated by miles and communicated through smoke signals. Pony Express riders carried mail across North America. Mail services could deliver documents anywhere in the country overnight. Email allowed a message to be delivered to the other side of the planet in a second.

PROGRESS
Does anyone want to go back to smoke signals?
VALUE
Collaboration represents a journey.

So what new change is upon us?

It used to be hard to publish information. You needed to know HTML or some complex web layout tool. At a corporate level, it was driven through a content management process that involved some workflow. Content that was needed was thoroughly evaluated, processed, formatted, approved, and diced and sliced with the rigors of the Veg-a-Matic.

Today people are publishing information about themselves, their interests, or anything they want to share easier than ever before.

In today's social networks, we can easily publish a picture, discuss the books we have read, the films we did not like, have a conversation, and blog about our day-to-day activities as a public diary. We can find others who have similar interests, skills, and responsibilities.

Social networks are super simple and easy to use. They also make it easy to connect and share with others.

Because people are able to connect with people and share information easier then ever before, there are going to be new ways in which people will interact.

My son forgot his homework one day, so I said to him, "Call up or email your classmate and get the homework—you NEED to DO IT."

Five minutes later I saw him writing on the kid's Facebook page. Why was he doing that?

"What are you doing? I thought I told you to call him or email him?"

"DAD, email is for your grandfather, this is the way he'll get it."

HUH!

Writing on someone's Facebook wall is the new way to openly have a discussion with your network.

We turned on a Twitter-like microblogging capability inside of IBM.

I microblog my status everyday at IBM. I won't give 500,000 people inside of IBM access to my calendar but I am quite willing to share basically what I am doing everyday and some milestones I want to broadly communicate. This river of news about what I am doing becomes part of my Profile.

Because of this, we are connecting with each other in ways we never could before. People inside of IBM can understand what you are working on and where. A sales representative could search and find any executives visiting their region and co-opt their trip to help or see their client. This is a big change in the way people are connecting.

When I started at IBM over twenty years ago, both my grandfather and father were also at IBM. I could look up their Profile on the mainframe through a 3270 EBCDIC Green Screen terminal and find their name and their phone number.

At IBM today, we have a rich view of employees that spans the basic business card type information to what they know and what they do. I can get to this information anytime, anyplace, and through any device.

We are leveraging this information to connect folks around the world and to best leverage our most precious asset—our people.

We are using capabilities like wikis, blogs, and discussion forums to best suit the interaction between people, no longer suffering an impedance match in collaboration requirements.

We are using these technologies in our intranet and extranet to build better relationships and do important work with our colleagues, clients, and partners.

With these new collaboration tools and ways to communicate, it is imperative to ask the question, "What will it do for business?" As I meet clients around the world, they have a lot of questions about the value of social networking to their business. And they ask many other questions as well: "Is there such a thing as Anti-Social Software?" and "If I allow people to use this technology, will they just goof around all day?"

Companies everywhere are using or considering using social software. In their evaluation, deployment, and adoption, they must learn much.

By reading Joey's book, you will learn about what social software is and how it can help connect people with people and people with information. It provides the details of the value we have seen at IBM in using these capabilities and a deep dive into the technology itself.

Joey's book will help you learn about the many facets of social software and develop a deep understanding of Web 2.0 technology. In it, you will explore programming models, APIs and standards, how these capabilities can integrate with portals, the ways to mashup information, the role of search, and so much more.

Take your next step in the collaboration journey. Read on.

—Jeffrey Schick
Vice President of Social Software
Lotus
IBM Software Group

Preface

Wow! When I started this journey, I really was not sure where it would lead. In many ways, Web 2.0 and Social Networking are just words, often referred to as buzz words as they gain more popularity within the industry. Behind those words, however, is a litany of patterns, ideas, and technology that can quickly overwhelm anyone who is trying to learn as much as possible. When learning any new technology, there are a couple of approaches one can take.

First you can take a broad approach and try to measure the length and breadth of choices and options that are available within a specific space. While this is an exciting approach, it can also be a bit frustrating (I speak from personal experience here), especially because most of the time technology is constantly evolving. These evolutionary steps can be exposed as small changes, such as a new standard or option, or perhaps new advances can expose themselves as entirely new areas, such as cloud computing.

Alternatively, you can take a "dive deep" approach into one or more of the areas or patterns that are available to try and understand intimate details about what options and concerns you might need to consider. This could, in theory, take you down a path where you can actually implement new products and applications within your organization. However, without a breadth of subject matter, you might initially start down the wrong path. A "dive deep" approach usually comes as a follow-up approach after you have a broader understanding and have determined in which areas you will initially focus.

This book provides a mix of both of these approaches. It definitely takes a broad swipe at many of the technologies and patterns that are available within Web 2.0 and Social Networking today. Almost anyone who is interested in understanding what is going on in the Web 2.0 space will gain some benefit from this approach. However, in some areas, I "dive deep" into the implementation details that will be helpful in guiding you through some of the many technical decisions that need to be made. Nontechnical readers can ignore these parts; although if you have a somewhat technical background, you can certainly wade through these parts to get a better understanding of some of the details.

While Web 2.0 technologies are not vendor specific, IBM has taken a specific approach in providing the applications and tools to implement good strategies within your own organization. Some of these patterns are not easily implemented within an organization without a product-based approach, such as using IBM Lotus Quickr or IBM Lotus Connections. For this reason, I have focused heavily on some of these products to illustrate the value they can bring both inside and outside the corporate firewall.

Included within most chapters are case studies that show how IBM has approached its own Web 2.0 growth. There are also interviews with IBM and industry experts on where some of the technologies are going and how best to use them. I think you will find this book as interesting to read as it was for me to write. I know you will find it informative. I hope you will find it useful.

Enjoy!

Acknowledgments

There is a very long list of people that I need to recognize who helped me finish this work, starting with my colleagues and coworkers who offered assistance and support for the endless hours of research and writing.

I would like to thank my manager Bennie Gibson, and other managers and executives including Ken Polleck, Mark Guerinot, John Allessio, and Tony Higham. Also, many thanks to Ted Smith and Dave VanVoorhis, who worked with me to figure out scheduling when I suggested alternatives.

There were many technical reviewers who helped me ensure that I wasn't too off track, starting with Julia Weatherby, who is the most savvy social networker I know. She really makes it work in her day-to-day life. I totally appreciate the efforts of my other reviewers, including Peter Blinstrubas, Chun Chan, Luis Benitez, David Byrd, Alex Sanielevici, Scott Davis, Richard Gorzela, Praby Ayyagari, Raghu Mancha, Saurabh Shukla, Carol Worthy, and Ron Lynn.

There are lots of examples and viewpoints within this book. The following people contributed their time and expertise to helping provide a well-rounded view of the technologies discussed: Jonathan Booth, Stefan Hepper, Rich Gorzela, Jason McGee, Usman Memon, Prabu Ayyagari, Marshall Lamb, and Adam Ginsburg. Thanks to Peter Burkhardt from Lotus Greenhouse. Also thanks to Bruce Elgort for letting me showcase IdeaJam and Steven Gerhardt from Ixion LLC.

Finally, many thanks to the IBM Press and Pearson team who really did a lot of the heavy lifting. Katherine Bull, it was a pleasure to work with you again. Hopefully we won't be working together for awhile (if you know what I mean). Also thanks to Ginny Munroe and Julie Anderson for the hard work they did editing my mess. On the IBM Press side, I should also mention Ellice Uffer and Steve Stansel, who are always ready to provide help and guidance as needed.

To anyone I might have left out by mistake: Thanks!

About the Author

Joey Bernal is an Executive IT Specialist with IBM Software Services for Lotus as a member of the WebSphere Portal Services Team. Sr. Certified with IBM as an IT Specialist, he has an extensive background in the design and development of Portal and Web Applications. His technical knowledge, management and methodology skills, leadership, and attitude have contributed to the successful completion of many major projects. Bernal is the author and coauthor of many popular books, including *Programming Portlets* and *Application Architecture for WebSphere*. He contributes to his popular blog; Portal in Action and has been awarded the designation of Professional Author by IBM developerWorks.

Bernal helps lead the Software Services team in many areas, including architecture and design, development of best practices, performance, and achieving operational excellence. He is currently focused on assisting clients with cross-brand challenges around WebSphere Portal. By its inherent nature of being a platform for application integration, WebSphere Portal projects require significant integration and cross-brand expertise. All WebSphere Portal projects have products from multiple brands, and many have products from all five IBM brands in the solution. Specifically, Bernal works to reduce the challenges presented by complex WebSphere Portal projects, especially those that make use of recent advances in technology such as Service Oriented Architecture and Web 2.0.

Prior to joining IBM, Bernal was the Director of IT for an incentive and performance improvement company. Bernal led the migration and upgrade of all desktop systems and a companywide conversion of the messaging platform, upgraded accounting and inventory systems, and integrated major systems with web based interfaces. Bernal was also the lead technical advisor and architect of multiple high profile Internet and Intranet applications for several Fortune 500 companies.

Bernal has a BS in Computer Science with a minor in Mathematics from the University of Montana. He is currently pursuing his MS in Software Engineering from Regis University. You can view the author's website at www.bernal.net.

I

Web 2.0 and Social Networking

Web 2.0 and *Social Networking*—what do those two technologies have in common? When looking at them independently, and from a purely technical point of view, you might think they don't have a lot in common. However, merge the concepts of two of the hottest technical advances to come around in a while, and you have the power to change the world. Not all at once, as change happens over time, but they do provide a framework and the opportunities for major change, which is a first step and much of what we discuss in this book.

Initial impressions are important. When you pick up a book like this and start to browse the contents in the bookstore, as the reader, you probably have some high expectations. Education is probably the top requirement that you expect from a technical book like this. However, at what level? Are you looking for an overview, a strategy, a design, or perhaps hands-on, do-it-yourself steps?

I struggle with what makes the most sense and what will provide you with the most value. This book attempts to give you some advice on all these levels; however, there is a fair amount of focus toward a hands-on approach. My hope is that you can use this book as a reference that provides some concrete guidelines for creating and then implementing a strategy for Web 2.0 and Social Networking integration within your group or organization.

Much of the focus in the Web 2.0 and Social Networking space has been toward customer interaction; that is, how to draw in or collaborate better with customers through blogs, forums, or Facebook and MySpace pages, how to increase brand or product awareness or drive sales with viral marketing campaigns, or how to increase customer satisfaction using Ajax so that pages are updated almost automatically. In this book, we look at these ideas and more. However, we also turn our focus inward to the enterprise to see how we can use new strategies and technologies to increase productivity, collaboration, knowledge management, and creativity of our employees and partners.

Web 2.0

By now, many people understand the use of the term *Web 2.0*, but it still requires some explanation in our context. For our purposes, we might define Web 2.0 as a set of enabling technologies that enable us to reach and provide services to end users in exciting new ways. The reality is that much of the hype around Web 2.0 already existed on the Web well before the term became popular with the media and within the industry, but the concept is helping to drive new innovation in the use of this technology toward better user interaction. At the core of these new technologies is the use of Asynchronous JavaScript and XML (Ajax) to provide a richer user experience to end users.

The term Web 2.0 was coined by Tim O'Reilly, founder and CEO of O'Reilly Media, Inc., and the term became better known across the industry after the O'Reilly Media Web 2.0 conference in 2004. The idea of Web 2.0 definitely has some technical aspects, with the implementation and innovation of new technologies and standards within the web platform. However, much of the focus of Web 2.0 is on new business models. Whereas the focus of Web 1.0 was on delivering products, Web 2.0 had created a paradigm shift to delivering services that can be used and combined with other services in new ways. Another key aspect is the growth of interactivity with end users in new ways, enabling users to drive what is important or of the most value.

Figure 1.1 illustrates the concept of Web 1.0, where there is a strict producer/consumer approach to delivering web content. The webmaster or content creators build and maintain the website for consumption by end users. The relationship is strictly unidirectional in this model, fixed and targeted based on assumptions made by the webmaster and content team.

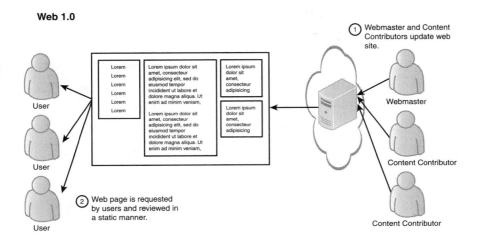

Figure 1.1 Web 1.0 paradigm

In contrast to this approach, in the Web 2.0 model, users actively participate and contribute to a website. This bidirectional approach enables users to interact with the site and each other in ways that provide for and foster a collective community. Users can create, edit, rate, and tag content at will, which provides other users with new information and guides the relevance of what is important to the overall community.

In addition to providing the underlying ability for communities to build momentum, obtain critical mass, and contribute to ongoing collaboration, services can be provided in the form of application programming interfaces (APIs), Representational State Transfer (REST) services, or Really Simple Syndication (RSS) feeds, which enable end users to merge and view data in ways that haven't even been imagined (see Figure 1.2).

Web 2.0 is not only about providing data in new ways, it is also about improving the user interface and enabling end users to view data quicker

Web 2.0

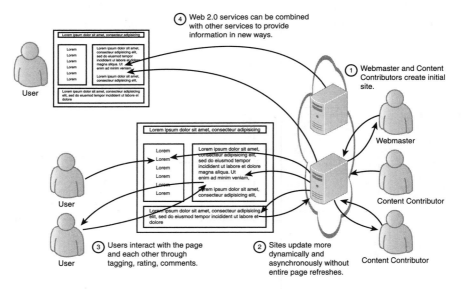

Figure 1.2   Web 2.0 paradigm

and in more dynamic ways through richer user interfaces using Ajax and other technologies.

Rich User Experience within the Browser

Although not always the case, the goal is to take advantage of the browser as the universal client and provide a richer interactive experience to the end user. Two core technologies that help provide this experience are Ajax and REST. There are lots of other frameworks technologies in this category that can also provide a browser-based rich user experience, such as Adobe® Flex® and Macromedia® Flash®. In addition, there are non-browser-based approaches, such as using an Eclipse framework based approach such as Lotus® Expeditor.

AJAX, now known more often as Ajax, has again brought JavaScript™ into vogue by providing a new approach to the language. Now you can leverage JavaScript using eXtensible Markup Language (XML), Representational State Transfer (REST), JavaScript Object Notation (JSON), and other technologies. The term *Ajax* is relatively new; although if you work with web technologies, you have undoubtedly heard of the term, but the underlying technologies have been around almost as long as the Web itself.

The key in Ajax is the term *asynchronous,* which enables the browser to provide services and features in simple but exciting ways. Ajax provides a new paradigm for interacting with the browser. Essentially, the browser can be updated in an asynchronous manner, which means that there need to be no more full-page refreshes that are so common with the Web. Take, for example, a simple stock ticker or some fluid piece of data. With the pre-Web 2.0 approach, the entire screen needs to be refreshed to update a potentially small piece of data. With Ajax and Web 2.0, that small piece of data can be retrieved behind the scenes at regular intervals and updated while users focus elsewhere on the page (see Figure 1.3).

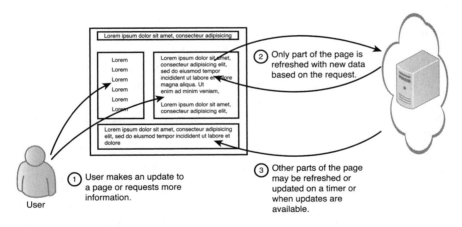

Figure 1.3   Ajax interaction model

The purpose of all of this is to provide much more dynamic web pages that not only respond quicker to user action, but that actually assist the user in working with the web page. Simple Ajax patterns include the following:

- **Type Assist:**   This enables a user to type into a text box while the system tries to figure out what word or phrase the user is looking for. As the user types, the text box continues to change with different values that can assist the user in getting the right value.

- **Form Assist:**   Another scenario is the concept of updating a list of options based on an earlier choice. Consider, for example, a user trying to fill out a form on the screen. Choosing one option from a list or drop-down box might trigger different options to appear, change, or prefill with additional values based on that choice.

- **Page Fragment Updates:**   Again, like in the stock ticker example, data can be retrieved behind the scenes and update small fragments of a page without requiring a full refresh of the page.

- **Sliding Palettes:**   This pattern is where a window appears or slides out on top of the page. This allows the user to choose from a picklist or set of displayed options.

More advanced examples of using Ajax are more obvious, where large sections of the page are updated based on options chosen. One example is a customer service type of application where the user can look up customer and order detail information in a single interface. A detailed example of this is in Chapter 3, "Ajax, Portlets, and Patterns." It has been said that the use of Ajax is nontrivial, which means that although it is simple to add basic examples to your web pages, more advanced works require advanced skills and additional design work to obtain good results. The results of this effort can be impressive as web pages become truly interactive for the end users.

Ajax and the Dojo Toolkit

The Dojo Toolkit is a JavaScript-based collection of libraries (hence the name toolkit) that enable you to build Ajax capabilities into your web pages. The Dojo Toolkit is more than just Ajax, but that is our primary focus in this book. In reality, Dojo is a DHTML toolkit. Because Dojo is open source, it is free to use in your projects, and many large organizations contribute to Dojo itself.

JavaScript, DHTML, and Ajax are complicated. Dojo encapsulates complex JavaScript capability with predefined components and APIs. Of course, Dojo has a learning curve; however, the gains obtained by focusing at a higher level of abstraction can be enormous. In addition, while some optimization can be obtained, using Dojo libraries implies heavier pages in the form of JavaScript libraries that need to be transmitted to the user's browser to enable all the cool functionality that you will build. It is worth the tradeoff, but I don't want you to think that you get something for free.

Several Ajax libraries are available on the market today. Many of them are open source. IBM® has opted to support Dojo by contributing to the community and building Dojo into WebSphere® Portal 6.1.

JSON

JSON is designed as a lightweight data-interchange format. Similar to XML but with the advantage of being easier for machines to parse and generate, in many cases, it can be much faster than using XML. JSON is language independent; however, it looks strongly familiar. Similar to pseudocode, JSON is built on the idea of name/value pairs that are often recognized arrays or lists of data. In addition, values are presented as ordered lists that can be recognized as arrays or lists of data.

The main idea is that these name/value pairs and ordered lists of data are universal to all programming languages and are easily translated into the common data structures. The following sample shows how a list of customers might be represented in JSON:

```
{"customers":
 {"@uri":"http://myhost/resources/customers",
  "customer":
  [
   {"@uri":"http://localhost/resources/customers/103",
    "name":"Atelier graphique",
    "city":"Nantes",
    "state":"",
    "zip":"44000"
   },
   {"@uri":"http://localhost/resources/customers/124",
    "name":"Mini Gifts Distributors Ltd.",
    "city":"San Rafael",
    "state":"CA",
    "zip":"97562"
   },
   {"@uri":"http://myhost/resources/customers/495",
    "name":"Diecast Collectables",
    "city":"Boston",
    "state":"MA",
    "zip":"51003"
   },
  ]
 }
}
```

Note that an object, which is an unordered set of name/value pairs, is represented by the left and right braces {} within the syntax. An array is an ordered set of values that are represented by brackets []. With that in mind, you can see that the preceding sample provides an array of customers. Similarly, the following example is the same data set represented with XML:

```
<?xml version="1.0" encoding="UTF-8" ?>

<customers>
<uri>http://myhost/resources/customers
</uri>
<customer>
<uri>http://localhost/resources/customers/103
</uri>
<name>Arelier graphique
</name>
<city>Nantes
</city>
<state />

<zip>44000
</zip>
</customer>
<customer>
<uri>http://localhost/resources/customers/124
</uri>
<name>MiniGifts Distributors Ltd.
</name>
<city>San Rafael
</city>
<state>CA
</state>
<zip>97562
</zip>
</customer>
<customer>
<uri>http://myhost/resources/customers/495
</uri>
<name>Diecast Collectables
</name>
<city>Boston
</city>
<state>MA
</state>
<zip>51003
</zip>
</customer>
</customers>
```

JSON works particularly well with JavaScript because it is actually a subset of the object literal notation of the JavaScript language. *Object literal* means that objects are created by literally listing a set of name/value pairs within the document. The debate continues to rage as to whether JSON is really the right approach as compared to XML. For work within the browser, it has some definite advantages, such as quicker parsing and being somewhat more focused on transferring data without worrying about much of the overhead of XML and the structure that it can often involve. The idea behind JSON is to strip down the data to a basic form for transmission to and within the browser.

There is no reason not to use XML, and in many cases, you might have to define XML as a standard in your organization (I'm big on standards) and let JSON be used in the exceptional cases where the application team can explain why JSON is a better fit. Another disadvantage on the JSON side is that it is not as readable as XML. That might be a preference for someone to decide, but the brackets and braces can be confusing, especially if the document is more squished together than what I have laid out here as an example. One big advantage of JSON is that it works well with the Dojo Ajax Toolkit that we use throughout Chapter 3 and other parts of the book.

REST

The term *REST* was first introduced by Roy Fielding in Chapter 5 of his doctoral dissertation titled *Architectural Styles and the Design of Network-Based Software Architectures*. REST focuses on the simplicity and efficiency of the Web as it exists today and leverages that simplicity to represent the state of data and resources within the Web. Like the Web, REST is a stateless protocol and is based on common HTTP verbs of GET, POST, PUT, and DELETE. This means that like many of the other technical aspects of the Web 2.0 approach, there are no additional standards required for providing REST services.

REST-provided services, often called RESTful services, are not based on any new standards, but are more of an architectural style that leverages currently available standards to deliver information and data about existing resources. Uniform Resource Identifiers (URIs) are used to determine what resource you are actually operating on. (Remember REST is resource oriented.) Reformatting data into the form of resources does take some initial effort, and with any design, you want to get as close as possible as soon as you can to the correct format. For our purposes, we look at some simple examples. Consider the following URI:

```
http://myhost.com/resources/customers
```

In this case, you can expect a list of customers to be returned as an XML stream from the server. Embedded within that data will probably be additional entity URIs so that you can retrieve information about a specific customer. Many of the URIs that would be used within RESTful services contain a combination of the location of the resource and the actual resource that we need. For example, the following URI should return a data stream with information about a specific customer:

```
http://myhost.com/resources/customer/103
```

The resulting data stream often takes the form of XML, which is defined to provide an understandable data set; however, other representations can be used such as JSON that we previously discussed.

So, why not use traditional web service technology such as Simple Object Access Protocol (SOAP) and Web Services Description Language (WSDL) to retrieve information? The debates continue about this question, but remember that REST is an architectural style designed to use technologies that are currently available. It can also be useful in simplifying much of the complexity that web services bring to the table. Figure 1.4 illustrates the difference between REST services and traditional web services.

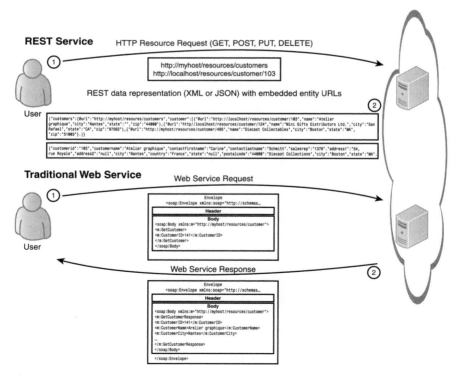

Figure 1.4 REST vs. traditional web services

Traditional web services, on the other hand, are complex because there is a focus on solving complex enterprise problems, which require robust and complex standards to ensure security, performance, and especially interoperability across the Web. Because of this, the standards around traditional web services are more complex and strict because they have to be. The caution here is for you to not think that they are necessarily easily exchanged or that one approach can be a complete replacement for the other.

Atom and RSS

Atom and Really Simple Syndication (RSS), previously known as Rich Site Summary but changed to Really Simple Syndication for version 2.0, might not seem like exciting new technologies. Anyone who has read a blog or news feed should be familiar with the RSS format. These are core technologies in the new Web. The ability to share news and information in a standardized format makes for easy integration in the Web 2.0 world.

Consider the simple case of a set of information around a particular topic. It could be a specific technology, industry, or perhaps political or scientific information. In the Web 1.0 world, readers would have to go to or log in to each website and see whether any information had been updated. As you can imagine, that approach doesn't scale well as users try to add new information sources to their resource pool. Imagine, in my case, where I am lucky to update my blog once a month during busy periods; readers would quickly lose interest in checking for new updates. Data feeds in a standardized format can be accessed and aggregated into a single tool or web page where users can see right away if new information is available. If a new update is available, even from a site where information is not updated as often, it can receive the same attention as the more prolific data sources.RSS is one such format for delivering content. Online news, blogs, products, and catalogs can be syndicated and delivered in a standardized way that enables readers to stay informed of existing and new information without the effort of constantly looking for new data.

Atom is another set of standards for providing the same capability. The Atom Syndication Format is an XML language that is used to provide web feeds similar to RSS. Atom provides the Atom Publishing Protocol (APP) as a way to update or publish to web resources.

Both of these services are readily available on many if not most websites. Usually they are offered together to enable consumers to choose the format that best fits their needs. You have probably seen the icons shown in Figure 1.5 embedded in many of the websites that you visit.

Rich Site Summary Logo   Atom Logo

Figure 1.5 RSS and Atom icons

When you click on one of these icons, you will probably see an XML-based representation of the content that is available on the site. Using a feed reader, you can import the URL of either feed to incorporate that data feed into your syndication tool.

Deciding upon a syndication strategy can be important to enabling the sharing of libraries and new content repositories in your organization. This strategy can help you understand how you want to expose information to other systems and end users. Let's face it, no organization has a single source of knowledge. Knowledge management experts have been working for years on trying to collect, organize, and share information and collective knowledge within the enterprise with limited success. The reality is that it is hard to keep up with everything going on in large organizations, and new knowledge sources seem to spring from the ground. Even beyond document repositories, which might be tightly controlled, blogs, industry news, and research, information can come from widely varied sources. Adopting a syndication strategy can help you avoid trying to control the knowledge and simply acknowledge that you can benefit from these new sources.

Situation Applications and Mashups

Another item at the heart of Web 2.0 is the concept of situational applications or a mashup. These are not the same thing exactly, but they are very closely related. The idea is that end users want to take control, to combine data and data displays to build new views that show information in new ways. Putting the user in control can drive many new ideas for how information can be delivered and used within your website. We typically think of situational applications as a short-term integration that will enable some growth or new understanding by the users.

There are several types of situational applications. IBM's WebSphere Portal comes to mind as a leader in this type of approach by building on the idea of composite applications. Composite applications are one of the core benefits that a portal can bring to an organization. The ability to combine portlets on a page displaying complementary data can allow you to provide a huge benefit to the end user. Composite applications can often be taken a step further and be combined with a business process engine to enable a workflow-type process around the use of these portlets.

Mashups are similar to composite applications, where data from multiple sources is combined into an integrated view. The most common example of this that you might find is data that is displayed on a map view, showing location information about a particular data set. These common types of mashups generally consist of a couple of views: one to help choose a particular item from the data set and a second view or section that actually plots the chosen data on the map. One example of this might be plotting customer locations, or sales reps, into a map of a specific area. You often see websites that display the closest store locations within a specific area, such as a ZIP code, or close to a specific address (see Figure 1.6).

Mashups can take several forms. Mostly the difference is around who actually creates the mashup. The enterprise can provide specific mashups to end users by combining business data from different sources into a unified interface. This type of mashup can also include data sources from external or public sources or APIs. Additional end users or consumers design their own mashups based on information of interest to them. From a business perspective, the idea of allowing end users to build their own mashups can be a powerful force. Technically, there are still governance, performance, and security issues to consider when allowing end users control to mash company data.

One of the key components in mashups is the idea that the user interface is separated from the data or service itself. This is what makes this type of situation application reusable, allowing fine-grained access to data through these reusable services. The idea is that reusability makes

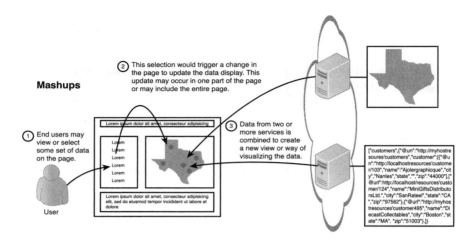

Figure 1.6   Using mashups

the business more agile and capable of building situation applications as required to respond to business criteria or questions.

We have to take some care when enabling end users to create situational applications or create their own mashups. Again, security, performance, and manageability concerns come to mind as end users take more control over how resources are used within the website. From an IT perspective that is responsible for the reliability of the site, it is important that these items not be compromised while trying to deliver new capability.

Social Networking

The lines between Web 2.0 and Social Networking are easy to blur here in the real world. We make a distinction, however, because much of the technology can be categorized within one of the two, although the end result is often due to a combination of both. For example, many of the Web 2.0 technologies that we have discussed so far assist in the delivery of Social Networking capability.

Social Networking involves the creation of a virtual community where users can share, discuss, collaborate, and even argue about topics of common interest. Within your organization the topics and nature of these communities can vary widely, providing the ability to collaborate on items such as technology, industry, or even product- or service-based topics. For the most part, communities are also self-establishing because the enterprise cannot always predict what will be important to their users. Allowing communities to be self-forming ensures greater acceptance by users and helps ad-hoc communities grow to critical mass.

File Sharing and Content Collaboration

File-sharing activities can be distinctly different depending on whether you focus within the boundaries of the enterprise or focus on public collaboration and access. Often, the two spheres utilize different types of files and information. The popular video-sharing site YouTube is a perfect example. A repository in an enterprise might not be able to reach critical mass when limited only to an employee base, but then again, it just might. In IBM, a system has been launched called BlueTube, which is designed to allow for the upload and sharing of internal video material. Although as of this writing, BlueTube is still in the trial stages of development and has not reached critical mass, IBM is uniquely situated to benefit from this type of repository. With more than 300,000 IBMers worldwide, many of whom are engaged in creating and sharing videos that illustrate new technologies, product demos, or video recordings of the dozens or hundreds of presentations that happen every day, there is a likely chance for overwhelming success.

Document-based content is probably a more common type of collateral that should be contributed to content repositories as much as possible. Every company struggles with the idea of reusability of assets and the sharing of expertise (e.g., proposals, estimates, presentations, design items, price lists, and offerings of services or products). In addition to the actual content is the meta information that comes along with this content. Such meta information includes categorization of content as formal or informal, and the tagging of content with specific keywords defined by end users.

Bookmarking and Tagging

A key benefit to gaining critical mass is to obtain large numbers of contributors to your site or application. A knowledge repository or application becomes more useful as it gains new information, and it is exactly this accumulation of information or knowledge that you are looking for. Of course, knowledge itself doesn't always have to be new content. It can also consist of identifying and tagging existing content to help separate the most useful information in the site. This is why it is important to enable users to add value in seemingly small ways, such as tagging, bookmarking, ranking, and leaving comments.

Tagging enables users to define content. People like to share, and they are opinionated about what they think is important and how content should be categorized. Making it easy for them to identify and categorize content can be a powerful way for others to better understand where things might fit or what other users consider important. This is a powerful for organizations that can then start to understand and react to tagged content in meaningful ways.

Tagging is a simple, yet extremely powerful concept. Tagging an item on the Web means to simply categorize that item with one or more category names. Ideally, people use similar names so that as more items are tagged, patterns can emerge based on these categories. Figure 1.7 shows one such pattern, commonly known as a tag cloud.

Figure 1.7   Sample tag cloud

A tag cloud is a list of categories that show variation on the tags based on popularity. The most popular tags become larger and darker in the list. Most tag clouds follow the power law curve, which results in the proportional scaling of a few large tags and many small ones. Other clouds follow a more linear scaling approach that smoothes out the power law curve. This type of list is often called a folksonomy. This is a true taxonomy of the content in the repository; however, instead of being defined by the knowledge management librarian, the structure is defined by common folks in the community.

The idea of knowledge management (KM) has taken some hard knocks during the past ten or so years. During the rise of the Internet in the mid-1990s, KM became a popular and important topic as sharing documents and organization knowledge became cheaper and easier to manage. With this increase, interest in document and content management within organizations and across the Web, identifying, tagging, and managing that content fell into the domain of KM. It made a lot of sense for organizations and industry domains to build what we call a taxonomy; within which documents and content can be stored to enable easier search and retrieval of that content.

Blogging and Wikis

Some of the more popular patterns in the Web 2.0 space are the blog and the wiki. This has been seen in the explosion of blogs and wikis (both internal- and external-facing) across the Internet. A blog, short for web log, is a personal log or journal shared with readers on the Web (see the Figure 1.8). Blogs typically focus on a certain area (e.g., technology, political, social).

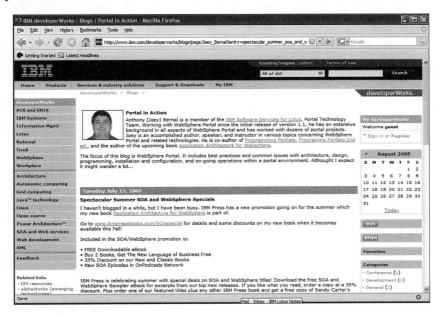

Figure 1.8 Author's WebSphere Portal blog

A blog can be a one-way mechanism to simply distribute information to an audience. However, the more powerful and popular blogs are those that elicit interaction between the blogger (the person posting the blog entries) and the readers. Reader feedback helps bloggers understand what readers really want from a blog author.

In many cases, internal blogging can be just as valuable to an organization as externally facing blogs. Internal blogging can help to drive innovation within the organization. At IBM, hundreds of ongoing blogs have been created for the technical force to share their knowledge and experiences. Many managers have blogs to post topics that interest them.

Whereas a blog is mostly a way for one person or a small group of people to share information, a wiki is much more collaborative. A wiki is a website designed for users to add, remove, or change content directly. In fact, most wikis are generally text-based content that is continually being added to or changed by the community of users who manage and use that wiki. This content is made directly available to end users who have the ability to update or add their own content to the site (see Figure 1.9).

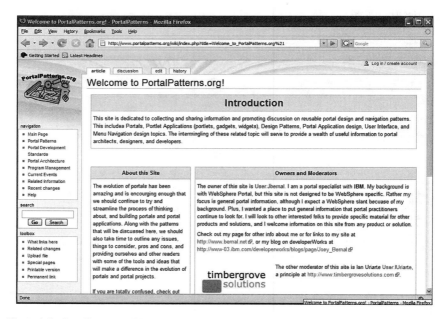

Figure 1.9 PortalPatterns wiki

Wikis are based on the concept that is should be easy to collaborate on content in real time and participate in the ongoing evolution of the material. Usually, you become a registered user of the site, and then you can add or edit content directly. Sometimes this content is reviewed by a moderator, which helps to ensure some continuity to the site; however, care should be taken to ensure that the moderators do not stifle the creativity and input from the field. I can think of at least one popular wiki where the moderators do sometimes take things a little too seriously. Wikis can be one of the most cost-effective ways for a community to collaborate, with the main requirement being people's time and willingness to participate in the effort.

Expert Location and Instant Messaging

Instant messaging (IM) has been around for awhile, both inside and outside the enterprise. Popular IM sites include AOL Instant Messaging (AIM), Yahoo! Messenger, and Microsoft® Windows® Live Messenger. For use within the enterprise, IBM's Lotus Sametime® provides full-featured IM and collaboration capability on the desktop. Figure 1.10 shows IM in action on the author's desktop.

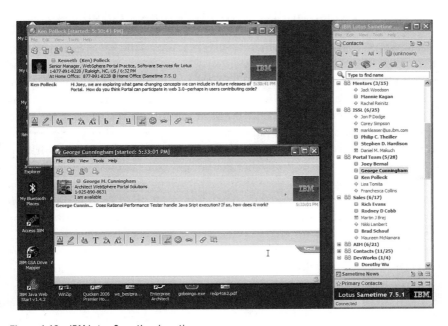

Figure 1.10   IBM Lotus Sametime in action

The ability to reach out and talk to other employees within your organization directly and instantly can certainly encourage and facilitate real-time collaboration within the enterprise. Instant Messaging has been around for several years and continues to grow in use as the technology gains wider adoption. Just as it is important to talk in real time with other colleagues, it is important to find the right person when you need to ask a question. Who are the experts for the particular question that I want to ask? This need to find an expert goes beyond the business and can reach into IT or even human resources questions as employees who need answers quickly, try to reach out and resolve problems. Recent advances in Instant Messaging, at least in the IBM realm, include the ability to embed IM awareness into web pages themselves. This ability extends the concept of expert location, or finding who the experts are, into the daily activities of end users. Consider, for example, the utility of a list of documents that contains an IM link to the author of each document. That same concept can be integrated into web page content to bring links within the web page to life, allowing you to trigger an IM to a content author directly from within a web page.

A Case Study: GBS Practitioner Portal

The GBS Practitioner Portal is shaping how IBM's Global Business Services (GBS) continues to evolve with their knowledge management needs. GBS makes up nearly half of IBM's global work force, with more than 150,000 practitioners worldwide. Delivering the right tools, templates, and practical information is a monumental task. The GBS Practitioner Portal team, in partnership with several other teams within GBS, is looking to leverage the latest in Web 2.0 and Social Networking technologies to try to address that challenge.

KM is nothing new to the GBS organization. An organization of this size has to be good at creating, capturing, and sharing information in order to streamline processes and obtain the repeatability required for effective delivery. KnowledgeView is GBS's worldwide knowledge-sharing solution and contains business solutions, engagement experiences, proposals, marketing materials, deliverables, practice aids, and thought leadership materials.

Even with a well-defined repository of documents and information, the Learning and Knowledge Management (L&K) team knew that they had to do more. Other repositories and libraries of information existed that needed to be tapped, searches needed to be federated across these other sources of information as well as within the primary source of KnowledgeView, and information needed to be tagged as to relevance and value it might bring to another user. From this was born

KnowledgeView Lite, or the GBS Practitioner Portal, which has several simple but wide-reaching goals. The primary goal of the portal is to improve the ability to find relevant, quality content and experts by

- Providing a simplified user interface.
- Utilizing a Google-like search functionality that includes content from all relevant IBM sources.
- Improving the culture of participation and leveraging the power of the organization via the integration of key social computing and expertise location tools.
- Proactively pushing content via available RSS feeds.
- Highlighting key practice content in business-driven portlets and providing a palette of available portlets to customize the user experience.

Beyond that, however, there are even higher goals to increase the search effectiveness by leveraging user feedback and applying social tagging, ratings, and bookmarks to items. This allows the portal to

- Promote quality content.
- Highlight key content within search results.
- Apply user interaction data to the content lifecycle to promote top quality and automated archiving.

GBS understands that the individual practitioner is one of IBM's greatest assets. The knowledge and collaboration capability that can be provided by each individual is essential in moving the art and science of service delivery forward. The GBS Practitioner Portal is a major step in making achieving that goal (see Figure 1.11).

How do you deliver targeted content to 150,000 service practitioners? No portal can be everything to everyone. No single portal instance, at least. GBS has more than 100 service lines ranging across multiple technologies and industries. Not every service line can be profiled as a top-level page and still maintain some sense of importance within the overall structure. The obvious approach is to attempt some form of personalization to target information to specific users based on job role, project, or position. However, that can have a tremendous performance and management impact on the portal. In addition, many practitioners might be assigned to a specific service line, but work on projects using a

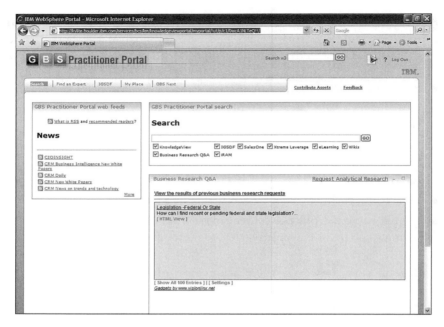

Figure 1.11   GBS Practitioner Portal

different technology or within an industry different from where they are usually assigned. The approach the portal uses to provide relevant information needs to be flexible depending upon practitioners' current needs.

The answer is to allow the end user to determine what is important by providing a palette of portlets that provide the targeted content based on service line. Users can drag and drop portlets that are important to their current needs to stay up-to-date with any particular service line (see Figure 1.12).

A portlet palette is a predefined feature within WebSphere Portal that allows end users to add portlets and customized the portal pages. The use of the palette is a classic approach for meeting the needs of such a large and diverse community of users. Practitioners in the automotive sector don't always care what is going on within the energy or HR practices, for instance. Users can customize their page using the dozens of predefined portlets that target information only to those who really want it.

Another useful feature for end users looking for qualified content is the Business Research Q/A portlet. Behind this portlet is a group of research librarians who are continually mining for important data and performing analysis based on information from research sources across

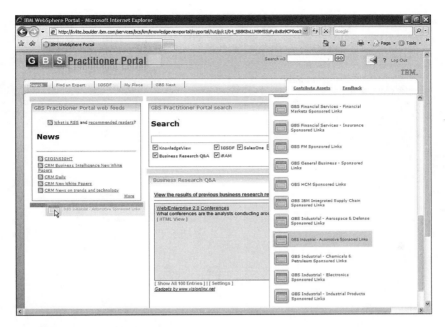

Figure 1.12 Using the portlet palette to manage service lines

multiple technologies and industries. User requests to librarians are usually conducted via email; however, by integrating the Business Research
portlet into the information already stored by librarians as it becomes
available, it becomes much easier for end users to understand what information is readily available. Most of this information is stored in IBM
Lotus Quickr and document libraries, which are fully discussed in
Chapter 5, "Team Collaboration and Content Sharing." Research librarians use Quickr libraries to answer once and save data for everyone. End
users can follow these links directly into the Quickr libraries to view
information that has been mined by the librarians. In addition, when
additional information is needed, research requests can now be initiated
via the portal.

One real star of the site is the ability to run a faceted search against a
number of existing repositories within the organization. This consists of
a federated or simultaneous search against a number of repositories. One
major problem with federated searches across multiple repositories is
that each repository has its own structure and taxonomy. Therefore,
search terms run against one repository might not get similar results
when run against a different repository. KVLite uses a different approach
that allows multiple classifications to be defined against content as it is

indexed. This provides much more consistent results when running the federated search. Figure 1.13 shows the search form with multiple repositories available for the federated result.

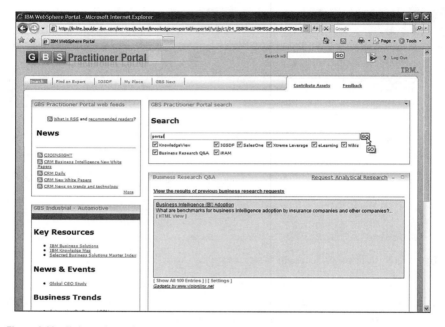

Figure 1.13   Federated search

The search results consist of a powerful interface that integrates the results from the federated search against eight defined knowledge repositories. These results go above and beyond the provided Google-like search interface. Figure 1.14 shows some sample results that integrate sorting results by end-user ratings, tagging counts, title, author, and relevance to the search criteria.

In addition, the search results are integrated within a tag cloud from IBM's Dogear technology. This tag cloud allows the search results to be refined based on the tags submitted by other users of the site.

There is a lot more to the KVLite portal then we can cover here. For example, the sites tried to distinguish between searching and finding. Suppose, for example, that you are searching for some briefing documents on a particular topic. There are 21 documents available on that topic within the various search repositories. It is unlikely that you could structure a query such that you would see all 21 briefing documents in a

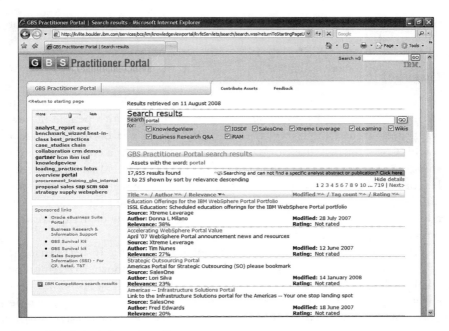

Figure 1.14 Federated search results

single search result. Much work is being done to help bring related information together into drill-down types of search. Dashboards are being created that illustrate industry and technology sectors where information can be *looked at* rather than *searched for*. All this is taking place in real time while end users continue to refine the quality of the content and enhance its value to the business.

Another consideration in the Web 2.0 world is the concept of continuous beta. Because KnowledgeView Lite runs on WebSphere Portal, the team can update, add, and test new features and functionality quickly and easily. In fact, one area of the site is strictly devoted to the delivery and testing of new functionality and ideas. This idea of the constant beta is pervasive throughout IBM, as you will see in additional case studies throughout this book.

External Social Networking Sites

Commercial Social Networking sites abound. These are not typically focused on the enterprise, but instead focus on end users or commercial activities themselves. However, they are important to the way that our user community views or expects to view and use technology. Some of these are discussed in the following sections.

Facebook

For many people, Facebook is the central Social Networking tool in their Internet lives. Facebook enables you to connect with people in new ways and interact on levels that normally would not occur in the real world. Consider my situation with using Facebook. As a consultant, I do some hardcore travel at times throughout the year. Most of my colleagues do the same. When we are not traveling, we work from our home offices. Depending on which city they call home, some people do go into a local office. The point is that I am lucky if I see some of my coworkers or even my manager in person once a year.

Facebook helps to bridge that gap of not working in a traditional office. I can see when my colleague Julia is running another triathlon or where other coworkers happen to be traveling to this week. This perspective fills a gap in the social fabric of our workplace that many people didn't even know existed. It enables us to get a new perspective on the daily lives that traditional office workers take for granted. It's our version of chatting around the water cooler and provides an insight into the human side of our business colleagues. At the same time, I can keep up with what is going on with my two sons in college, other friends, family members, and previous coworkers from around the globe.

Although Facebook allows us to network and connect in an organizational context, it is not the place to conduct internal corporate business. One would not (or perhaps should not) use this application to try to move up the corporate ladder. Unless you are actually trying to interact with the general public, there should be limits to what your employees are discussing on a public site. Chapter 9, "Managing a Changing Social World," goes into more detail on this topic. You can try to re-create Facebook within the confines of your organizational firewall, but you probably do not want an exact duplicate. There are features of Facebook that can be emulated, and the building and collection of profiles has benefits within most business organizations; however, the lure of Facebook is not confined to those areas, and there are other approaches to building a social network that can add direct business value.

In addition, Facebook's status as an external application adds to its appeal. Having the people I enjoy connecting to within a single place provides me a direct benefit in terms of the time and effort that would normally be involved with maintaining contact with such a diverse group of people. Were I to have to choose between connecting internally or externally, or worse have to manage several different systems based on multiple sets of users, I would have to carefully consider how much effort I wanted to expand on each system. This is an important factor in deciding to build a Social Networking application within the enterprise. If you build it, will they really come?

Flickr

Several months before writing this chapter, I was a presenter at a conference in Sydney, Australia. This was a small internal IBM conference that included participants from across the Asia Pacific (AP). Several of my U.S. colleagues and I had flown over for the event to help train our coworkers from Australia, Japan, Malaysia, India, and other countries. More important, it was an event designed to make connections with experts from all across the world that would enable us to communicate and collaborate better in the future.

As you might expect, everyone had a camera and was taking pictures (e.g., of event happenings and group photos with new friends). As the week progressed, it became apparent that everyone had photos that needed to be shared with the larger community. Thumb drives and SD cards were flying around between participants. However, the main issue was knowing what each person had and figuring out which photos we wanted.

Flickr to the rescue! By posting those photos on a shared community site, access to the greater community was easily provided, something that never could have been accomplished by this diverse of a team using other methods. The community was just too geographically dispersed, and trying to set up a custom site, communicating the information to access the site, and keeping it up and running would have been logistically problematic. Flickr is a well-known, easy-to-use, free service that met all those needs with minimal setup.

Conclusion

We have talked a little about some of the business aspects of how Web 2.0 might be leveraged within a business organization, but the reality is that in most cases, a business case must be used to determine and drive all aspects of IT. It does not make sense for the development team to start building new interfaces unless there is some business driver and a known return on investment. Defining the business goals and requirements should be a first step with any approach. Some amount of learning and testing new technologies should be encouraged within any IT organization; however, business drivers outweigh resumé building by the development team.

In contrast, one of the goals that should be set is to fully acknowledge the feedback gathered from our users as they interact with the tools we provide. Without a complete feedback loop, much of the effort might be wasted. One significant benefit of Web 2.0 and Social Networking is that it is now so easy to find content that is interesting, relevant, or just popular. Tagging and rating allow "good" content to rise to the top of any list, and comments allow us to understand whether other users have found things useful. This aspect is changing the way we work with the Web and others.

References

O'Reilly, Tim (September 30, 2005), "What Is Web 2.0, Design Patterns and Business Models for the Next Generation of Software," at http://www.oreillynet.com/pub/a/oreilly/tim/news/2005/09/30/what-is-web-20.html.

ECMA-262 (December 1999), ECMAScript Language, at http://www.ecma-international.org/publications/files/ECMA-ST/Ecma-262.pdf.

Fielding, Roy T. (2000), "Architectural Styles and the Design of Network-Based Software Architectures," at http://www.ics.uci.edu/~fielding/pubs/dissertation/top.htm.

Smith, Gene (2008). *Tagging: People-Powered Metadata for the Social Web*. New Riders Press.

developerWorks Links

Thinking XML: Using the Atom format for syndicating news and more, Uche Ogbuji, http://www.ibm.com/developerworks/xml/library/x-think24.html.

2

Portals in the Enterprise

Portals are proving to be somewhat of a unique piece of software within the enterprise, rapidly replacing the standard website as a more standard framework for delivering information and functionality to end users. The key word here is *standards*. These portal standards are in the enterprise as software for web interfaces and in the framework that is made up of and leverages industry standards across the board. In addition, there is a sense of longevity as portal software continues to evolve along with the capabilities and demands of the enterprise. This enables IT to easily deliver new functionality through a standardized interface without having to consistently build and support new approaches to reach the end user.

Exceptional User Interfaces

One factor that contributes to the strength and use of portals within organizations is that they have longevity. Unlike traditional web pages, portals can more easily adapt to the organization as needs and requirements change over time. IBM's own intranet, w3, is a great example of that; it has evolved over the past 10+ years into the core user interface engine that it is today. This concept holds because of the ability of portal technology to provide an integrated and cohesive interface across all applications in the organization and beyond.

An early promise of portal technology was to provide the integration of people, content, and applications. This idea rings true even more today as portal technology continues to expand with new capabilities for the enterprise. The evolution of portals beyond content includes growing into additional spaces such as collaboration, workflow, and now Social Networking.

Portal technology has always been about the user interface. Sometimes people become caught up in the fact that portals are often based on application server technology, and so much of the robust capability is also available in the portal environment. That means that when building a portal application (portlet or set of portlets), you can build a complete robust application that lives in the portal framework. The portal framework provides a consistent set of features such as navigation and branding that end users can rely on, while the portlets provide new functionality and integration with external systems.

Originally, portals were considered somewhat clumsy in the user interface department. This was an obvious problem, but one that was fairly easy to work around. It wasn't so much that the technology didn't allow for customization; rather, it was the idea that IT expected or asked for an easier way to customize the interface with their desired look and feel. With an HTML-based site, this is pretty easy because you start from scratch to build up the desired look and feel. A portal framework, however, provides much of the navigation and control that you might otherwise have to build yourself. However, much of that plumbing is wrapped in the user interface, so customizing the look and feel means having to learn the correct approach for optimum effect and efficiency. The reality is there is not a look and feel that cannot be replicated in the portal. In fact, I am often amazed when I see sites that have taken the portal to new extremes. Figure 2.1 shows a simple example that is discussed in more detail later in this chapter. A simple search of the Web for WebSphere Portal sites reveals many more public examples.

IBM's w3 is a company intranet, but there are basically three main types of sites that organizations build with portals:

- **B2E:**   Business to employee, or corporate intranets

Figure 2.1 Portal user interface

- **B2B:** Business to business, often known as business partner or dealer portals
- **B2C:** Business to consumer, or Internet sites

This might not be new knowledge to anyone who has worked with the Internet for awhile, but each of these has its own challenges, sometimes dealing with security and exposing business functionality outside the corporate network, and other times dealing with things such as volume and performance. Portal technology has to be flexible and robust enough to fit in any niche in the organization that is required.

Portals Evolution in the Enterprise

This flexibility is often a direct result of new portal innovations. Figure 2.2 shows this innovation over the past few years as portal technology continues to evolve both as a product and as a technology. Originally portals were thought of as a way to replace the standard HTML pages of the early Internet. Maintenance and adaptation of these pages was difficult, and portals provided a framework that included easy-to-manage navigation and access control to different sections of the website. The other obvious benefit was the introduction of portlets, or what are often called portal applications (as mentioned earlier).

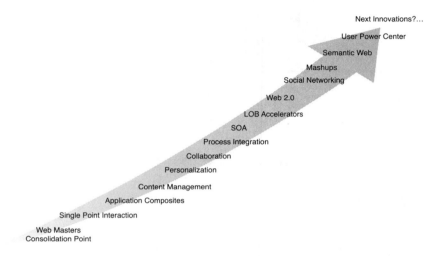

Figure 2.2 Portal innovations

Composite applications and the idea of integrating applications on the glass (at the browser) quickly became a core concept of portal technology. This enabled organizations to see the true business value of portals, which was the idea that many of the disparate applications across the company could not only be combined within a single user interface, but that in some cases, they could work together and share information on a level that enabled a measurable increase in productivity for end users.

Delivering targeted and personalized content to end users is another aspect of portals that becomes important to the enterprise, although in no way is it any less important. At their core, many portals are information and content delivery vehicles and in no way should we take for granted that this is an easy step in the evolution.

In Chapter 1, "Web 2.0 and Social Networking," we introduced the idea of folksonomies and the approach of letting end users drive the categorization of content in a site. In many cases, however, content needs to be targeted to specific sets of end users based on location, job role, or the type of relationship that person has with the company. It is not an easy job for the business to create a set of categories or taxonomy for the enterprise. In the old days (about ten years ago), an organization would have had a team of knowledge management experts helping to define an official taxonomy. Often this was based on industry standards, but usually there were areas specific to the way a company did business. Face it; even organizations in the same industry have internal variations on how they manage customer and business partner relationships.

The idea then is to categorize both the content and the portal user who will view that content. Along with this categorization effort is the work toward defining the rules that match up content and users to determine when a user sees a particular piece of content or a document.

Personalization should not be confused with the concept of user preferences. End-user preferences are when a user specifically chooses to receive information of a particular type or format. This is the same idea of picking specific categories of information. You might choose to receive different types of news such as financial, medical, retail, or technology. Preferences are driven by the choices that the users themselves make toward the delivery of content. Personalization is driven by the *organization* making choices on what information they want the end user to see or have access to.

For consumer (B2C) types of portals, personalization is not as important because much of the content is designed for public consumption. However, for portal implementations where you know and can categorize a user (B2B and B2E), personalization can play a huge role in ensuring that content is targeted toward correctly to a user and not shown to those who do not need to view it. If you think about it, that is the point of personalization in the first place: to provide "personalized" content to the viewer.

Not all portals are content driven, although many have content as a major contributor. However, for portals to be truly useful across the enterprise, they have to be able to participate as a full member of the business processes that drive most organizations. Many of the process-driven activities in an organization have specific tasks or points where human intervention is necessary (a human task)—for example, to review and approve a loan application. This is a step that might occur within a larger loan application process. Portals make an obvious choice as the user interface in which to surface those human tasks to the approval officer in an automated way. Generally, a human task requires some supporting information or access to other applications with which to

evaluate and complete that specific task. For example, when assessing a
loan application for possible approval, the approver will probably need
access to the original loan application, the applicant's credit information, and other important pieces of information. In addition, he might
need to access another application in the enterprise where the approval is
actually performed.

Portals are already set up to provide this type of interactivity, combining information and application access from different vertical sources
within the organization. Access to various pieces of information usually
comes from legacy sources; however, as service-oriented architectures
(SOA) became more popular, it also became obvious that portals could
consume and provide information and access to users through standardized service protocols such as web services, Java® messaging services, and
even through remote Enterprise Java Bean (EJB) invocation. Again, the
portal is proving to be the ultimate consumer, providing one-stop shopping for all end-user and organizational needs. It comes as no surprise
then as technology continues to evolve that portal technology evolves
right alongside it. Current trends in collaboration, Web 2.0, and Social
Networking are perfect additions for portal integration because all of
these activities are user-centric and require some type of vehicle to
deliver information to your users. Often, portals can be used to provide
summary information to end users and then provide direct access to
other applications for more detailed information. In this way, the portal
maintains its status as the central gateway into the enterprise.

Attacking the Desktop

It is probably not realistic that a single portal can become everything
to everyone; however, as you have seen, portal technology itself has no
real limits in the type of functions that it can provide. At times, there
might be technical challenges, but these are rarely something that cannot be worked out, and often these challenges go way beyond the portal
technology itself. The goal of many portals is to make the end user's job
(or perhaps life) easier by providing the single place that the end user
can go to for some aspect of his or her day-to-day job. Figure 2.3 shows
the desktop that many of us are familiar with in our day-to-day lives.
(This is no joke, as we continue to get crushed by all the information
and activities that surround our lives.)

One goal of a portal can be to bring some calm to the chaos around us.
Not only can a good portal implementation make things easier, but it

Figure 2.3 Common end user's desktop

can also pay off in productivity benefits as activities and tasks are
streamlined and the right information is readily available. Figure 2.4
illustrates the idea of bringing order to chaos using portal technology.
Contrast that with the chaos displayed in Figure 2.3 and you will get an
idea about how improvements can be made using a well-designed portal.

Figure 2.4 Bringing tasks and activities to the end user

Notice that I am focusing on the idea of application integration, end-user productivity, and line-of-business acceleration, which involve automating business processes or providing access to applications and information. This is an obvious step in the evolution of portals, not only within the industry but also within your organization. Growth is always slow, and many organizations need to let portal technology bake in the enterprise before they can really begin to take advantage of the technology. If you are new to portals, let me state this again: Start slow and let the portal grow into your organization. Large projects often fail. Large portal projects are no exception. Collaboration and Social Networking are obvious next steps in the evolution and are what this book is all about, but setting the stage is important, and understanding more about your options can help you meet business goals.

WebSphere Portal in the Enterprise

Portals are an investment that must be taken seriously, but the return on investment (ROI) can be substantial. From an enterprise perspective, it really comes down to cost and the value gained from investing in the technology. Note that a portal framework is not necessarily a lightweight component that you bolt on to your existing infrastructure. Instead, it is an investment in ensuring that your foundation is solid and secure for the future. That said, the purchase of your portal framework is just the first step. As applications get added into the framework, mishaps can occur. Faulty application code can severely hamper portal performance and stability, just as if an electrician were to mis-wire a home.

WebSphere Portal is a full-featured enterprise portal solution that can achieve all the goals that have been discussed so far in this chapter. New features are being continuously added and make the portal technology much more adaptable to Web 2.0 and Ajax integration. This makes the prospect of what we can achieve with portal technology exciting as we continue to build new features on top of an already solid technological base. Figure 2.5 shows an overview of the architecture features in WebSphere Portal.

This rich set of features and functions can also be what makes portal technology somewhat daunting as technology teams try to take advantage of all that WebSphere Portal has to offer. Although we won't examine every aspect of the architecture, the major functional areas probably require discussion. Figure 2.5 indicates several main functional areas, as follows:

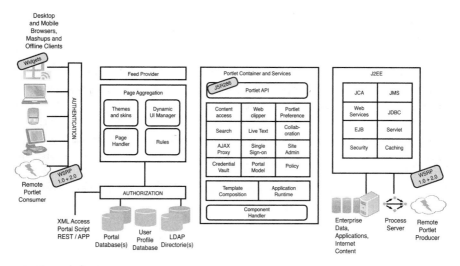

Figure 2.5 WebSphere Portal architecture

- **J2EE:** J2EE services are essentially inherited from WebSphere Application Server. WebSphere Portal is an application framework, albeit very comprehensive, that runs on WebSphere Application Server (WAS). Therefore, we can take advantage of much of the functionality and services available with WAS itself.

- **Portlet Container and Services:** The portlet container and portal services are the services that are provided on top of WAS by the framework itself. WebSphere Portal provides a portlet container where you can run your portlets and a number of growing services that can provide enhanced functionality to your application. Note that the portlet container for version 6.1 does support JSR 286, which is discussed in the next section in this chapter. Much of the functionality provided here is for back-end integration and portal business logic functionality.

- **Feed Provider and Page Aggregation:** Page aggregation is about the user experience. Page aggregation and theme support enable you to provide a comprehensive yet flexible view to end users. Portals can provide a customized set of pages to every user based on access control rules and user preferences.

- **Authentication and Authorization:** WebSphere Portal provides a comprehensive set of authentication and authorization services. Much of the authentication is built on WebSphere security, which provides a comprehensive security solution. WebSphere Portal's authorization and access control system is designed to allow maximum flexibility in ensuring that you are targeting the right pages and information to the right people.

The prevailing advice is to take it slow and build up your skills and the vision of what you can accomplish with portals in your organization. It is exactly this framework that drives the build versus buy decision between WebSphere portal and some homegrown framework. The thousands of hours that have been invested in creating a robust and feature-rich framework would be extremely difficult to reproduce in the enterprise, and it would be (or should be) difficult to justify the cost. The reality is that this rich set of functionality should be very exciting because the possibilities are almost limitless.

Accelerating Business Value

In addition to the portal framework, IBM has released a variety of business accelerators that should be thought of as snap-in products to the portal. These enable you to accelerate the delivery of solutions for specific business goals. Figure 2.6 illustrates the accelerators available at the time of this writing.

Each of these accelerators includes additional feature-rich products or sets of products that can be used within WebSphere Portal, or often independently as their own products. Of particular importance to this book are the Collaboration and Content accelerators:

- **Collaboration accelerator:**   As of this writing, the Lotus Collaboration accelerator includes the use of Lotus Sametime Standard 8.0, Lotus Quickr 8.1, and Lotus Connections 2.0. Later chapters examine these products in more detail. Together they provide a comprehensive collaboration package that includes instant communication, Social Networking, and team collaboration.

- **Content accelerator:**   The Lotus Content accelerator includes Lotus Web Content Management 6.1 (as of this writing), Lotus Quickr 8.1 (for document management), and IBM OmniFind™ Enterprise Edition 8.5. Together these products create a comprehensive content and document management system and provide enterprise search capabilities with OmniFind.

Portals are very feature-rich web presentation frameworks. It would take an entire book to talk about all the features that portals have to

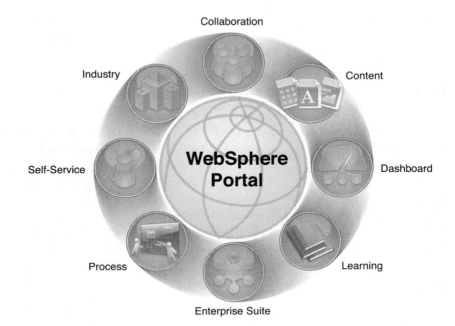

Figure 2.6 WebSphere Portal accelerators

offer. Adding to that are things like accelerators that can provide even more value to your application. Unfortunately, we only have one chapter here, so it is important to focus on basic development skills to build up a base for later discussion.

Portal Applications

I like the term *portal applications* because it much more accurately describes what you are creating. The term *portlets* suggests something lightweight, which might actually be the case, but it does not always seem to be correct. Our portlets often take on a life of their own and grow beyond our control. Strong application architecture, including well-defined standards, is almost always needed, yet rarely provided to portlet developers who are building new applications. Too often, this aspect of the job just gets lost in the fray of trying to deliver a portal project.

When building WebSphere Portal applications, you are really building WebSphere applications. I start with this point because building good WebSphere applications requires more than just a basic level of experience. Some initial guidance is available in my book *Application Architecture for WebSphere.*

Internal and External Standards

As with most of the WebSphere brand of products, WebSphere Portal has made a concerted effort to work with many of the standards that are becoming common in the industry. This is important because standards enable organizations to find experienced developers and provide some confidence that they are not getting entrenched in a single vendor's technology. Although I often make the case that it is important to take advantage of vendor-specific options where they provide value, it is also important to ensure that standards are followed as much as possible. This includes both industry standards and organizational standards.

Java Portlet Specification

You might hear the terms *JSR 168* and *JSR 286.* These numbers refer to specific working specifications of the Java Community Process sponsored by Sun Microsystems. The Java Community Process (JCP) enables all parties with an interest in the growth of the Java programming language a way to take part in shaping the future of Java.

This approach is important to specifications such as the Java Portlet Specification we are discussing right now. One of the major ideas behind the initial specification, called JSR 168, was to provide for the interoperability of portlets across portal servers from different vendors. If you think about it, this was an important step for the industry in terms of portal development. First, as a developer, you can now focus on a standard application programming interface (API) for developing portlets. Of course, there are always nuances and extensions that are provided by each vendor's product, but the core specification will remain the same. As an organization, there is a similar reward in that it is easier to find practitioners with skills that are necessary to help with your portal project. Another advantage is the interoperability of the portlets themselves. From a high level, you could conceptually build your application on one vendor's portal and then migrate fairly easily if switch to another portal product later. From a business point of view, switching platforms is probably not the best use of business dollars unless you have strong justification. In fact, you are probably better off leveraging some of the nonstandard features of your current platform to enhance your application's performance, security, or functionality (as necessary).

No, the advantage here goes to third-party vendors themselves who might build portlets that allow for the integration of their specific products. Using a standard-based approach can minimize the effort and enable the portlets to run on any platform that supports the standard. Figure 2.7 shows the Java Community Process page for the version 2 of the portlet specification.

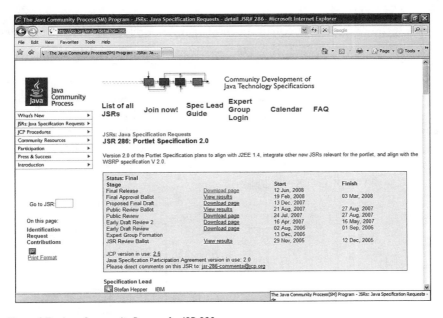

Figure 2.7   Java Community Process for JSR 286

So what's important about the numbers in the Java Community Process? Nothing especially, but it is easy to get confused. The numbers refer to different specification versions for each JSR. What is important is that each version can contain different features and standards, so when you are building your portal, they can become more interesting. Review of the specification is necessary if you are trying to understand what application functionality you can provide within your own portal. The following specifications are available:

- JSR 168 is the initial specification that covered the basic portal lifecycle and API. This specification should be called the Java Portlet Spec 1.0.

- JSR 286 is the latest enhancement to the specification and builds upon version 1. This version includes enhancements such as portlet events, which are discussed later.

Note that JSR 286 is the second release of the specification and is more commonly known as the Java Portlet Specification 2.0. It is referred to this way throughout the rest of this book.

How Do Portlets Work?

More important than what they are is how portlets actually work on the portal server. Figure 2.8 gives you an overview of the important parts of the concept. Remember that portlets are applications that get combined on a page. These portlets can stand alone or work together as composite applications, as necessary. This is important because the design of the portlet should be such that it works in many different circumstances. In many cases, you should not assume that your portlet will be used in any particular way. This is especially true of content-type portlets that might be used many times to show different types of content in different areas of the page.

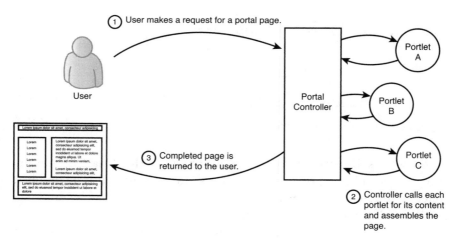

Figure 2.8   How portals work

In Figure 2.8, the user makes an initial request for the page, but it is the portlet controller that sets up the portlet on the page. The portlet controller calls each portlet either one at a time or in parallel and asks that portlet for its particular content or markup. The portal controller can then aggregate the returned markup into the resulting page, which is then sent back to the requesting user.

During the initial view of the page, which is shown in this example, more than likely the view mode of the portlet is being requested. This mode provides the markup or content for the current portlet state as defined during the render process of a portlet.

The portlet itself is built as Java code that conforms to the portlet specification. What does this mean? Well, the portlet has to understand what commands it is being given by the portlet container. When is the container asking for render markup versus when an action is being performed by the end user. The simple code example that follows is probably the most basic portlet that you can create:

```java
package com.ibmpress.portlet.helloportlet;


import java.io.*;
import javax.portlet.*;

public class HelloPortlet extends javax.portlet.GenericPortlet {

  public void init() throws PortletException{
    super.init();
  }

  public void doView(RenderRequest request, RenderResponse response)
   throws PortletException, IOException {

    //output some markup here!
    response.getWriter().println("Hello Cruel Portal World!");

  }
}
```

Notice that this portlet only has an init() method and a doView() method. The init() method is called when the portlet is initially created and initialized by the container. Then when a request is made for a page that this portlet lives on, the render portion of the portlet is called via the doView() method.

Portlet Definition

Under the covers, portlets can be confusing components. That is because they are designed for flexibility within the system. The ability to use a portlet on multiple pages or to allow administrators or end users to customize specific portlet features is important for maintaining a good portal environment. Figure 2.9 illustrates this flexibility in defining different parts of the portlet components.

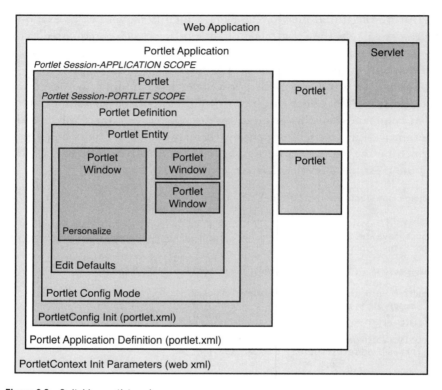

Figure 2.9   Switching portlet modes

You can see that portlets are actually deployed as a web application. This is similar to servlet packaging and deployment. A web application is often packaged as a .war file for deployment into the application or portal server. Sometimes the .war is packaged as a subcomponent of a larger enterprise application, but in most portal applications, the .war is the most common component. Within the web application is the actual portlet application itself. This portlet application can be joined together with other more common Java components such as servlets if necessary.

A portlet application contains one or more portlets that can be deployed together on a single page or separated across pages within the portal. It is a common question to ask how portlets should be combined within the portlet application. They are usually grouped by functionality. For example, a set of content portlets might be deployed together even if they are used in different circumstances. Because there is probably some overlap in the design of these types of portlets, this allows for the similar functionality of these portlets to be managed together within the development environment.

The portlet definition, portlet entity, and portlet window are used to logically separate instances of the portlet so that preferences and configuration information can be managed independently for the portlets themselves. The configuration options for each of these entities are defined at a different level of scope, depending on whether you need to define options for a single user, single portlet, or for all portlets within the portal.

Portlet Modes and Window States

Another concept is the ability for a portlet to provide different modes, and be viewed in different window states. A portlet mode enables a portlet to show different views depending upon how it is being used. The most common of these is view mode, where the portlet simply displays the content or functionality to the end user as desired. Remember, however, that portlets are unique components in that they can be installed and configured to work in different places on the portal. Because of this, they provide additional modes that enable the end user or administrator to confirm they are working as desired. The basic specification calls for three main modes: *view*, *edit*, and *help.* In addition, the specification allows custom modes to be provided by the vendor as desired. WebSphere Portal provides two additional custom modes within the portal (see Table 2.1).

Table 2.1 WebSphere Portal v6.1 Portlet Modes

Mode	Mode Type	Description
View	Standard	As mentioned previously, view mode is the common state for any portlet. It is here that all the business presentation work is done. The official definition is this is where the portlet generates markup that reflects the current state of the portlet.
Edit or personalize	Standard	Edit mode allows for a single user to make changes to the preferences of the portlet. For example, a user of a news portlet may choose the categories of news that interest him or her (financial, technology, or business, for example).
Help	Standard	Help mode is a way for the portlet developer to provide additional help information to the end user.

Table 2.1   WebSphere Portal v6.1 Portlet Modes

Mode	Mode Type	Description
Edit defaults	Custom	Edit defaults mode is similar to edit mode, but these preferences are set by an administrator and apply to all users of that portlet.
Configure	Custom	Configure mode is similar to edit and edit defaults mode, but on a much more global scale. Configure mode allows you to set preferences on a portlet instance that will be shared across multiple pages and users. In addition, you might view configuration mode as modifying the plumbing of a portlet (that is, setting core integration properties such as which back-end service or application this portlet should be connecting to).

Note that although these modes are available, it is up to the developer to use these modes within the portlet. Within WebSphere Portal, an administrator or end user can switch between these modes using the Portlet menu (see Figure 2.10). Modes can also be switched programmatically when necessary. This is especially important if the portlet requires some user information before it can display the initial markup.

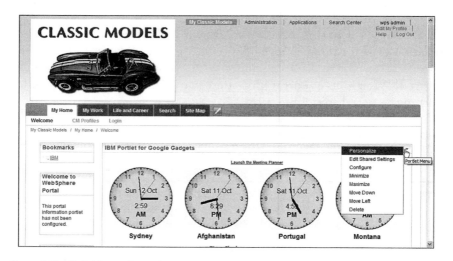

Figure 2.10   Switching portlet modes

The portlet window state is another aspect of portlets that is not often found in other types of web interfaces. Because portlets often share space on the page, it is sometimes necessary for a portlet to expand to fill the entire page or shrink to take hardly any space at all, enabling other portlets to expand. This is called minimizing and maximizing a portlet. Normally, portlets take some space on the page. However, this is a shared space where all the portlets live together on the page in harmony. Figure 2.11 shows several portlets sharing the same page. When a portlet is on the page in this manner, it is said to be in *normal* mode.

For the most part, normal mode is the preferred state. However, the ability to modify a portlet's window state is important in some cases. Minimizing a portlet means that only the title bar is shown on the page, which leaves room for other portlets to expand and display more functionality or information on the page. This is good for portlets that take up a lot of space or for portlets that are not used as often within the page.

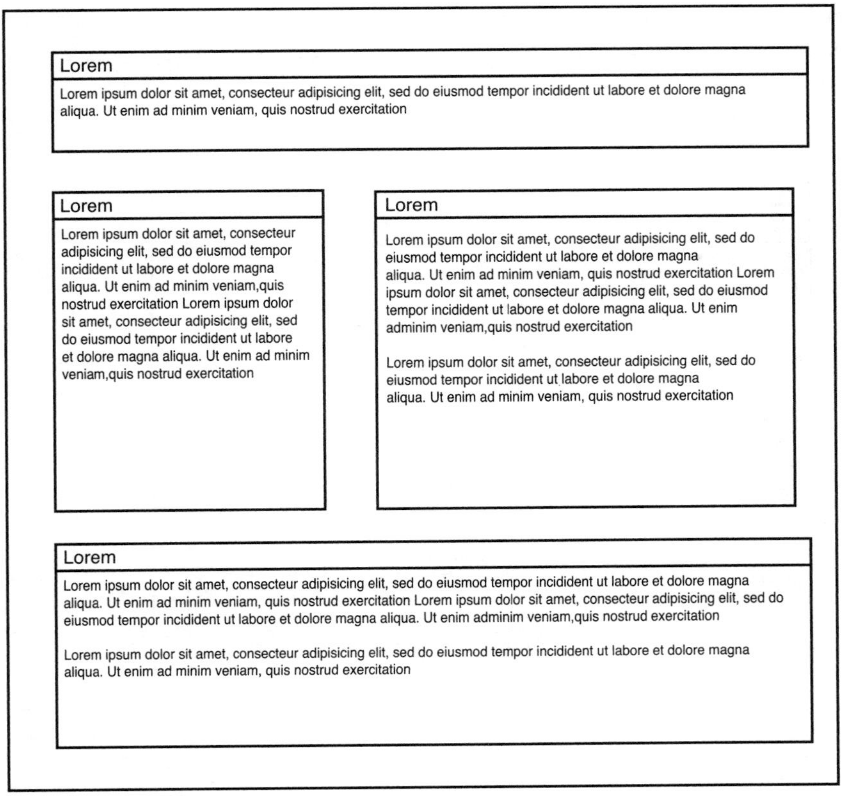

Figure 2.11 Normal portlet view

Figure 2.12 shows the top and bottom portlets minimized, which enables the middle portlets to use more space on the page to show more information.

Another option is to expand a single portlet to take up the entire screen (see Figure 2.13). In this mode, all the other portlets on the page are removed entirely as a single page is displayed. This is an important window state for when you need to focus on a single application.

Although an end user can initiate a window state change with menu options, it is sometimes important for the application or portlet to initiate the change itself. For example, consider a portlet that allows a user to enter information into a form. Often, the portlet window will not be big enough to display the entire form on the screen. If you know the portlet will share the page with other portlets, you can have the user enter just some initial information, and when this information is submitted the portlet can programmatically maximize to fill the entire page. This just-in-time approach to changing window state is a great

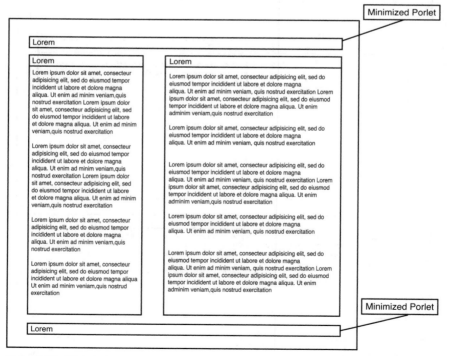

Figure 2.12   Minimized portlets

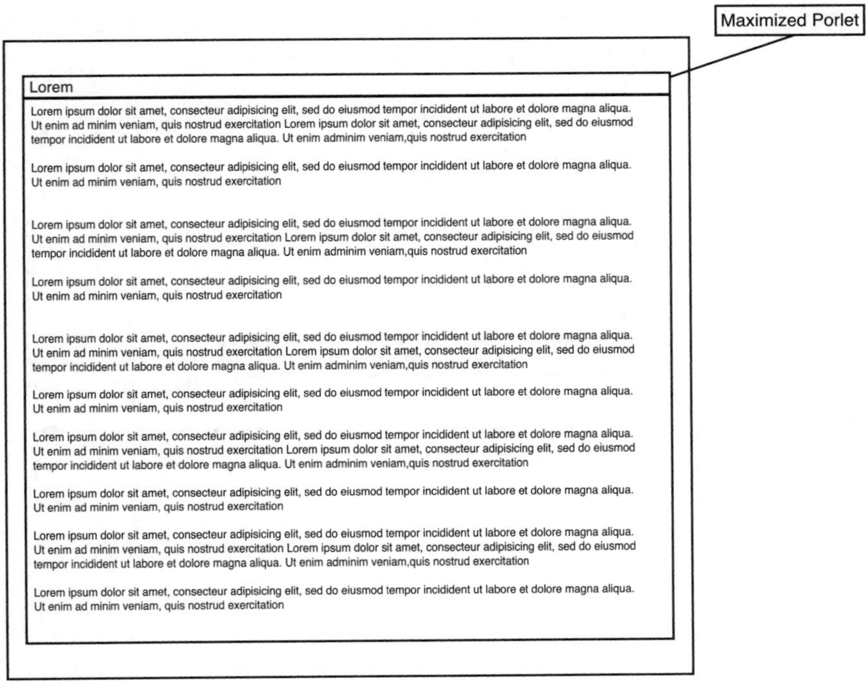

Figure 2.13 Maximized portlet

way to deliver the right capability to your end users as they need it, and does not require you to anticipate what users will do.

Action and Render Phases

During normal operations of a portlet, two main lifecycle phases might occur: the render phase and the action phase. You might think of these as something similar to the GET and POST methods on a servlet, similar but different. In a servlet, you would call these two methods independently depending on the type of request you were attempting. A POST is usually used for an update, or some form of input, whereas a GET is used as a standard type of request for content from the servlet. This does not have to be the case, and many exceptions apply, but those are common conventions for servlet development.

With a portlet, it is slightly different. A render method is called when the portlet is asked to display some content on the page. This occurs almost always when a user views a page and set of portlets for the first time. Figure 2.14 illustrates this occurrence.

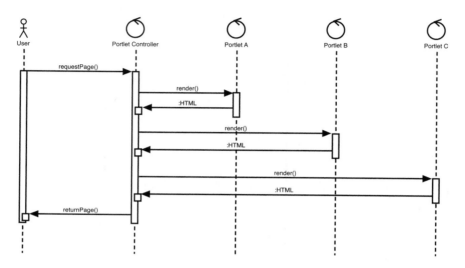

Figure 2.14   Portlet render phase

In this case, the user requests a page from the portal. The portal or portlet controller then calls the render method for each of the portlets that will be displayed on that page. After all the portlets have returned their section of the page, the controller can assemble or aggregate that information and return the completed page to the initial user.

Contrast this with an action that needs to occur within a particular portlet. Remember that each portlet can be a separate application, so portlets have to be able to operate independently, yet still work together on a shared page. If a user requests some action from a portlet, he will request it specifically for that portlet on the page. Other portlets will not be involved in the initial action phase of the portlet. However, the concept of the action phase allows other portlets, even those on other pages, to get involved if necessary. Consider the example in Figure 2.15 where a user initiates an action on portlet A. This request is again made to the portlet controller, which calls the processAction() method on portlet A.

Portlet A then processes the request. However, it needs to communicate some event information to portlet C. This event management

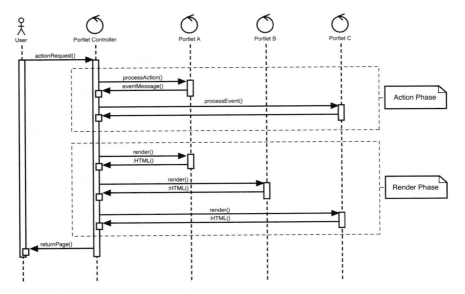

Figure 2.15 Portlet action and render phases

occurs during the action phase also, because the render phase cannot start until all the underlying processing and messaging is finished.

Why is this important? Consider that portlet C may actually be on a different page. In this case, portlet A needs to process the action and send a message to portlet C. When the render phase begins after all this has occurred, it may be that the rendering is happening on a different page from where the user started based on the flow of the application.

Additional Specification Features

To be successful with WebSphere Portal and building portlets, you need to understand many features. Your investment in this technology is such that it is much less expensive to use what is available than it is to try to address requirements with custom solutions. After all, if you don't know what is available, you may be constantly reinventing the wheel. This is a huge waste of business and IT dollars. It might also be the case where the specification or WebSphere Portal addresses some requirement but in a slightly different way. This is where the discussion begins around this question: Do you modify the requirements or build expensive custom functionality to address those requirements?

Portlet Language Options

Portlets can now be written in almost any popular development language and with many different frameworks. Bridges and wrappers enable your code to be deployed to the portlet container and run just like any other portlet that conforms to the specification. The question is this: Should you write your portlets with another language or framework? There are many tradeoffs embedded in this discussion.

Standards are one good decision criteria in helping to determine which framework or language you might consider. Some options such as JavaServer™ Faces are more standards based and have support from multiple vendors and organizations. Other options such as Struts are not necessarily standards based; however, they have a large support base across the industry as a whole.

Options such as SpringMVC, Grails, or JRuby can muddy the waters a bit when you are trying to make a decision. Although they all have a strong following, there can be supportability problems, or difficultly finding the right expertise when it is needed. Am I willing to bet the business that this approach is better than what the industry as a whole is moving to? Am I willing to spend valuable IT dollars to learn a new technology just because it is the latest thing?

Some amount of learning and exploration is necessary for the growth of any organization. However, planning a mission-critical portal application might not be the right venue for this type of effort. Another category of development framework is the more proprietary frameworks such as Flex and WebSphere Portlet Factory. These are more graphical in nature and are fully supported by a single vendor.

WebSphere Portlet Factory

WebSphere Portlet Factory (WPF) has come a long way in recent years, fueled by continued interest in quickly developing portlets that can leverage existing systems within the enterprise. WPF uses a model-driven approach that allows developers to generate code based on input to the model through the use of builders. Components within WPF called builders are literally the building blocks of an application and are combined and wired together within the model (see Figure 2.16).

Although initially targeted toward non-Java developers who might be coming from a background of development in Domino®, Microsoft, or other

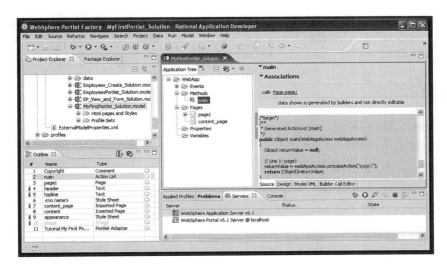

Figure 2.16   WebSphere Portlet Factory

scripting or visual types of languages, WPF has gained acceptance as a main-stream development platform on the WebSphere Portal platform.

The one major issue one might have with WPF is that is it not based on industry standards. Although this might be important to some organizations, the speed with which someone can prototype and deliver robust applications may far outweigh this issue. The core issue is possible migration of WPF components on competitive platforms. This argument might not be compelling for your organization given the cost of development that can be saved by using WPF initially, and adding the ROI disadvantage of switching platforms at a future date.

As with any language, a ramp-up time is necessary for developers to get up to speed and learn a new language. With such a development paradigm shift, this can be anywhere from a few weeks to several months to become somewhat expert on the framework. Again, however, the benefit of being able to quickly build new applications may greatly outweigh this initial cost and ramp-up time. And, the ramp up is not more severe than what it would take to learn JavaServer Faces (JSF) or another Java-based presentation framework.

WPF is based on the concept of using builders to identify discrete pieces of functionality. These builders are added to a model and tied together to create necessary application flow. At last count, more than a hundred basic builders are available that can provide much of the core functionality of any application. The Portal Factory InfoCenter provides a preview of the many out-of-the-box builders that are available. Available builders include the following:

- Ajax Type-Ahead
- Applet
- Breadcrumbs
- Button
- Calendar Picker
- Collapsible Section
- Cooperative Portlet Source and Target
- Data Page
- Date / Time Formatter
- Dojo Inline Edit
- Dojo Tooltip
- Domino Data Access
- Domino View & Form
- EJB Call
- Excel Import
- File Upload
- Flash
- GreenPoint WebCharts
- HTML
- HTML Event Action
- Image
- Image Button
- JMS Message
- JSP Tag
- Link
- Linked Java Object
- Lotus Web Content Management Access
- Page
- PeopleSoft View & Form

- Portlet Adapter
- Radio Button
- REST Service Call
- SAP View & Form
- Siebel View and Form
- SQL DataSource
- Web Service Call

This makes it glaringly obvious that WPF can do much of the routine work behind the scenes. However, using WPF does not absolve you of using good design and development techniques; it's just that you need to focus them to take advantage of the framework.

Dashboards

WPF has become the base technology for a number of initiatives and product offerings during the last couple of years. Included in this list are HR-based self-service accelerators for WebSphere Portal, the dashboard framework components for quickly building dashboards within the enterprise, and mashup builders that enable you to easily build mashup components for Lotus Mashup Center (see Figure 2.17). IBM Mashup Center is discussed in detail within Chapter 6, "Mashing Up Data and Applications."

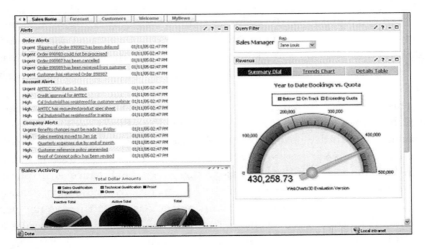

Figure 2.17   Dashboards built on WPF

Dashboards can be used to quickly categorize and identify trends in almost any type of data. After the initial dashboard is in place, getting new monitors in place can become a regular event as the need arises. Although dashboard technology does not strictly depend on the portal framework, that is the most common platform for displaying dashboard technology to end users. The dashboard framework is based on a set of builders that enable the quick integration and display of data sets in a graphical way. This enables all users to identify trends and then quickly drill down into the data itself when necessary.

IBM's w3 Company Intranet

For IBM, like most organizations, the company intranet has quickly become the initial go-to place for employees looking for information. Employees often start at the main intranet, what we call w3, whether they need to perform daily activities (e.g., fill out time sheets, submit expenses, or book travel), need to search the major document repositories for information relevant to their project, or just want to see the latest buzz.

With an average rate of more than 1.5 million page views per day and almost 200,000 searches per day, not only does this environment need to be highly scalable, but highly functional to meet the needs of IBMers worldwide. The demand for this level has not grown overnight; instead, it has built up over the past 10+ years. Figure 2.18 illustrates the growth in functionality of the system over the past 20+ years.

Until the mid 1990s, IBM, similar to most organizations, was providing many of the HR and employee functions via mainframe-based applications. With the introduction and mainstream adoption of the Internet, IBM was one of the first organizations to jump on and start to help its employees get on the Web.

This effort has evolved into the On Demand Workplace (ODW), a one-stop shop where IBM employees can get the help and information they need to achieve day-to-day goals. There is not just a single team involved in this activity. IBM's w3 is the front end to the entire global organization and as such has the responsibility to ensure that strict governance is in place. Technical responsibilities fall to architects, operations, and support teams across the globe. In a worldwide company such as IBM, there is no such thing as downtime. Even in maintenance mode, a static site alternative is available so that employees can find what they need.

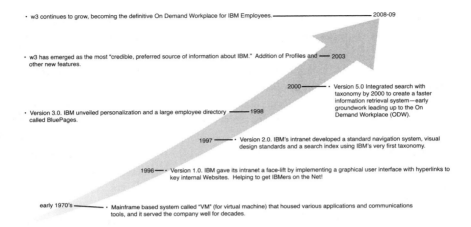

- w3 continues to grow, becoming the definitive On Demand Workplace for IBM Employees. ——————— 2008-09

- w3 has emerged as the most "credible, preferred source of information about IBM." Addition of Profiles and —— 2003
  other new features.

                                                                2000 ——— · Version 5.0 Integrated search with
                                                                          taxonomy by 2000 to create a faster
                                                                          information retrieval system—early
- Version 3.0. IBM unveiled personalization and a large employee directory ——— 1998   groundwork leading up to the On
  called BluePages.   Demand Workplace (ODW).

                                          1997 ——— · Version 2.0. IBM's intranet developed a standard navigation system, visual
                                                     design standards and a search index using IBM's very first taxonomy.

                          1996 —— · Version 1.0. IBM gave its intranet a face-lift by implementing a graphical user interface with hyperlinks to
                                    key internal Websites. Helping to get IBMers on the Net!

early 1970's ——————— · Mainframe based system called "VM" (for virtual machine) that housed various applications and communications
                       tools, and it served the company well for decades.

Figure 2.18 Evolution of w3

However, technical responsibilities are not the only area where focus is required. Many of the nontechnical aspects of w3 have dedicated teams, including the following:

- **User experience:** This group works to create a working environment that helps IBMers live and practice the company's values and help their colleagues and the company to succeed. An important foundation for that is a productive and consistent online experience across the intranet, accomplished through such disciplines as design, information architecture, information management (including search and enterprise taxonomy), and research and measurement.

- **Strategic messaging:** Provides up-to-date, candid, and strategic news and perspective to help IBMers understand and advance IBM's business, strategy, and values. This is accomplished through both original editorial content and information resources drawn from across IBM. This includes external news and analysis of IBM, coverage of the competition, and how IBM stacks up against them.

- **Workforce enablement:** Facilitates IBMers' abilities to find and make use of the resources (including content, applications, processes, and colleagues' expertise) available through the On Demand Workplace to accomplish their role-specific work and to live and practice the company's values.

The investment in w3's growth and value is substantial, but the return is obvious given that any employee can function independently from management and HR when working remotely or out in the field with customers. The use of personalization is kept fairly light; however, end users can customize the views and content that they receive based on their preferences. This allows for the tradeoffs that need to occur, between providing a highly personalized experience and managing the infrastructure that is required to support 350,000+ employees and contractors.

In anonymous mode, w3 has three tabs: Home, Work, and Career and Live. These tabs or key site areas are common to the intranets within many organizations. Because so much of the day-to-day information is available on these three tabs, it can be the case that users do not have to log in to the portal itself at all times. This saves on processing power of the system if not all users have to log in. Contrast this with other portals where everyone is required to log in to see the right information.

If a user chooses to log in, however, the information provided is much richer than otherwise. Profile and targeting metadata is used to identify additional content and tabs that become available to a specific end user. Note on Figure 2.19 that an additional tab titled SWG (Software Group) Development appears based on my current job within IBM.

The idea of running a constant beta is one of IBM's more visible approaches to the continuous advancement of technology use within the enterprise. Chapter 1 talked about the Global Business Services Knowledge View portal and the idea of providing a continuous beta. In addition, much of the development effort is undergoing a continuous beta program where customers can download the latest development version on a regular basis.

w3 is no exception, as the ODW Next portal attempts to provide new features and functionality to end users and to help determine what the next version of w3 will contain. Using buttons at the top of the pages shown in Figure 2.19 and Figure 2.20, users can switch back and forth between the current stable version of w3 and ODW Next.

A continuous beta approach allows IBM to continue to keep the main site stable and keep employees as productive as possible, while still testing new features and functions as the technology continues to move forward. There is no substitute for real users to determine what works and what does not work in a website.

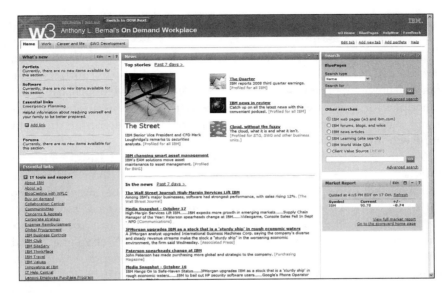

Figure 2.19   The author's w3 page

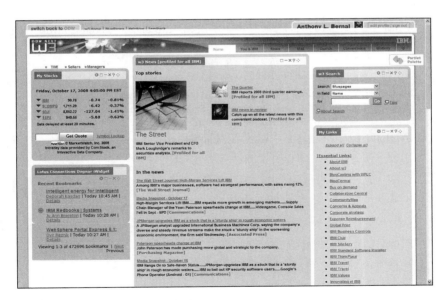

Figure 2.20   Continued growth with ODW Next

Conclusion

This has been a bit of an eclectic chapter, but with a primary focus on portals and their core components, which are, of course, portlets. You can see how important portlets are to deploying new information and functionality to your end users. Because of this, there is a lot to understand and a lot of decisions to make when trying to determine the right approach for your environment.

The reality is that choosing a portal platform as the basis of your user interface is an easy decision. Implementing that decision is where the real work begins as services and application begin to be integrated into the core platform for distribution to end users. There are no easy answers to making this all work together. The technology is just too complex and is moving forward at a constant rate. However, WebSphere Portal has shown that it can continue to evolve with this constant change and provide a platform that you can build upon into the future.

References

Bernal, J., *Application Architecture for WebSphere*, ed. K. Bull. 2008, Boston, MA: Pearson plc as IBM Press. 336.

JSR286. *JSR 286: Portlet Specification 2.0*. 2008; 2.0: Available from: http://jcp.org/en/jsr/detail?id=286.

InfoCenter. *WPF InfoCenter - Builder List*. 2008; Available from: http://publib.boulder.ibm.com/infocenter/wpfhelp/v6r1m0/index.jsp?topic=/com. bowstreet.designer.doc/designer/r_builders.htm.

w3. *IBM w3 Guidelines*. 2008; Available from: http://w3.ibm.com.

3

Ajax, Portlets, and Patterns

Understanding your basic development options is important when deciding which technical approach to take when building a solution. This is especially true when using a portal framework and building portlets. This chapter outlines the basic options and provides some decision points to help you choose the correct approach for your project or organization. Using Ajax within your portlets is another area where understanding the basics is important. Knowing how to make the right choices in your design is very important. This chapter outlines some of the basics patterns for using Ajax within a portlet.

Portals and Portlets as a Platform

The primary focus of this chapter is on developing portlets, with a slight twist. You will learn the basics of portlet development, but the focus will be on displaying data on the client or browser within the application. Chapter 2, "Portals in the Enterprise," outlined the basic portlet specification and options for developing different types of portlets. In this chapter, we actually expand on that idea and build a simple usable portlet for data display. In addition, the display will concentrate on using Web 2.0 technology to update the screen quickly without requiring a complete page refresh in the browser.

Ajax in WebSphere Portal

With the release of IBM WebSphere Portal 6.1, Web 2.0 has become a major theme within the framework. It is one thing to include Web 2.0 technologies such as Ajax in your stand-alone web pages. However, when you work in a defined framework, such as WebSphere Portal, you sometimes need a little help. It often comes down to the fact that portals provide a shared space for applications that need to reside together on the same server. You'll read more about this shared space in which applications can reside. For now, you need to know that although this is a benefit, it can also be the source of much confusion. We keep alluding to the fact that developing for a portal is somewhat different from nonportal development.

Q. Why can't you just code your portlet like a stand-alone application?

A. Because if everyone took that approach, nothing would work together. Portals insist on slightly different rules to ensure that the shared space is meaningful.

Figure 3.1 illustrates the example of using Ajax in the portal environment. Ajax is behind most of the capability that allows for a partial-page refresh in real time. This creates an environment that is almost alive in its ability to respond to your requests or interaction. Click on a link and the associated information immediately changes, or enter a search string and watch the page attempt to complete the request with type-ahead capability. Type-ahead is when you start typing in a text box on a page and the system then attempts to complete the words you are typing. This is something that you regularly see in search pages today.

From a performance standpoint, this capability can take a tremendous load off your system by preventing full-page refreshes with every request. Portals are dynamic in nature, so the performance impact is already heightened as the portal server aggregates different portlets based on the current user's role and context. This is powerful stuff that has become mainstream within the development community. Understanding and enabling these details around using Ajax within your organization can help you to present a more modern and flexible presentation to your end users.

What do we mean by role and context? A user's role is fairly understandable. It can equate to a number of factors, but mostly it is about the relationship of the user with or within the organization. Is the user a

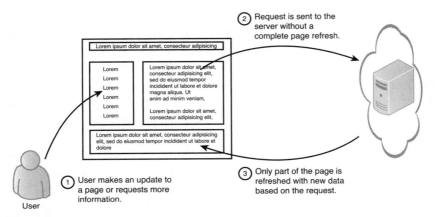

Figure 3.1 Simple Ajax interaction

manager, customer, supplier, or something else entirely? You can think of a role as a logical representation for the actual groups of which a user is a part. Generally, a role equates to one or more groups, which determine physical access to portions of a website.

A user's context is a more complex question to answer because it depends on a number of factors. Generally, you can think of context as what the user is doing at that particular time in the site. Is the user performing a search, viewing content, or interacting with some business functionality or application? Figure 3.2 shows a simple context around the example that we will be building within this chapter.

Figure 3.2 should be Users → assigned to → Groups → mapped to → Roles/Profiles.

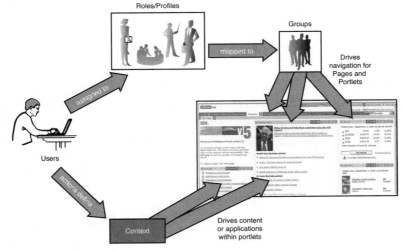

Figure 3.2 User role versus context

The customer example is a portlet or set of portlets that interact to display information about the Classic Models customer list. Classic Models is a dataset that is used for many of the examples used within this book. It is a fairly standard set of information about a fictitious company that can be adapted to almost any situation. This idea of a customer list is but one simple example, but there are many applications. Products, employees, and locations are all items that a user might need to browse, examine, or modify as part of some business process.

Although simple, this customer list example is complete enough to get a feel for how this would work in a real application. Displaying information from a large dataset in a usable manner is something that can be complex to design and build. In this chapter, we will build this example in a couple of different ways and take advantage of tooling and frameworks to simplify the effort yet still deliver a quality user experience. Figure 3.3 shows the example that will be discussed. Information is displayed in a general customer list, and then as a user clicks on a customer, more detail about that customer displays.

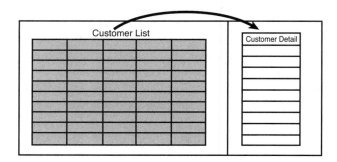

Figure 3.3   Customer Ajax portlets

The real-time update of the data is another area where we need to illustrate how this approach can both improve the user experience and at the same time allow for better capacity growth within the site infrastructure. It is truly rare that those two often-competing goal coincide. Essentially, the portlet will display a grid with summary type of information about each customer. This grid will be loaded via Ajax after the initial page load. This enables the server to deliver the page to the browser without having to wait for the data to be queried within the application. This wait is often a bottleneck, or at least cause a delay. The second interaction will occur when a user chooses or clicks a customer from the initial list; when that occurs, the complete data will load in the customer detail portion of the portal in real time.

Start with the Service

Chapter 1, "Web 2.0 and Social Networking," outlined the idea of REpresentational State Transfer (REST) services and their usefulness in Ajax environments. For the first example, we need to build a service to use within our portlet. We actually need the following two services:

- A Customers List service that returns some type of list of customers. This is possibly a summary set of information about all customers or some set of customers.
- A Customer service that returns more detail about a specific customer.

Because we are focusing on using URL-based REST services, these are pretty easy to mock up for our example. We must decide how the data is represented when it is returned. We have a few options, and the most common is Extensible Markup Language (XML) based on JavaScript Object Notation (JSON). In this case, let's use JSON because it can be handled easily within the JavaScript code later within the portlet. We know that a REST service is resource oriented and follows the web protocol. So the end result of our service should be accessible via a straightforward URL. Figure 3.4 shows the end result of our Customer service. By accessing the service URL of http://myhost/.Customer/resources/customer/114, we are directly requesting information about customer number 114. By changing the ID or number of the resource, we are requesting to receive information about other customers.

Services such as this are so simple to build that not much is needed. Of course, we are looking only at the initial GET request for some data.

Figure 3.4 Customer REST service

Updating, inserting, and deleting data requires some additional complexity. Here we will build a simple servlet-based REST service to return the requested data as JSON. If you are familiar with servlet programming, this code will be recognizable. Specifically, this servlet will be deployed along with the portlet itself. Note that we are importing the ClassicModelsService in the servlet. This service provides the data access functionality to the servlet, so we don't have to bother with all the Java DataBase Connectivity (JDBC) access. The code for this data service is included with the chapter examples:

```
package com.cm.portlet.customer;
```

```
import com.ibmpress.cm.model.Customers;
import com.ibmpress.cm.service.ClassicModelsService;
import java.io.IOException;
import java.io.Writer;
import javax.servlet.Servlet;
import javax.servlet.ServletException;
import javax.servlet.http.*;

public class CustomerResource extends HttpServlet implements Servlet
{

public CustomerResource() {}
```

The magic for our example happens in the doGet() method of the servlet. Remember that REST services follow HTTP, and so we can map directly to the methods available within a common servlet, such as doGet(), doPut(), and doPost(). The first part of the doGet() method is the most interesting. Although the code might not be the most formalized, it gets the job done in a simple manner. Essentially, the customerID comes from the request and then calls the ClassicModelsService to return the data for that customer:

```
protected void doGet(HttpServletRequest request, HttpServletResponse
response) throws ServletException, IOException
```

```
{

    Writer out = response.getWriter();

    try {

    String customer = request.getPathInfo();
    customer = customer.substring(1);

    int customerID = Integer.parseInt(customer);
    System.out.println("CustomerResource-GET cid=" + customerID);

    ClassicModelsService cmService = ClassicModelsService.getInstance();

    Customers cust = cmService.findCustomerById(customerID);
```

The second part of the method, shown below, is all output to the servlet response based on the data that was returned. Notice that the data is formatted to adhere to the JSON specification so that it can be easily used by the client. I consider this the poor man's way of creating JSON and a REST service, but it works, and it helps you fully understand what we are trying to achieve:

```
    out.write((new
StringBuilder("{\"customerid\":\"")).append(cust.getCustomernumber()).append
("\",").toString());

    out.write((new
StringBuilder("\"customername\":\"")).append(cust.getCustomername()).append(
"\",").toString());

    out.write((new
StringBuilder("\"contactfirstname\":\"")).append(cust.getContactfirstname())
.append("\",").toString());

    out.write((new
StringBuilder("\"contactlastname\":\"")).append(cust.getContactlastname()).
append("\",").toString());

    out.write((new
StringBuilder("\"salesrep\":\"")).append(cust.getSalesrepemployeenumber()).
append("\",").toString());

    out.write((new
StringBuilder("\"address1\":\"")).append(cust.getAddressline1()).append("\",
").toString());

    out.write((new
StringBuilder("\"address2\":\"")).append(cust.getAddressline2()).append("\",
").toString());
```

```
out.write((new
StringBuilder("\"city\":\"")).append(cust.getCity()).append("\",").toString(
));
            out.write((new
StringBuilder("\"country\":\"")).append(cust.getCountry()).append("\",").
toString());

out.write((new
StringBuilder("\"state\":\"")).append(cust.getState()).append("\",").
toString());

out.write((new
StringBuilder("\"postalcode\":\"")).append(cust.getPostalcode()).append("\",
").toString());

out.write((new
StringBuilder("\"phone\":\"")).append(cust.getPhone()).append("\",").
toString());

out.write((new
StringBuilder("\"creditlimit\":\"")).append(cust.getCreditlimit()).append("\
"}").toString());


}catch(Exception ex){

System.out.println("CustomerResource-GET: " + ex.getStackTrace());
}

}
```

Java gurus will notice that the code is creating a new object for each line instead of using a single `StringBuilder` to append all output. This type of optimization should definitely be considered as this code moves into a product-ready mode.

For completeness, the `doPost()` method shown here is included within the servlet code. However, nothing is implemented at this point:

```
protected void doPost(HttpServletRequest httpservletrequest,
HttpServletResponse httpservletresponse) throws ServletException,
IOException {}


}
```

The end result, shown next, is a nice normalized set of data that can be easily consumed by a JavaScript or Ajax client. As noted, this approach can be implemented for almost any data type where you need quick and easy integration and access:

```
{
"customerid":"114",
"customername":"Australian Collectors, Co.",
"contactfirstname":"Peter",
"contactlastname":"Ferguson",
"salesrep":"1611",
"address1":"636 St Kilda Road",
"address2":"Level 3",
"city":"Melbourne",
"country":"Australia",
"state":"Victoria",
"postalcode":"3004",
"phone":"03 9520 4555",
"creditlimit":"117300.0"
}
```

As mentioned previously, the data can also be represented via XML, or even both types can be represented for the most flexible approach.

Standardized REST Services

As with most technologies, full adoption comes at a slower pace. Serious adoption can occur only with standardization. For REST standardization, it comes in the form of a standard called JAX-RS (JSR000311), which is the standard for a REST-style service implementation framework. There are currently several implementations of this specification. However, none have yet become the leader in the field. This will change over the next couple of years as REST becomes standardized within the industry. Organizations that naturally gravitate toward industry standards will be able to adopt whichever implementation emerges.

As of this writing, we are in the early adoption phases of some emerging JAX-RS implementations, and it is unsure which of these will emerge as the final set of standards. In the meantime, review the specification for JAX-RS (some light reading) to be sure you are up to speed on the direction of this important technology.

Writing Dojo Portlets

In this recent release for version 6.1, Dojo is the Ajax framework that has been incorporated into WebSphere Portal. There are several strong Ajax frameworks. However, as suggested, standardization is important, and IBM has standardized on Dojo for the portal platform (see Figure 3.5). For this reason, it is important to see how to work with this particular framework and the portal to build Ajax portlets. Remember that portals are shared frameworks, and so if everyone just did his or her own thing, you might quickly have problems.

Figure 3.5   Dojo toolkit

This does not mean, however, that your organization cannot decide that another framework fits your needs better. It is actually not that difficult to incorporate other frameworks into your portal environment. But this brings me to rule one: Don't fight the framework.

This rule is an important one. We all have our own preconceived ideas about how things should be done. We also all know that we could do things better given the chance. Trying to retrofit a design outside of the portal framework is a dangerous choice and goes against why we made the decision to use a portal framework in the first place. A business requirement often leads to a decision that a different approach is necessary. Meeting the business need is the goal. However, there can be ways to meet the business goals without rewriting the whole portal framework. The tradeoff is often between customization and functionality. However, when there is no other way, you'll be ready dig in and redesign with the best of them.

Where Are We Headed?

Nothing helps a project succeed like a good design. Fully understanding not only the requirements but also the technical approach enables a developer to move at full speed without having to stop and ask a lot of questions. Unfortunately, this is not reality in most projects.

In this example, we want to use the dojox.grid component, as shown in Figure 3.6, to display a list of customer data. In addition, we will use other Dojo widgets to display detailed customer information in real time as a user clicks on different customers in the grid.

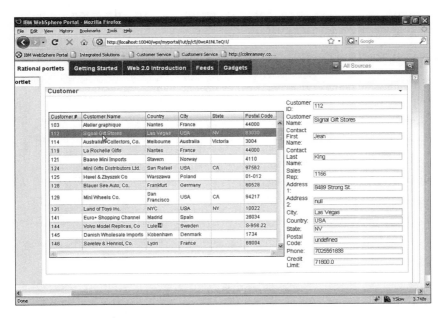

Figure 3.6 Dojo portlet example

Another goal is to build an Ajax portlet using the Dojo toolkit that is *built into* WebSphere Portal. The key here is leveraging the Dojo implementation that is provided with portal. It's easy to package your own version of Dojo and other libraries in the portlet .war. This helps to avoid any package or version conflicts. However, this is not always the correct approach. Suppose every portlet packaged dependent libraries within its individual .war file. You would potentially have dozens of copies of the same libraries loaded within the JVM.

The final project in the IDE is a straightforward Web or .war project. Within the source (src) code directory, there are three Java files:

- **CustomerPortlet.java:**   This is the actual portlet code. It doesn't do much, as you will see, except call the .jsp file to display the data.
- **CustomerResource.java:**   This is the REST service for a customer. We built this service in the earlier example.
- **CustomersResource.java:**   This is a REST service for a list of customers. This example is used in the file portlet.

Figure 3.7 shows these three listed in the .src direction under the package com.cm.portlet.customer.

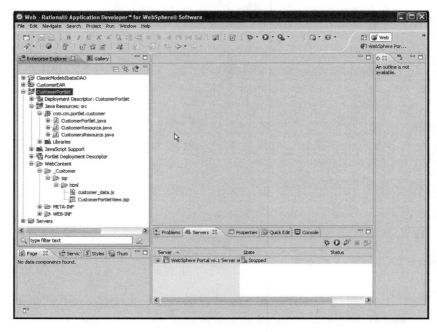

Figure 3.7   Dojo portlet RAD project

Figure 3.7 also shows two important client-side files in the WebContent directory:

- **Customer_data.js:**   This is a sample static data file that is used to initially load the grid in the sample code. In the final code, we remove this and load the grid directly from the service in real time.
- **CustomerPortletView.jsp:**   This is the view Java Server Page (JSP) that is used to display the Dojo components and interact with the end user.

The only missing piece from this puzzle is the data access service that is also provided as part of the sample code. Unfortunately, this is not the focus of this book. However, in previous books, such as *Application Architecture for WebSphere*, I have outlined how to build these services in detail.

How Should the Portlet Work?

Remember in an Ajax application that the business logic moves to the client in the form of JavaScript. In a non-Ajax application, you normally make a call to the server for every action, which would then return a new page with the data that is being requested.

The flow is similar in a client-side application. However, the implementation is different. We still need to determine the logic and which methods or JavaScript functions will need to be called. Figure 3.8 outlines the flow of logic that occurs when a user clicks on a customer listed in the grid.

This flow is a mixture of Dojo and non-Dojo functions, which enables us to easily define the business logic yet leverage functionality from the Dojo toolkit when required. Let's look at the flow in some detail.

Initially, the page is loaded with an empty grid; however, the onLoad() method runs right away, and the customer grid data is displayed. This happens before the sequence displayed in Figure 3.8 even begins. The user cannot click on a customer until the customer list data is loaded. Let's follow the sequence in Figure 3.8 more closely:

1. The sequence begins when a user selects a customer or row from the grid in the portlet display.
2. When this occurs, the CustomerSelect function is called by the grid. This is done by defining the onRowSelect on the grid object.

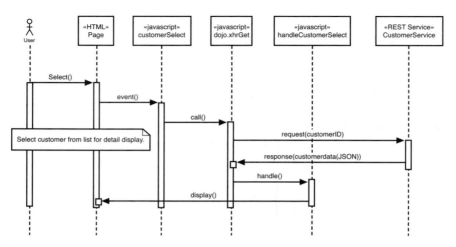

Figure 3.8 Initial customer list display

3. The CustomerSelect function is told the customer number of the row that was selected by the user and creates a URL using this customer number that can access the REST service.

4. The dojo.xhrGet command is called using the defined URL to call the REST service and handle the result.

5. If successful, the handleCustomerSelect function is called and passed the result from the xhrGet. The function handleCustomerSelect then populates the table containing the fields, which display the customer detail. If the xhrGet is not successful, an error is thrown, and an alert is shown.

It's always a bit confusing at first, but understanding the flow of events helps you trace how the page interacts with the user. Admittedly, this seems backward, but you can see how the page reacts to user actions. The second (or rather the first) flow (see Figure 3.9) shows how the customer data actually gets loaded in the first place.

For the initial load, we need a trigger similar to the onRowSelect used to load the customer detail. Let's look at the flow in detail:

1. We use the dojo.addonLoad function to trigger the initial data load. This function is called when the portlet is loaded on the page.

2. The addonLoad function calls the getCustomerList function to set up and retrieve the customer data.

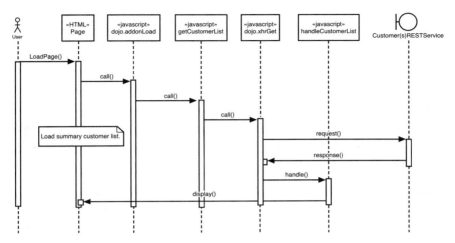

Figure 3.9 Customer detail display

3. Embedded within the getCustomerList function is a dojo.xhrGet function, which calls the customers service and retrieves the result.

4. If the call is successful, the handleCustomerList method is called, which loads the grid with the new data. If it is not successful, an error is called.

The flows are similar, but with different triggers. After you understand the overall approach, it will become second nature to start this way and then build as your experience grows.

Namespace Requirements

Portlets normally share space on a portal page, and additional rules often go along with this aspect of portlet development. One of those rules is the idea of namespace encoding any variables that might clash with a different portlet. You might think that the value you are using to identify the customer ID is unique, but another portlet on the page could easily be using a similar name.

Most of the time, it is actually hard to clash values with another portlet on a page, but it can happen. For this reason, you want to namespace encode your variables so that no clash occurs with other portlets. You will see within the JSP the following line early in the code:

```
String namespace = renderResponse.getNamespace();
```

The namespace `String` can now be used to distinctly name all the variables and functions within your code.

Writing a Portlet

Chapter 2 discussed how portlets work and some of the specifications for portlet development. This chapter looks at how the portlet is written, and then moves into the important Dojo stuff. A portlet is similar to a servlet except for the major point that it has to live in a shared space. When you think of a portlet, you might imagine a web archive or .war file as the portlet. However, another way to think about a portlet is as a particular Java class that extends the class `GenericPortlet`. This portlet contains the core methods that are called when a portlet needs to be rendered or some user action has occurred.

The beginning of the file is general package naming and standard portlet imports. The `CustomerPortlet` extends the class `GenericPortlet`, which enables it to inherit portlet-based objects and implement the standard portlet methods such as `doView()`:

```
package com.cm.portlet.customer;


import java.io.IOException;
import javax.portlet.*;

public class CustomerPortlet extends GenericPortlet
{

    public CustomerPortlet() {}

    public void init()
        throws PortletException
    {
        super.init();
    }
}
```

The `doView()` method is where all the action occurs within this class file. This method is not exciting. It simply identifies the main view JSP and then includes that JSP within the request dispatcher. Basically, this method calls the view JSP, which will do all the work:

```
    public void doView(RenderRequest request, RenderResponse response)
        throws PortletException, IOException
```

```
    {
        response.setContentType(request.getResponseContentType());
        PortletRequestDispatcher rd =
getPortletContext().getRequestDispatcher(getJspFilePath(request,
"CustomerPortletView"));
        rd.include(request, response);
        return;
    }
```

The rest of the code is also unexciting. Several helper methods are
used to determine the markup and location of the JSP files. This is standard code generated by the portlet toolkit within Rational® Application
Developer:

```
    private static String getJspFilePath(RenderRequest request, String
jspFile)
    {
        String markup = request.getProperty("wps.markup");
        if(markup == null)
            markup = getMarkup(request.getResponseContentType());
        return (new
StringBuilder("/_Customer/jsp/")).append(markup).append("/").append(jspFile)
.append(".").append(getJspExtension(markup)).toString();
    }

    private static String getMarkup(String contentType)
    {
        if("text/vnd.wap.wml".equals(contentType))
            return "wml";
        else
            return "html";
    }

    private static String getJspExtension(String markupName)
    {
        return "jsp";
    }

    public static final String JSP_FOLDER = "/_Customer/jsp/";
    public static final String VIEW_JSP = "CustomerPortletView";
}
```

Finally, note that two static values are defined, which identify the
location and name of the view JSP. These constants are typically used to
provide consistent naming within the portlet code.

Writing the JSP

Working through the JSP code will be a bit of an exercise. The first
step is to outline all the different parts of the JSP in the hope that it

makes sense when you see how the complete code example fits together. Initially, this is a pretty standard JSP file that requires standard Java includes for the code to run:

```
<%@page session="false" contentType="text/html" pageEncoding="ISO-8859-1"
import="java.util.*,javax.portlet.*,com.cm.portlet.customer.CustomerPortlet.
*,java.net.URL;" %>
<%@taglib uri="http://java.sun.com/portlet" prefix="portlet" %>
<portlet:defineObjects/>
```

The next section creates some basic housekeeping variables that will be used by some of the function calls. The namespace encoding variable is one, but we also generate the URL for the REST services being deployed with this portlet. It is true that a service such as this one does not need to be deployed within the portlet .war file. These services can be deployed and managed separately. This is especially important if a service needs to be shared across multiple portlets or clients.

Next in the following sample, we provide some setup information that defines the look and feel of the grid component within the page. Dojo components can follow predefined themes, one of which is the tundra theme. This is what makes all the widgets look and feel very similar:

```
<%
//some basic housekeeping and setup.

String namespace = renderResponse.getNamespace();

String HostURL = renderRequest.getScheme() + "://" +
renderRequest.getServerName() + ":" + renderRequest.getServerPort();

String custURL = renderRequest.getContextPath()+"/resources/customer";
%>

<style type="text/css">
@import "<%=HostURL%>/wps/themes/dojo/portal_dojo/dojox/grid/Grid.css";

@import "<%=HostURL%>/wps/themes/dojo/portal_dojo/dojo/resources/dojo.css";

@import
"<%=HostURL%>/wps/themes/dojo/portal_dojo/dojox/grid/_grid/tundraGrid.css";

  body {
    font-size: 0.9em;
    font-family: Geneva, Arial, Helvetica, sans-serif;
  }
  .heading {
    font-weight: bold;
    padding-bottom: 0.25em;
  }
  #grid {
    border: 1px solid #333;
```

```
    width: 35em;
    height: 30em;
  }

</style>
```

Although some of the Dojo libraries are included within the portal theme, or at least they should be, not all of them are. Some tradeoffs are involved in this process. The Dojo libraries should be included within the theme to ensure that all the portlets can share the same set of functions. The out-of-the-box (OOB) example is included with the Web 2.0 theme in WebSphere Portal 6.1. However, the Dojo toolkit consists of a lot of functionality; and to help reduce the amount of data that is downloaded to the client, not every library needs to be included.

The grid component requires a set of client-side libraries so that it can function properly. We include those libraries in the JSP. In truth, we are not using all these libraries within our example. However, it could easily be the case that you are building a complex grid component and would need all of these features:

```
<script type="text/javascript"
src="<%=HostURL%>/wps/themes/dojo/portal_dojo/dojox/grid/_grid/lib.js">
  </script>
  <script type="text/javascript"
src="<%=HostURL%>/wps/themes/dojo/portal_dojo/dojox/grid/_grid/drag.js">
  </script>
  <script type="text/javascript"
src="<%=HostURL%>/wps/themes/dojo/portal_dojo/dojox/grid/_grid/scroller.js">
  </script>
  <script type="text/javascript"
src="<%=HostURL%>/wps/themes/dojo/portal_dojo/dojox/grid/_grid/builder.js">
  </script>
  <script type="text/javascript"
src="<%=HostURL%>/wps/themes/dojo/portal_dojo/dojox/grid/_grid/cell.js">
  </script>
  <script type="text/javascript"
src="<%=HostURL%>/wps/themes/dojo/portal_dojo/dojox/grid/_grid/layout.js">
  </script>
  <script type="text/javascript"
src="<%=HostURL%>/wps/themes/dojo/portal_dojo/dojox/grid/_grid/rows.js">
  </script>
  <script type="text/javascript"
src="<%=HostURL%>/wps/themes/dojo/portal_dojo/dojox/grid/_grid/focus.js">
  </script>
  <script type="text/javascript"
src="<%=HostURL%>/wps/themes/dojo/portal_dojo/dojox/grid/_grid/selection.js">
  </script>
  <script type="text/javascript"
src="<%=HostURL%>/wps/themes/dojo/portal_dojo/dojox/grid/_grid/edit.js">
  </script>
```

```
  <script type="text/javascript"
src="<%=HostURL%>/wps/themes/dojo/portal_dojo/dojox/grid/_grid/view.js">
  </script>
  <script type="text/javascript"
src="<%=HostURL%>/wps/themes/dojo/portal_dojo/dojox/grid/_grid/views.js">
  </script>
  <script type="text/javascript"
src="<%=HostURL%>/wps/themes/dojo/portal_dojo/dojox/grid/_grid/rowbar.js">
  </script>
  <script type="text/javascript"
src="<%=HostURL%>/wps/themes/dojo/portal_dojo/dojox/grid/_grid/publicEvents.
js">
  </script>
  <script type="text/javascript"
src="<%=HostURL%>/wps/themes/dojo/portal_dojo/dojox/grid/VirtualGrid.js">
  </script>
  <script type="text/javascript"
src="<%=HostURL%>/wps/themes/dojo/portal_dojo/dojox/grid/_data/fields.js">
  </script>
  <script type="text/javascript"
src="<%=HostURL%>/wps/themes/dojo/portal_dojo/dojox/grid/_data/model.js">
  </script>
  <script type="text/javascript"
src="<%=HostURL%>/wps/themes/dojo/portal_dojo/dojox/grid/_data/editors.js">
  </script>
  <script type="text/javascript"
src="<%=HostURL%>/wps/themes/dojo/portal_dojo/dojox/grid/Grid.js">
  </script>
```

Along with the grid component, we use a set of text box widgets for display of the customer detail information. Next, we need to set up all the required widgets that we will use. Again, for this example, we are not using all these components. However, you can experiment with different dojo.dijit elements to see how they work within a page:

```
<script type="text/javascript">

  dojo.require("dijit.form.TextBox");
  dojo.require("dijit.form.Button");
  dojo.require("dijit.form.DateTextBox");
  dojo.require("dijit.form.ValidationTextBox");
  dojo.require("dijit.layout.TabContainer");
  dojo.require("dijit.layout.ContentPane");
  dojo.require("dojox.grid.Grid");
  dojo.require("dojox.grid._data.model");
```

Setting up the grid is one of the most important elements of the page. Grid components require a layout definition and a model definition. The layout definition defines the rows and columns that the grid will display. The model definition is the set of data that will be displayed within the layout. A layout can be quite complex, with rows and columns embedded within other rows and columns to be expanded as required. The layout is set up as an array of views. This example shows a simple set of columns that correspond to some summary customer data:

```
var data = null;
var model = null;

// this simple view lays out the columns in the grid.
var view1 = {
  cells: [
    [
      {name: 'Customer #'},
      {name: 'Customer Name', width: "150px"},
      {name: 'Country'},
      {name: 'City'},
      {name: 'State'},
      {name: 'Postal Code'}
    ]
  ]
};

// a grid layout is an array of views.
var layout = [ view1 ];
```

Next, you write out the required functions. The first function is designed to handle the customer list data that comes when the page is loaded. Because the customer data is returned as JSON, it is easily translated into a format that can be used by the grid. In this case, we set the variable of data to the responseObject, which contains the returned set of data. Then, the model value is set to a Table representation of that data. Finally, we parse the page element where the grid is contained to allow the grid to display the data:

```
function handleCustomerList(responseObject, ioArgs){
  data = responseObject;
  model = new dojox.grid.data.Table(null, data);
  dojo.parser.parse("<%=namespace%>CustomerData");
}
```

The function getCustomerList() is called by the addonLoad() function to get the initial customer data for the grid. This function calls the dojo.xhrGet() on the customers REST service and then handles the result. If the call is successful, it calls the previous handleCustomerList() function to load the data, as shown here:

```
function getCustomerList(){
  var targetURL = "http://localhost:10040/.Customer/resources/customers";
  dojo.xhrGet({
    url: targetURL,
    handleAs: "json",
```

```
    load: handleCustomerList,
    error: handleError
  })
}
```

The handleCustomerSelect() function is similar to the handleCustomer
List() function. They are called by different methods, but are both used
to manage the data returned from a successful xhrGet() call. In this case,
the function is used to display the retrieved detail customer data from a
user selection.

In this next part, the function simply goes down the list of text boxes
and sets the display value to the elements in the data result that we
received from the server:

```
//this function displays the customer data in the side fields.
function handleCustomerSelect(responseObject, ioArgs){

  var customerid = dijit.byId("customerid");
  customerid.setDisplayedValue(responseObject.customerid);

  var customername = dijit.byId("customername");
  customername.setDisplayedValue(responseObject.customername);

  var contactfirstname = dijit.byId("contactfirstname");
  contactfirstname.setDisplayedValue(responseObject.contactfirstname);

  var contactlastname = dijit.byId("contactlastname");
  contactlastname.setDisplayedValue(responseObject.contactlastname);

  var salesrep = dijit.byId("salesrep");
  salesrep.setDisplayedValue(responseObject.salesrep);

  var address1 = dijit.byId("address1");
  address1.setDisplayedValue(responseObject.address1);

  var address2 = dijit.byId("address2");
  address2.setDisplayedValue(responseObject.address2);

  var city = dijit.byId("city");
  city.setDisplayedValue(responseObject.city);

  var country = dijit.byId("country");
  country.setDisplayedValue(responseObject.country);

  var state = dijit.byId("state");
  state.setDisplayedValue(responseObject.state);

  var postalcode = dijit.byId("postalcode");
  postalcode.setDisplayedValue(responseObject.portalcode);

  var phone = dijit.byId("phone");
  phone.setDisplayedValue(responseObject.phone);
```

```
  var creditlimit = dijit.byId("creditlimit");
  creditlimit.setDisplayedValue(responseObject.creditlimit);
}
```

The handleError() function is used by both of the xhrGet calls. In reality, you might not want to use the same function. However, in this case, an alert box is displayed to inform us that an error occurred. The error function is defined in the xhrGet method as the appropriate error handler. Note that the error handler might also be called by the load handler if an error occurs in that part of the process. In other words, the xhrGet() function might be successful. However, if a problem occurs in handling the result, an error might be thrown. Also shown is the customerSelect() method, which is called when a user selects a row in the grid:

```
//simple error handler when something goes wrong.
function handleError(responseObject, ioArgs){
  alert("error");
}


//this function retrieves the customer data when you click on a grid row.
//when successful the function 'handleResponse' takes over.
function customerSelect(event){

  var activeCustomer = data[event.rowIndex][0];
  var targetURL = "<%=custURL%>/"+activeCustomer;

  dojo.xhrGet({
    url: targetURL,
    handleAs: "json",
    load: handleCustomerSelect,
    error: handleError
  })
}
```

The addOnLoad() function is key to starting the interaction when the page is initially loaded. This function calls getCustomerList() to initiate the process:

```
//this function triggers the initial loading of the grid data.
dojo.addOnLoad(function() {
  getCustomerList();
});

</script>
```

At this point, the main JavaScript is complete, and we need to set up the actual page elements for the display. The <div> element wraps this entire portion of the JSP and is used to trigger the parse event for the grid data loading. The grid is a Dojo extension (dojox) element and is pretty easy to set up after all the dependent functions and the model have been created. Note how the div id has been namespace encoded to prevent conflicts with other page elements:

```
<div id="<%=namespace%>CustomerData" >


<table border="0" cellspacing="3" cellpadding="3" width="100%">
<tr>
<td>

      <!— setup the grid to display the data. —>
      <div jsid="grid"
           id="grid"
           dojoType="dojox.Grid"
           autoWidth="true"
           onRowClick="customerSelect"
           model="model"
           structure="layout">
      </div>

</td>
<td>
```

The table layout for the detail customer information is a standard HTML table embedded with Dojo text components.

With this example, all the elements in the form shown here have been configured as dijit.form.TextBox elements. However, different elements are available to provide a richer experience for your users:

```
<!— Lay out the table for the customer detail information. —>
<table border="0" cellspacing="3" cellpadding="3">
<tr>
<td>Customer ID:</td>
<td><input id="customerid" type="text" name="customerid"
dojoType="dijit.form.TextBox"/>
</td>
</tr>
<tr>
<td>Customer Name:</td>
<td><input type="text" id="customername" name="customername"
dojoType="dijit.form.TextBox"/></td>
</tr>
<tr>
<td>Contact First Name:</td>
<td><input type="text" id="contactfirstname" name="contactfirstname"
dojoType="dijit.form.TextBox"/></td>
</tr>
<tr>
<td>Contact Last Name:</td>
```

```
<td><input type="text" id="contactlastname" name="contactlastname"
dojoType="dijit.form.TextBox"/></td>
</tr>
<tr>
<td>Sales Rep:</td><td><input type="text" id="salesrep" name="salesrep"
dojoType="dijit.form.TextBox"/></td>
</tr>
<tr>
<td>Address 1:</td><td><input type="text" id="address1" name="address1"
dojoType="dijit.form.TextBox"/></td>
</tr>
<tr>
<td>Address 2:</td><td><input type="text" id="address2" name="address2"
dojoType="dijit.form.TextBox"/></td>
</tr>
<tr>
<td>City:</td><td><input type="text" id="city" name="city"
dojoType="dijit.form.TextBox"/></td>
</tr>
<tr>
<td>Country:</td><td><input type="text" id="country" name="country"
dojoType="dijit.form.TextBox"/></td>
</tr>
<tr>
<td>State:</td><td><input type="text" id="state" name="state"
dojoType="dijit.form.TextBox"/></td>
</tr>
<tr>
<td>Postal Code:</td><td><input type="text" id="postalcode"
name="postalcode" dojoType="dijit.form.TextBox"/></td>
</tr>
<tr>
<td>Phone:</td><td><input type="text" id="phone" name="phone"
dojoType="dijit.form.TextBox"/></td>
</tr>
<tr>
<td>Credit Limit:</td><td><input type="text" id="creditlimit"
name="creditlimit" dojoType="dijit.form.TextBox"/></td>
</tr>
</table>

</td>
</tr>
</table>

</div>
```

That's it! There is still a lot of behind-the-scenes detail involved with using Dojo and embedding Ajax within the portal framework. However, this example should provide a great head start in building your own portlet applications. One thing that we did not do was provide name-space encoding on the example Dojo ID elements. This is actually necessary for portal applications to ensure that your elements do not interfere with another set of elements created by someone else. We left those out to keep the code sample easier to understand and read.

Using WebSphere Portlet Factory

Building a similar type of application using WebSphere Portlet Factory (WPF) is also an option for creating applications that provide client-side interaction. WPF has quickly become a key framework for portlet development of all kinds. The approach is a little different when building with WPF, and considerations should be made around which development framework you use.

With the WPF approach, the set of models can work together to provide the required functionality. Specifically, four core models are built, and then a fifth model ties everything together for testing. Figure 3.10 illustrates how the models work together. There are two customer user-facing models, and then two models that work behind the scenes. In this example, the customer list and the customer detail are created as two separate models, with another model to share events between the two so that the customer detail can be updated on demand. The data itself is loaded from methods provided via the data service model. The service

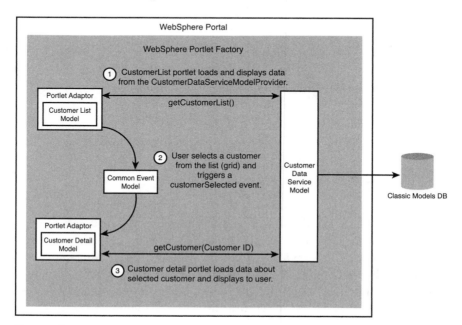

Figure 3.10   WebSphere Portlet Factory (WPF) model overview

provider model is a common pattern for WPF applications, with one model providing information to other models that show the data to the end user.

Looking at the project from within the Eclipse Project Explorer (see Figure 3.11), you can see how the models have been created with the WPF project (WPFProject). Again, this setup is common with WPF projects and follows a best practices approach for building WPF applications. WPF uses components called builders that are wired together to create functionality within a model. Builders range in complexity from a simple Structured Query Language (SQL) call to a complete view and form within a model.

The CustomerServiceProvider model provides two main data services to the application (see Figure 3.12). These services correspond with the REST services that were created in the Java example. We can reuse those existing web services if we deploy them independently from the portlet. WPF provides builders that enable you to use REST services and JSON data. The services provided by the CustomerServiceProvider model include the following:

- **GetCustomerList:** This service provides a complete summary list of customers.

- **GetCustomer:** This service provides detail information about a single customer.

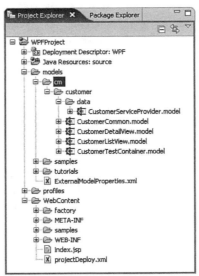

Figure 3.11 WPF project and models

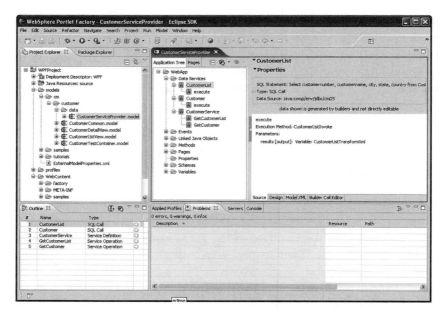

Figure 3.12   CustomerServiceProvider model

The builders used in this model consist of two SQL call builders, which make calls to the database to retrieve customer information and two service operation builders, which expose the service to the outside world or other models.

Getting models to work together requires some type of signal to be passed between them at runtime. In this example, you can build a separate model that can be imported into other models and provide some shared functionality. The CustomerCommon model is designed to provide that function in the form of an event, which can be triggered when necessary (see Figure 3.13). This model uses only the event declaration builder to provide this event service.

The main part of the user interface is the CustomerListView model (see Figure 3.14). This model is used to display the customer summary list to the user. It uses the Imported Model builder to import the CustomerCommon model, which provides the event sequencing.

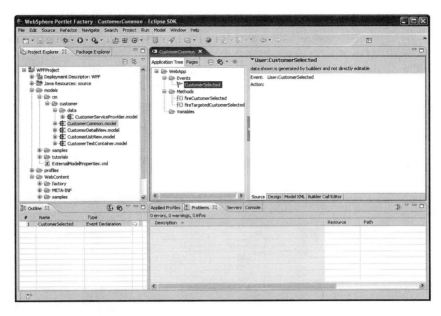

Figure 3.13 CustomerCommon model

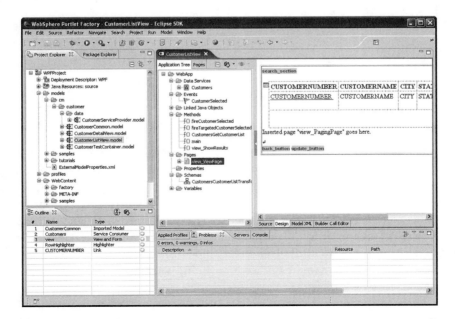

Figure 3.14 CustomerListView model

Multiple builders can be combined to create more advanced functionality. For example, the Highlighter builder is used here to highlight the row within the grid when a user moves her cursor over the row.

The CustomerDetailView model provides the end result for the data the user is looking for (see Figure 3.15). This model displays a complete list of information about a specific customer based on the customer ID that was clicked in the CustomerListView model. This display update is triggered by the CustomerSelected event.

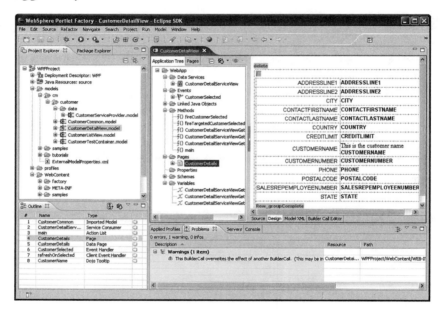

Figure 3.15   CustomerDetailView model

WPF is a model-driven programming framework, which means that it can run in many different environments or on different application servers. When a model is to be provided as a portlet, a portlet adaptor builder is actually added to the model and configured to run within the portal container. This adaptor enables the portlet to look and behave like a JSR 168 portlet to the portlet container. The CustomerTestContainer model is designed to allow you to test how different models will behave when placed on the same page without being within the portal environment itself (see Figure 3.16).

There are many advantages to actually testing in the portal environment, especially when you are testing a specific application programming interface (API) or service provider interface (SPI) that may be

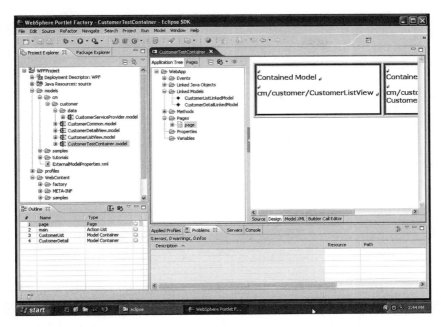

Figure 3.16 CustomerTestContainer model

provided by the portal. For simple testing, however, a Model Container builder enables you to do simple testing within a servlet container, such as that provided with WebSphere Application Server Community Edition.

Running the CustomerTestContainer model provides a view similar to the Dojo example that was created in the first part of this chapter (in the "Writing Dojo Portlets" section). The look and feel is slightly different, but both approaches are customizable to adopt whatever type of them or branding is required for your project (see Figure 3.17).

You can see how building client-side applications can be done using a completely different approach, while using practically no Java. Although in our simple example, there isn't any Java code, this is not always the case. Sometimes some actual Java code is needed to help a builder that is not exactly the right fit for your application. Overall, however, we have generated the same type of user experience using a different set of components: WPF builders rather than Dojo widgets.

You might now be asking this: Where is the Dojo? Several builders are available within WPF that provide actual Dojo functionality.

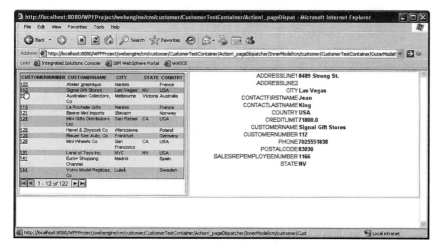

Figure 3.17 WPF customer portlets example

Figure 3.18 shows the Dojo Tooltip builder for adding core user interface functionality. Adding this builder to the model and then mapping to a page and a tag within that page enables the tooltip to be used at runtime.

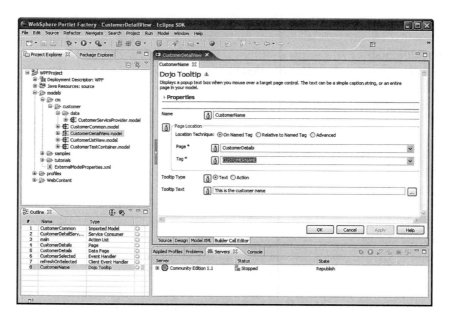

Figure 3.18 WPF Dojo Tooltip builder

Figure 3.19 illustrates this builder in action. By moving your cursor over the correct component, the Dojo functionality is triggered to provide the tooltip to the user.

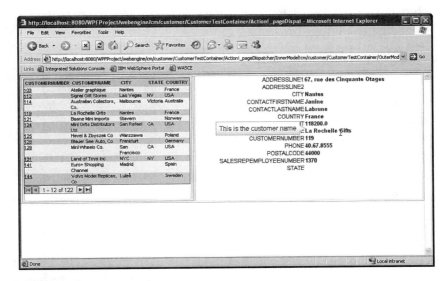

Figure 3.19 WPF Dojo Tooltip in action

This can get you started with building up a dynamic user interface that both looks good and reacts in a way that the user can understand. Although in WPF, we would use a builder to add some Dojo functionality, the Java example can also be extended to add similar capability. Consider our first portlet example built using Dojo. We could modify the example code in the CustomerPortletView.jsp with the following additions:

```
<tr>
<td>Customer Name:</td>
<td><input type="text" id="customername" name="customername"
dojoType="dijit.form.ValidationTextBox" promptMessage="Please enter the
Customer ID" /></td>
</tr>
```

This syntax works better when you are creating a form that allows the user to create or update some data, but you can begin to see how you can extend Dojo to build richer user interfaces.

Comments from the IBM Labs

To get some perspective on portlet development, the following includes comments from leaders in portlet development at IBM. Included in this discussion are Jonathan Booth, Chief Architect of Portlet Factory, and Stefan Hepper, JSR 268 Spec Lead. The goal of this discussion is to provide some additional insight to help you decide on a portlet development framework.

How would you position your main development framework with other frameworks? What are the technical or organizational advantages to a specific approach?

Stefan:

I personally don't have a main development framework. I'll use whatever best fits the needs of the application. That may be pure JSR 286, Portlet Factory, JSF, or Dojo.

Jonathan:

The big technical difference between Portlet Factory and most Java development tools is that Portlet Factory uses a model-driven approach, with "builders" that automate software design patterns, whereas other tools use a more conventional direct Java coding approach. Portlet Factory's model-based approach insulates developers from the technical details behind the design patterns that are implemented by the builders. This can enable very quick development. Portlet Factory also includes builders that support integration with a wide variety of enterprise data sources such as SAP, Domino, web services, and REST services, and I think this integration support is often a factor for organizations deciding to use Portlet Factory. Another unique feature of Portlet Factory is its ability to generate multiple variations of an application from a single source model ("dynamic profiling"), which can be important for many customer scenarios. And one more feature I should mention is that with Portlet Factory, you can use a single set of tools and code (models), and then deploy as portlets, as stand-alone servlet-based applications, as widgets for IBM Mashup Center (as of Portlet Factory 6.1.2), and as components for Lotus Notes® 8.x.

What questions should an organization ask of itself to help decide on a particular framework or direction?

Jonathan:

As you know, IBM offers two advanced tools for portlet development, WebSphere Portlet Factory (WPF) and Rational Application Developer

(RAD). Both support rapid development and automatic deployment of portlet applications, and both tools enable developers to quickly build rich Web 2.0-enabled portal applications that support all the features of the WebSphere Portal framework such as SSO, personalization, and run-time customization. Both are excellent choices for building both portal and nonportal applications.

As far as how to decide which tool to use, I'm afraid I may not have one simple answer to this, though obviously I have a natural bias toward Portlet Factory for most organizations. Certainly the existing developer expertise within the organization should be considered, since any framework involves an investment in learning. We've heard some customers relate that they've had a lot of success using Portlet Factory with development teams that are very new to Java and JEE/J2EE, although I think most teams using Portlet Factory have JEE expertise. Organizations should also consider the importance of key framework features, which for Portlet Factory includes the ones I mentioned such as enterprise data access and dynamic profiling.

I will also acknowledge that there's a personal preference factor when comparing the two development styles offered by WPF and RAD. Some developers seem to have an inherent preference for working directly with the code, while others are happy working at a higher level with Portlet Factory builders.

Stefan:

I agree with Jonathan, in real life these decisions are often triggered by the skills of the team implementing the solution. In general, I think the following questions are important:

- What are the skills of my developers?
- Will the development team also maintain the code (if not, it would be an argument to use more high-level frameworks like WPF)?
- Is the framework a standard?
- What is the best framework for my application?
- Does the framework support JSR 286?

Is there a case when an organization or development team should not consider using your framework?

Jonathan:

In general, we haven't seen many portlet development scenarios where Portlet Factory couldn't work well, as long as the development team is comfortable with the tool. Given that Portlet Factory involves automation of design patterns, I suppose that if there's a highly specialized portlet that doesn't match the design patterns available with Portlet Factory builders, you might consider a hand-coded approach.

We have seen how Ajax has grown to become a top-level technology with support and tooling being provided. How is your framework prepared to handle the next big thing?

Jonathan:

That's one of the things I have appreciated the most in working with Portlet Factory's automation approach: The framework is extremely flexible and can accommodate code generation for any kind of technology. This has included technology ranging from back-end data access and services to the complex client-side and server-side code involved with Ajax. Regardless of the technology, we can create builders that present a simple wizard-like interface for developers to work with, and the builders generate all the code. This makes me very confident about our ability to handle the next big thing, and the one after that, and the one after that.

Where do you see the technology in two years?

Stefan:

I think in the next two years, we'll see the ability to mix client-side and server-side frameworks so that they can communicate data and events. Thus programmers could program with their favorite framework, either client-side or server-side, and you will still be able to create composite applications out of those that span the client-side or server-side frameworks.

Jonathan:

We have a very strong and experienced team working on Portlet Factory, and there are a range of enhancements we'll be delivering in the product. We'll continue to add builders to support new technology and to provide even more automation. One area I know we'll be expanding a lot is support for Web 2.0 and rich client-side UI. Another is application integration and services support, with things like FileNet support and new service-oriented tools. We'll also continue to enhance the developer experience in areas such as graphical development and general usability features.

Another whole area where Portlet Factory-based technology is expanding is in portal "accelerators"—there are more and more of these being created on top of Portlet Factory's automation technology, and they provide companies with very quick "time to value" for specific types of applications, such as dashboards or health care.

Where do you see the technology in five years?

Jonathan:

In this business, it gets hard to predict all the specifics as the time-frames get further out, but I would make some general points. As I mentioned, I feel very good about the ability of our automation framework to provide high value in building any kind of software, so I think you'll see our tooling adapt to provide excellent support for whatever the most important new technologies are. I know we'll continue to add more and more automation (new builders), we'll continue to enhance the developer experience, and we expect to see more and more "accelerator" automation frameworks built on top of our tooling.

Stefan:

In addition to what Jonathan said, I think it may also be the case that we'll be able to model UI flows more like workflows and thus be able to generate the flows automatically and integrate them with business workflows.

Any final comments?

Stefan:

I think that base standards, like JSR 286, will become more important as they allow to bridge between different framework technologies. With JSR 286, you can send events between a struts portlet, a portlet factory portlet, a JSF portlet, and whatever custom portlet framework you have.

Jonathan:

I guess I'd just like to mention the active developer community that's grown up around Portlet Factory, since I think a developer community is a key factor in the success of any development paradigm. The Portlet Factory developer community has a strong web presence, including very active forums and wiki, and there are a couple of books devoted entirely to Portlet Factory, and a number of companies provide services and training for Portlet Factory.

Conclusion

Although there is a lot of information in this chapter, it just scratches the surface on using the Dojo toolkit, WebSphere Portlet Factory, and building client-side applications. There are many complete books on these topics. For a good introduction on using WPF with WebSphere Portal, consider *Programming Portlets, 2nd Ed.* (IBM Press).

One main area to consider is the technical approach you choose for developing your Ajax applications. This is a huge responsibility and you owe it to your organization to make the right decisions. Your choices should be based on many factors, such as current standards, ease of use, available skills within your organization, and any existing or future business requirements.

All these need to factor into your framework decision. Because there are advantages and disadvantages to every option, carefully consider your options on which approach to choose.

References

JSR 000311 (Java Community Process). *JSR-000311 JAX-RS: The Java API for RESTful Web Services.* Accessed Dec. 11, 2009 at http://jcp.org/aboutJava/ communityprocess/final/jsr311/index.html.

4

Social Software for the Enterprise

Social Networking! You can't stop it! Surely you realize that by now. You can try to protect yourself and your organization by putting firewalls and rules in place to keep your employees from doing it, and to help keep the bad guys out, but people find ways to work around these blocks. They are out there using personal computers, unsecured firewalls, and because of the ubiquitous cell phone, people are connecting in ways that we don't even know about yet.

One option is to embrace it, support it, and control it. This approach can provide several advantages. By controlling it, we can ensure that security is a key part of information flowing into and outside of our network. Another advantage is that it just might help your organization. Increased productivity, connectivity, interaction, and knowledge sharing are all part of the social experience. In this chapter, we look at some products and tools that will help expand collaboration in the enterprise, specifically through the use of user profiles, blogs, communities, social bookmarking, and activity-centric computing.

As of this writing, early adoption has already begun as organizations start to learn how to transform their businesses into more collaborative organizations. IBM has been on this path for several years now and has some good ideas about how this works and how to grow adoption and collaboration within an organization.

Lotus Connections

Social software for business can provide a unique opportunity to empower employees, customers, partners, and others to create and join dynamic networks to share information and collaborate over new ideas. Lotus Connections is a set of tools that can be used individually or together to enable people to connect in new and exciting ways. These tools include the following:

- **Activities:** Tools for collecting, organizing, sharing, and reusing work that is related to a project or goal
- **Blogs:** Online journals that you can use to deliver information in real time
- **Communities:** A place where people who share common interests can interact with one another and share resources
- **Dogear:** Social bookmarking tool for saving, organizing, and sharing Internet and intranet bookmarks
- **Profiles:** Directory of the people in your organization, including expertise and interest information you need to form and encourage effective networks

These five tools, along with the integration into your enterprise systems that Lotus Connections provides, can revolutionize the way that business is done in your organization. In addition, the recently released Lotus Connections version 2.5 adds two additional capabilities of File Sharing and Wikis. Figure 4.1 shows the main Lotus Connections home page, where users might start with their Social Networking efforts.

The home page component of Lotus Connections is optional. Actually, all the features of Lotus Connections are options. For a seamless integration of Connections for your users, you can also integrate Lotus Connections into WebSphere Portal.

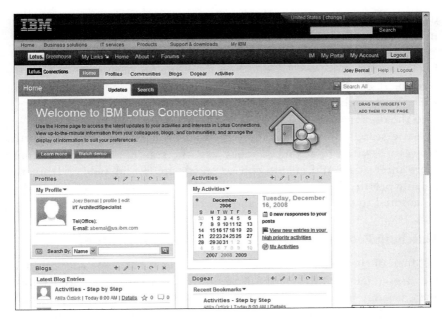

Figure 4.1   IBM Lotus Connections

Managing Your Profile

People are more than titles and phone numbers. Most of us get this and understand that there is a lot of known information about people that can be cataloged and made available. Information such as your department and management chain can tell us where your area of expertise lies. Add a title with some relevance, and you are on the way to creating a useful profile. At IBM, we have a repository called Blue Pages, shown in Figure 4.4 later in this chapter. This comprehensive user repository provides a wealth of information about people at IBM and allows employees to find and connect with colleagues across the globe. This directory of people in the organization shows not only the basic information, but also people's interests, activities, and how and when to contact them. This can enable you to quickly get in touch with people when you need them.

A profile can contain all the stuff that an organization doesn't know or at least doesn't have readily available. For example, a profile might indicate what teams an employee belongs to or what products or services a person works with. It hardly makes sense to bug someone in HR if he does not have experience with payroll, benefits, relocations, or whatever information you seek.

Figure 4.2 shows the initial profile screen for Lotus Connections. Lotus Connections provides one-stop shopping for people in your organization. It enables users to showcase their abilities and interests, along with the more basic information about who they are and where they fit into the organization.

Basic search allows for searching based on name or using keywords. However, switch to advanced mode and the search capabilities become more interesting and enable you to search on several fields within the default profile. Customization is an important factor, as profiles need to be tailored to the organization and not the other way around.

Matching People Through Interests or Responsibilities

Much of the effort is about awareness. Who is out there that can help me or give me the information I need? How can I become better known and share my expertise with others? Another question you might ask is this: Do I or do others have the right skills to accomplish this goal?

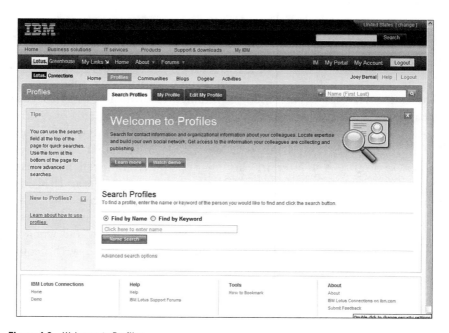

Figure 4.2 Welcome to Profiles

Profiles can help answer those questions in a way that lets you become more approachable to others (see Figure 4.3). If you take the time to advertise your interests and expertise, that must suggest that you are open to sharing this information with others.

Making a Connection

Making a connection is often a matter of whom you know. Often, you can ask someone who works in a particular area, or whom you think might be able to point you in the right direction. The *Tipping Point*, by Malcom Gladwell, uses the following terms to identify people within your organization's social order:

- **Connectors:**   Networking at many levels and in many spheres; the "hubs" of a social network that connect different groups.
- **Mavens:**   Know about many things, or know where to find out; subject matter experts.
- **Salespeople:**   The persuaders or evangelists around an idea or technology.

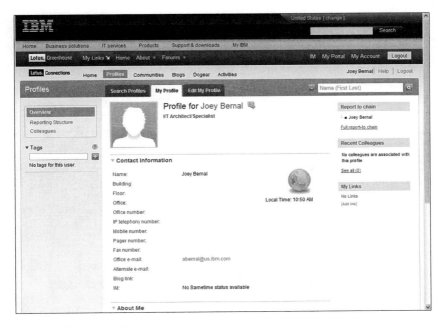

Figure 4.3   Viewing a profile

People will make connections and build their networks differently depending on what type of person they are. Making connections can be tremendously valuable in many situations. Organizations never know where an opportunity might arise for valuable collaboration. IBM has cultivated this type of growth for years through a number of efforts. Obviously, for IBMers, Blue Pages can be the primary source when looking for individuals. Often, a name is mentioned in casual conversation, and a trip to Blue Pages can fill in the details of a possible connection. Figure 4.4 shows the author's Blue Pages entry.

For services and sales teams, a photo can prove invaluable when people are going to meet for the first time or when teams are working remotely. It can be comforting to have some idea of what your coworker looks like, even if you have never met face to face. Also, if you are meeting a coworker for the first time at a meeting or even a customer location, knowing who you are looking for can be invaluable.

As IBM evolves, so does the profile repository or Blue Pages. In fact, there are ongoing studies to determine what information is most valuable when creating new connections. Many times, information, such as about interests or areas of expertise, can be provided only by participants

Figure 4.4   My Blue Pages profile

themselves. However, sometimes information can be readily integrated from other sources such as blogs or wikis.

Sharing Ideas with Blogs

Everyone likes to share their expertise and knowledge. Contributing to the greater community is a natural extension of making connections. Okay, maybe not everyone likes to share information. Some try to hide what they know so as to gain more power, or perhaps for job security. I think there is a new generation of users coming up where this is not the norm, but just in case I thought I would mention it here.

These situations sometimes involve subject matter expertise, and other times they involve a leader who wants to communicate more broadly to a team or organization. In the simplest case, a blog is an online journal, diary, or technical notebook and an effective way to quickly share information with the world. Sometimes it can be commentary that informs a general audience about specific happenings or events. Lotus Connections make blogs and blogging a central part of the functionality, which makes it easy for authorized users to create and maintain a blog on any subject (see Figure 4.5).

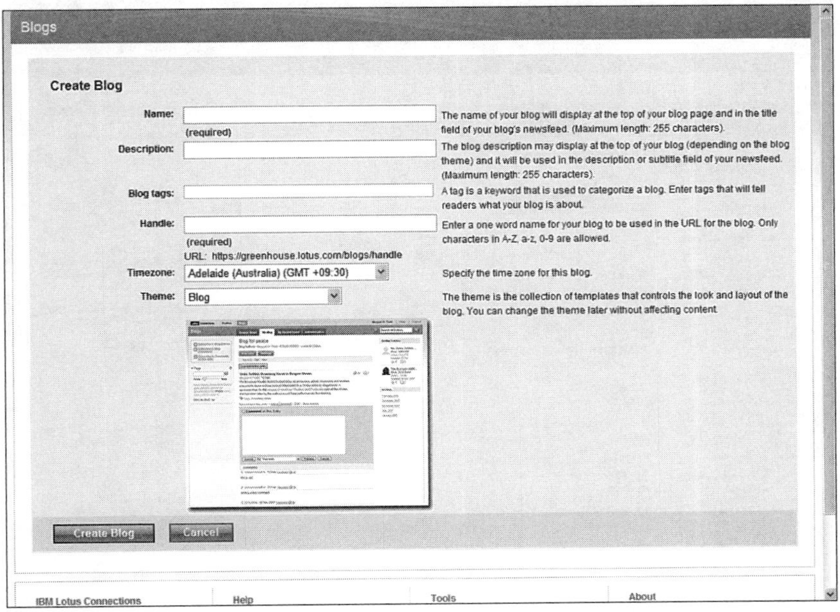

Figure 4.5   Creating a new blog

Ideally, after a blog is available, it should be easy for other users to find and subscribe to it. Within an organizational structure, there are often a lot of top-down types of blogs where managers are looking for an easy way to communicate with a large block of their employees. In addition, experts from many areas often create blogs to share their particular subject matter expertise.

Team blogs have also gained some popularity, especially at IBM. Keeping a blog fresh can be a daunting task, especially when you have real work to do. Partnering up with a number of your coworkers to share the load can be a smart approach and help to provide a broader perspective to your blog. Lotus Connections provides a Blogs component that is shown in Figure 4.6.

In some cases, blogging is not internal, but is about sharing information with your customers. In my case, I started a blog several years ago mostly because I had a lot to say (see Figure 4.7). There were many areas I was exploring, and the only real avenue to share that information was though magazine or journal articles. Because it is much more work to actually write an article, many of the topics were getting put on the shelf and not being shared with anyone.

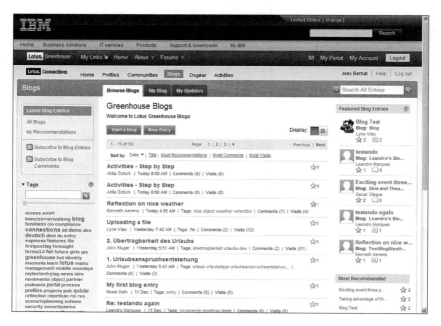

Figure 4.6   Greenhouse Blogs

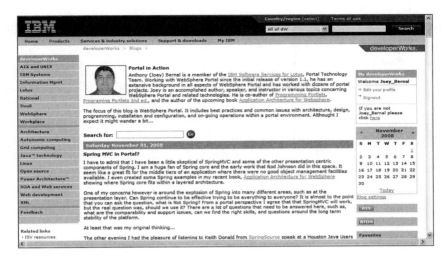

Figure 4.7   The author's portal blog

My blog helped to fix that problem. It was an easy way to share some information that would not make it as a fully fledged article. It was also a way to say something once and then refer others to that entry, instead of digging up the same stuff repeatedly. Wikis actually work better for organizing different information, but a blog keeps a record. I often get questions about information I might want to share with others, so instead of replying directly to the questioner, I write a blog entry and refer them to that instead.

Dogear Your Favorites

The same way some people turn down the corner to mark their favorite places in a book, you can save a collection of bookmarks for future reference or for sharing with others. After all, the Web is a pretty big place. Think about it as a galaxy where your organization's intranet might be considered a planet or even a solar system depending on its size. Keeping track of all the inhabitable planets, or in our case usable information within a sea of noise, can be a daunting task. We all have our bookmarks for frequently used pages or sites that we need to reference in the future. Sharing those bookmarks, however, can prove a bit troublesome, especially when others want to save those links and references in their own system. Figure 4.8 shows the main screen for the Dogear component of Lotus Connections.

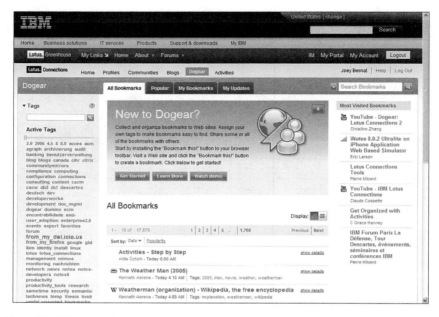

Figure 4.8   Welcome to Dogear

Getting started with Dogear is slightly more involved than other
aspects of Lotus Connections. However, it is fairly easy. The key is
installing the plug-in that can then be used to start bookmarking your
favorite web pages (see Figure 4.9). After the plug-in is installed, it is as
simple as clicking the Bookmark This! button when you see something
that you think might be useful to others.

The act of bookmarking something provides a good set of options.
Bookmarks can be made public or private and can be added to other
Connections features, such as to a community or an activity. This makes
these bookmarks immediately useful to others who share the same passion or goal.

Tagging is another component of bookmarking and blogs. Tagging
allows you to assign keywords to a bookmark. This allows you to search
on tags to find related information or to refer to tags in a tag cloud or
list as you refine your search.

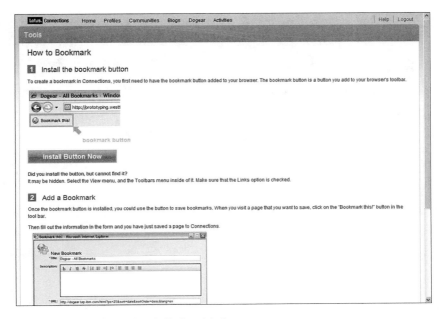

Figure 4.9 Installing and using the Bookmark button

Join In on the Activities

Lotus Connections provides the concept of an activity. Activities are part project management tools and part document repositories. In the past, Lotus Notes users would often set up a team room database to store and share information. With Lotus Connections, this has evolved into a web-enabled approach to managing your team's activities. Activities can be pretty much anything from building a new product to on-boarding new employees. It's the idea of a shared space for collaboration that you can think about in terms of cloud computing for the enterprise. Activities enable you to stay organized as you manage people and actions in a collaborative manner. All of this is stored and shared from a single place available from the Web.

What does that mean? With activities, the information and tasks are stored somewhere on the Internet, or in IBM's case the intranet, and cloud and end users simply need access to the network to participate in the activity. Figure 4.10 shows the main Activities screen where you can search, start, or work on your own activities.

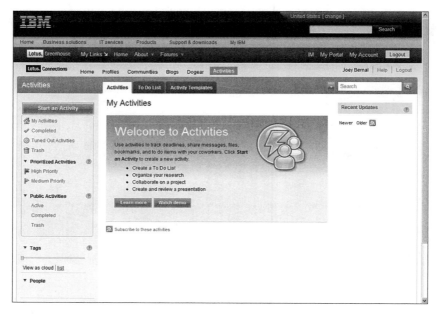

Figure 4.10　Welcome to Activities

Every organization is different, and each has different types of activities. Consistency is important when performing routine tasks across an organization. Activity templates are available to help maintain consistency whenever you start a new activity. For example, when on-boarding a new employee, the steps are often the same or similar. In this case, a template can be created that defines those routine tasks and action items for you (see Figure 4.11).

Of course, you should not be forced into using a template if a specific activity is unique. Templates should be used as a convenience or as a starting point for helping to predefine the tasks within an activity for you. In some cases, they might be highly recommended, especially where some degree of consistency is required based on organizational norms.

In most cases, someone will start an activity and then add or invite additional participants to join. Email is the most common approach for communicating what new tasks and entries have been added to an activity (see Figure 4.12).

Activities are about collaboration and using a shared space to achieve a common goal. Having the right tools enables teams to see what actions are assigned and to review documents and entries provided by other participants. In short, it enables everyone to be more productive.

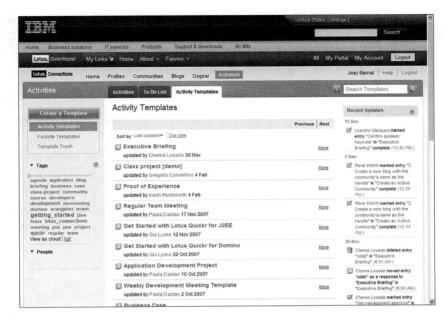

Figure 4.11 Activity Templates

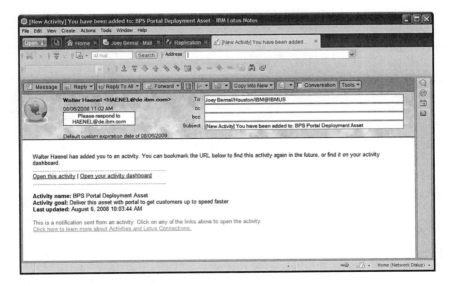

Figure 4.12 Inviting users to an activity

Organizationally, activities are easy to manage and use. Components of an activity can be broken down into sections. For example, in a project, you might make sections for infrastructure and development, or add sections based on the phases of the project. In addition, contributors or the project leader can add an entry or a to-do to the activity or to a section:

- **Entry:** This is typically a piece of content or a link to some information.
- **To-do:** A task that is assigned to someone on the team. It can be left open for a participant to choose. Target dates can be assigned to the to-do to help keep the effort on track.

Figure 4.13 shows the Activities page in action. It provides an example of how activities can be created quickly and easily so people can start to collaborate asynchronously on a project or set of tasks.

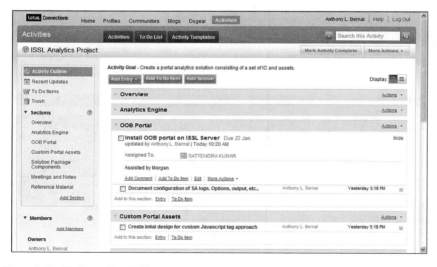

Figure 4.13 Working with activities

Activities can also provide a history of what collaboration has taken place which allows for tracking of tasks and reuse of any information that was gathered or created. Figure 4.14 shows a view of completed activities, each one of which contains a wealth of information to be harvested or reused within the organization.

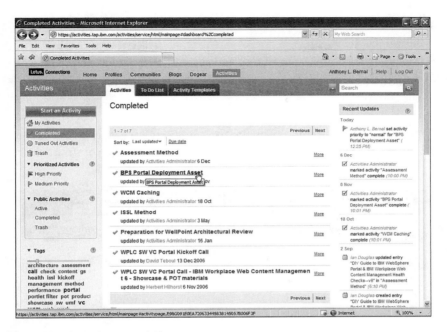

Figure 4.14   Reviewing your activities

It is easy to imagine how powerful activities can be within any organization. The idea of a team room or place to collaborate or share information is not really new. However, activities provide the base platform and functionality along with integration into other Connections features.

Building Your Communities

Communities are a way for people with similar interests to collaborate and share information on an ongoing basis. These people share a common interest in an event, a product, or a topic. They provide a way for members to stay in touch on the topic, see what is new or interesting about that topic, and meet other members with this common interest. Communities consist of a number of components for information sharing and discussion:

- Forums are asynchronous discussions that allow community members to talk about a particular topic.

- Feeds display information from different sources such as newsgroups or blogs.

- Members make up a community and share information and ideas.

- Bookmarks tag content across the Web that is of interest to members of the community.

Together, these items can make up a powerful set of tools for a community to work with. Figure 4.15 shows some available communities.

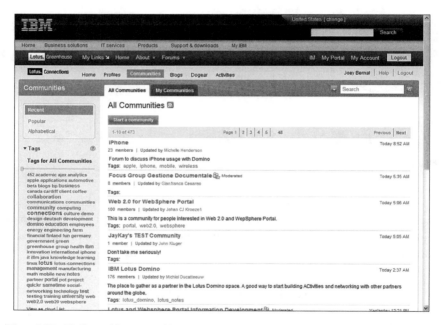

Figure 4.15   Finding public communities

Understand that all these pieces combined can make up a powerful set of features for your organization. Many organizations already have sets of communities targeted to interests both inside and outside of organizational responsibilities. Consider whether your organization has a local speakers club, where members meet on a regular basis to learn and improve their public speaking ability. A strong case can be made that this type of activity is beneficial to employees within the organization, because as their skills grow, so does their value to the team.

Additional communities can be more company focused, based on product lines, industry, or internal or customer projects. The list is endless, and no one can predict the exact value that can be gained from these communities. Consider a community hosted by HR around the on-boarding of new employees. Managers who join this community will easily find information on creating an activity using the on-boarding template. This makes the task of finding and completing all the right steps as seamless as possible. Joining public communities is as simple as searching through the list to find something of interest (see Figure 4.16).

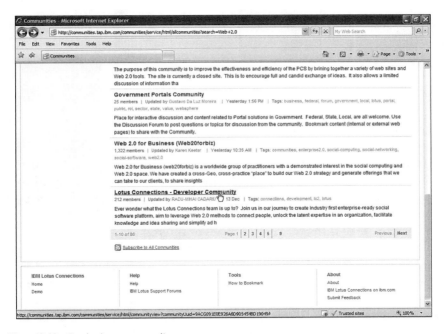

Figure 4.16   Previewing a community

At the top of each community, a button enables a user to join or request to join a community (see Figure 4.17). Much of the information about a community is readily available even for the casual browser (showing what any specific community is about, what goals it hopes to achieve, and even how active members are within the community).

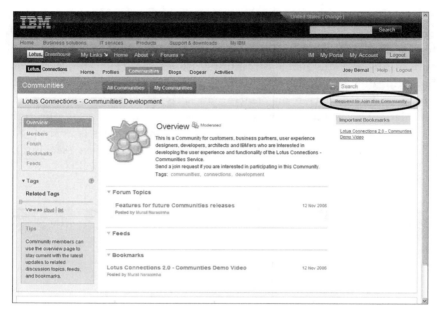

Figure 4.17 Joining a community

As a member of a community, you can participate in and help the community to achieve its goals and grow. Bookmarks can be added to a specific community when you create them through Dogear. This enables you to either target your links to your private bookmarks library or to share them with different communities of interest.

In addition, you can incorporate feeds into your community, which pull in data from blogs or other sites in the Internet. This data feed will update items of interested in a regular manner and keep the audience from having to search the entire Web again. Forum topics are another area of collaboration. Every community has areas that need to be discussed and debated. Forums provide just that medium where questions can be asked and considered. You can even use it as a place to share recipes. Community members always know what the latest postings are about because they are listed on the community's home page.

A user may subscribe to a number of communities, as shown in Figure 4.18. As community interest and participation grows, these communities become important stopping points in the search for knowledge.

Starting a new community is also a simple task (see Figure 4.19). Proximately placed is a Start a Community button on the listing page. You can define the level of access for a community, such as the following:

Figure 4.18 Listing your communities

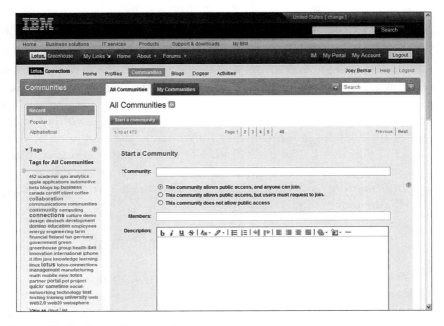

Figure 4.19 Creating a new community

- **Public access:** Allows anyone to join a community on his or her own
- **Public access with a request to join:** Allows users to join a community with the owner's permission
- **Private access:** Does not allow public access and is not searchable, but provides invitation-only access to the community

Communities are one of the most powerful of all the features within Lotus Connections. I say this because communities enable true ongoing collaboration across different departments or business lines within the company. An activity often uses a team-based approach, and can be limited in terms of the size and scope of the project. Even though the team members may cut across different lines of the business, they are still focused on a specific set of tasks. A community, on the other hand, often provides an open invitation for others, anyone really, to search, join, and participate, in the true nature of collaboration. One parallel that can be drawn is that of a Facebook page designated to a particular cause, event, or product. Joining that link is similar to joining a Lotus Connections community to collaborate at the highest level.

Integration with WebSphere Portal

As with all or most IBM software products, one size does not fit all. IBM Lotus Connections provides a JSR 168-compliant portlet that allows integration into WebSphere Portal. By placing this portlet on a portal page, as shown in Figure 4.20, all the capability of Lotus Connections can be displayed within the portal context.

One or more portlets can be placed on the same page to duplicate some of the home page functionality illustrated at the beginning of this chapter in Figure 4.1. Not every feature of Lotus Connections is enabled through this portlet. However, it does provide much of the initial display information, and then allows you to launch into Connections directly when more interaction is required.

Planning a Connections Deployment

When jumping into Social Networking for your organization, do not overlook some of the considerations in terms of deployment options. Lotus Connections runs on WebSphere Application Server and therefore requires planning. Figure 4.21 outlines the different deployment options.

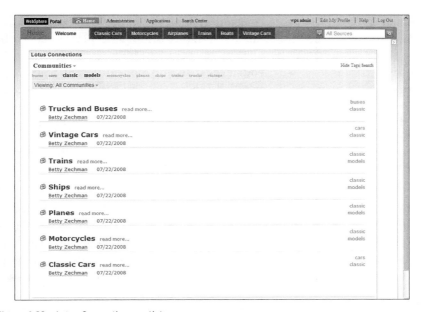

Figure 4.20   Lotus Connections portlet

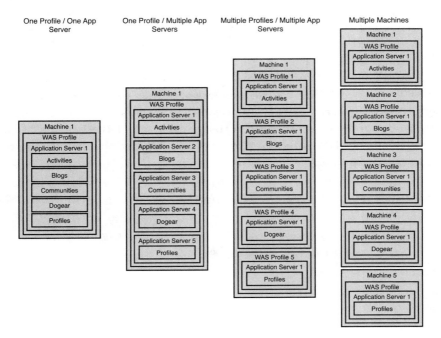

Figure 4.21   Deployment options

Each option provides additional scalability, but at the cost of additional infrastructure investment. A sizing should be performed to be sure that you make the best use of your available infrastructure and that the system can grow with your needs. In addition, different features of Lotus Connections can be installed separately, and not all features need to be installed. If features are installed separately, they can also be managed or updated without affecting other features that are installed on different servers or machines.

Conclusion

It is understandable if you are still skeptical. All of this might sound interesting, but most organizations need to identify concrete returns on investment, especially one of this scale. Currently, the tangible nature of social networks is difficult to pin down, but there is a lot of empirical evidence that they work. This is measured mostly through the increased ability of employees to communicate and share knowledge across organizational boundaries. These boundaries can be departmental or geographical in nature. As communities and connections grow, greater informational sharing can take place, and best practices or examples can be requested on a greater scale. And as more experts become known as they complete their profiles, it is possible to reach a wider audience or pinpoint a subject matter expert in any particular area.

Lotus Connections takes Social Networking and collaboration to the next level by allowing you to integrate activities with other enterprise efforts and systems. After Connections is integrated into your user repository and end users begin to take advantage of the benefits of an integrated Social Networking platform, real productivity and collaboration can begin to happen.

References

Gladwell, Malcolm (January 7, 2002). *The Tipping Point: How Little Things Can Make a Big Difference*. First Edition, Black Bay Books.

5

Team Collaboration and Content Sharing

Organization and team collaboration of documents and information has become mainstream within the enterprise. It has actually been a bit of a progression from the early days of knowledge management and enterprise taxonomies to the current trend of tagging content with what makes sense to the individual allowing us to find content where it lives across the enterprise and the Internet. Much of the formality has been replaced with the ability to share and collaborate in an almost effortless manner, while still keeping some structure in place and enforcing security concerns.

Lotus Quickr

IBM Lotus Quickr opens up a new generation of file-sharing and collaboration capabilities. Where Lotus Connections provides a complete set of Social Networking options, Quickr offers the ability to create, manage, and share information at a whole new level through the use of *places*. These places are designed for creation and provisioning by the end user based on a set of predefined templates within the product. Each place also provides for its own security structure that can also be controlled by the end user. A Quickr place is like its own website that provides the base for your project, library, or team. A place consists of pages and components, which make up how your place will be used. Core features of Lotus Quickr include the following:

- A content library is one of the primary features of Lotus Quickr. A content library is a component that resides on a page within your place. This is one of the first components that come to mind when evaluating Lotus Quickr. However, it is just the beginning. A core piece of functionality, the library component provides the basis for many Quickr places. Libraries allow you to easily upload, store, and share content.

- Team places enable you to create an online place for your project or team. These places contain more than just a library component. Team places also contain a blog and a wiki to share information, along with a library for documents and media files.

- Quickr connectors enable you to integrate Lotus Quickr places with other applications that you might be working with (e.g., IBM Lotus Notes, Windows Explorer, and Microsoft Office products, Lotus Sametime, Lotus Symphony™, and Microsoft Outlook®). This allows for easy check in/out of documents and editing and uploading of documents as they are used within your daily routine.

Lotus Quickr Places are customizable; so when looking at the possibilities that Quickr provides, you will see that this is only the beginning. In addition, Lotus Quickr provides several prebuilt templates to get you up and running right away. Figure 5.1 illustrates how Quickr might be presented after you log in for the first time.

The main screen in Figure 5.1 is empty because this user (the author in this case) has no favorite places defined. However, by clicking on the tabs across the top, the users would normally see different views of places that are available to them.

It should be mentioned that Lotus Quickr is offered in two versions;

- A Lotus Domino-based version that replaces Lotus QuickPlace®
- A WebSphere Portal-based version that leverages the capability and power of WebSphere Portal and Lotus Web Content Management

Figure 5.1   IBM Lotus Quickr

This chapter looks at the portal version of Lotus Quickr, which is Lotus Quickr Services for WebSphere Portal; however, both versions are similar. Why offer two versions? With any type of enterprise software, one size never fits all customers. Many organizations have a high set of skills and operations around Lotus Domino, and Lotus Quickr Services for Lotus Domino can fit nicely into the infrastructure. Similarly, many WebSphere and WebSphere Portal shops can leverage existing infrastructure and skills to add new capability into the organization.

Creating Your Own Place

The main page enables you to view places, but also to create places and manage those you have created or have permission to manage. Place management is important. However, the real work is done within the places themselves. By clicking on the Create a Place button shown in Figure 5.1, you can navigate through the Place Creation Wizard to start creating your own place. Figure 5.2 shows the first step in creating your own place within Lotus Quickr, which is choosing a template on which to base your place.

Figure 5.2   Create a Place

There are several templates to choose from depending on the function that the Quickr place will serve. In this case, the user chooses Custom as the type of place to create. However, many users will choose a predefined template that will automatically populate the place with the required components. There is also the opportunity with the right permission to create new templates or save your current place as a template. This makes a lot of sense if you are using a similar design for multiple places. Consider, for example, a team room customized to your working style or organization. A team room is a common Lotus Domino concept where multiple users can share information. You can think of places as information stores of ideas or personal knowledge such as can be shared via a blog or wiki, or as documents and media that can be stored in a content library. A place can be of a personal or single-user design, or it can focus on team collaboration. Either way, many of the components are the same, they just vary slightly in the way content is authored or shared.

The process of creating a new place is simple, as illustrated in Figure 5.3. It is mostly a matter of identifying the name and URL of the requested place and providing a good description of what the place would be used for. Although seemingly minor points, these items help to define the overall context of places within an organization. For example, naming conventions might be applied so that Quickr Places do not grow out of control without some semblance of taxonomy for identifying places that are created for specific uses within your organization.

Figure 5.3 Creating a custom place for information sharing

For example, suppose you are a project manager who will be creating a place for each project that you manage, or to put this in a broader context, maybe there is a predefined template that all project managers should use when creating a place for specific types of projects.

After the place has been created, it might appear similar to Figure 5.4. In this case, the place is empty because we choose a custom place. However, in other cases where a predefined template is chosen, pages and components will already be in place ready for use.

Now you are ready to customize this place. There are two ways to go about customizing a place in Quickr, as shown in Figure 5.4. The easiest is to use the built-in customization tool to create pages and add components to the place. The second approach is to use the WebSphere Portal administration features to customize your place.

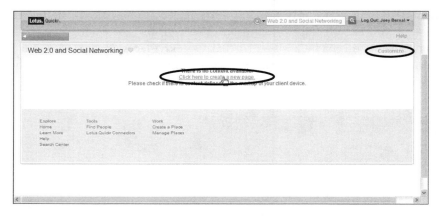

Figure 5.4   Uncustomized Quickr page

Customizing a Place

As previously mentioned, Lotus Quickr is built on top of WebSphere Portal and Web Content Management. This provides the base functionality to build a full-feature collaboration application, such as Quickr. Because of this, Quickr inherits lots of functionality that is regularly available in WebSphere Portal. In fact, the message in Figure 5.4 that states there is no content available is a standard portal message that you might find on any blank portal page. The preferred way to populate a Quickr place is to use the Lotus Quickr components pallet and the drag and drop capabilities (see Figure 5.6). A secondary approach is to use the portal features. Clicking on the corresponding link will bring you through a series of portal pages shown in Figure 5.5

These pages are standard portal administration pages that provide complete customization of your page and layout. The drawback of this approach is that some portal administration skills are really necessary. In some cases, this might not be a problem because basic page layout and composition is not very difficult. For the normal end user, however, this might be too much to learn, and we want to get started quickly. Notice that three pages display in Figure 5.5. The first allows you to define a new page for your Quickr; from there, you can define the layout and add specific portlets to the page. This approach implies a different level of knowledge, as the user must understand which portlets need to be placed on the page.

Figure 5.5 Manually creating your Quickr page

A more comfortable approach for users would be to use the Quickr Customizer. Figure 5.6 illustrates a much more user-friendly way to customize your place using the Quickr Customizer.

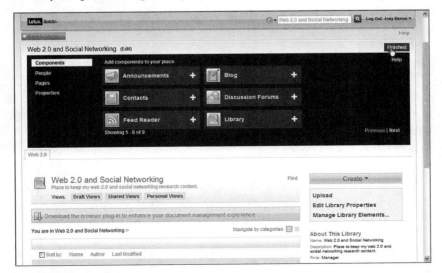

Figure 5.6 Using the Quickr customizer

If you click the Customize link in the upper-right corner of Figure 5.4, the Customizer will display. This provides a much more usable approach to designing your place and laying out your pages. Among other things, the Customizer enables you to do the following:

- Create new pages.
- Add components to your pages.
- Add and manage users of your Quickr place.
- Configure general properties for your place.

Within a few minutes, most people can have a place configured. Maybe less after someone has done it a few times, or of course if you use a template to create your place from, there is no customization at all except perhaps for adding additional users. Figure 5.7 shows a fully customized place.

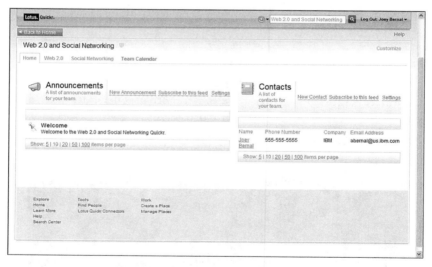

Figure 5.7   A fully functional Quickr place

Figure 5.7 illustrates that four pages have been created each with different components set up on the page. The setup is similar to a team type of space configured as follows:

- The home page is set up with an Announcements and a Contacts component.

- The Web 2.0 page is set up with a Library component to store Web 2.0 content.

- The Social Networking page is also set up with a Library component to store Social Networking content.

- The Team Calendar page is set up with a Calendar component to share information about important dates and events. At this point, your Quickr place is ready for use by yourself or a team (starting with uploading or creating documents in your provided libraries).

Working with Quickr Libraries

One of the key features of Quickr is the ability to store and share documents and other media. These files are stored in a library that can be made public or private and enables you to organize your documents and information in any way you can imagine. Figure 5.8 shows a new library that is ready for you to start uploading or creating documents. You can see that most of the document creation and management features appear to be readily available. However, Quickr goes a bit further by providing a browser plug-in for documents. Later we discuss how to use Quickr connectors to make working with libraries even more seamless through the desktop; but when working with the library directly through your browser, the plug-in can improve the experience.

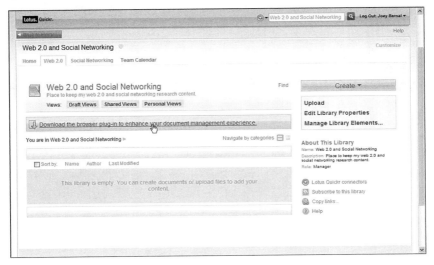

Figure 5.8 Working with a Quickr library

This plug-in installed just like any other browser plug-in. In most cases, this installation is pretty seamless. Clicking on the download link will bring up a new page with instructions on how to install the plug-in.

After the plug-in is installed, a new area appears on the library page, in the lower-right corner (see Figure 5.9). This circular area is a target where documents can be dragged from the desktop or Windows Explorer to be automatically uploaded to the library.

This is an easy way to upload your preexisting content to a library. As you drag documents onto the hot spot, they will automatically be uploaded into the library via the plug-in that is installed in your browser that activated the hotspot.

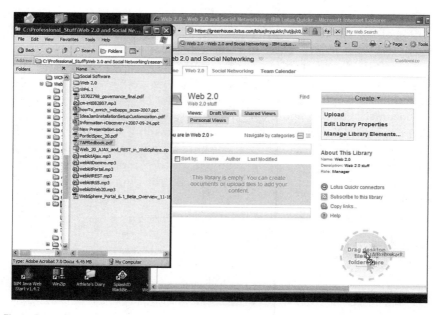

Figure 5.9   Uploading documents to a library

Working with Documents and Folders

Of course, uploading documents is a key part of Quickr libraries, but the ability to create new documents within your place can take collaboration to the next level. The Create menu on the right side of the library page enables you to create new documents, as well as folders and views of your documents (see Figure 5.10).

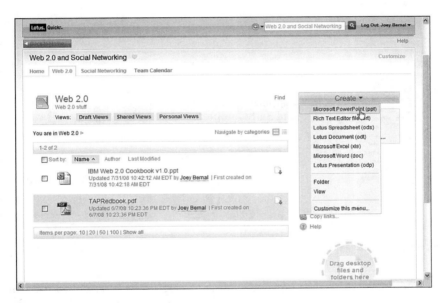

Figure 5.10   Creating a new document with Quickr

Folders allow you to organize your document structure, similarly to how you might organize a directory structure on your local system. Views allow you to provide a single view of a complex folder structure without having to navigate into each one.

Editing or viewing an existing document can be accomplished easily via a similar menu structure (see Figure 5.11). When you choose to work with a specific document, you can display that document directly within the page if it is of a compatible file type. You can also download that document or check it out as you make changes.

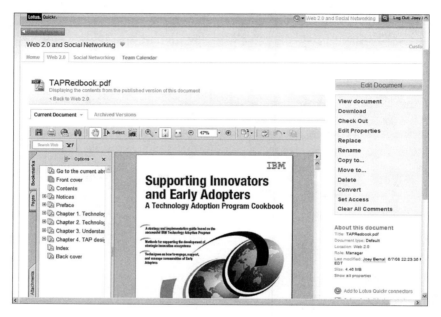

Figure 5.11   Working with a document

There are additional options such as replacing or renaming a file, or even deleting that file if necessary. Access permissions can also be set to determine who has specific access to a file, such as editor or read-only access.

Everything that has been shown so far has been using the Web 2.0 interface that comes out of the box with Quickr. As you can see, this in and of itself is pretty compelling functionality that can add great value for users within your organization. However, even more compelling value can be added by integrating Quickr with desktop applications and custom applications. The use of Atom feeds and Quickr connectors helps streamline that process.

Working with Quickr Connectors

Quickr places enable users, teams, and organizations to share documents and information seamlessly across the entire enterprise, but the web interface that Quickr provides is not always the most convenient way to interact with Quickr libraries. Quickr connectors enable you to integrate document repositories with Lotus Notes, Lotus Sametime, Windows Explorer, and Microsoft Office applications. This integration enables your users to work the way that is most productive for them, yet still share and collaborate in new ways.

Figure 5.12 shows the main Quickr Connectors screen, which outlines the benefits of Quickr connectors and enables users to get started downloading the application.

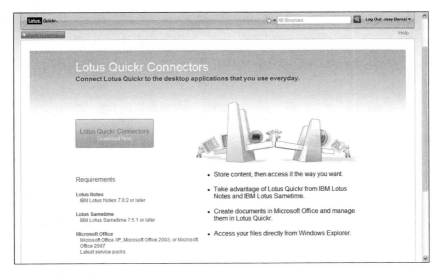

Figure 5.12   Quickr connectors

Quickr connectors are applications that run on your desktop and provide the integration needed to the libraries that you determine you need to work with. Installing Quickr connectors is a standard process, as shown in Figure 5.13. As mentioned previously, connectors are available for a number of standard applications, and users can choose which applications need to be connections enabled.

The installation process includes a Welcome screen and then terms and conditions that must be accepted. Next the connectors that the user wants to be installed are listed and can be modified if a specific application is not available on the user's desktop. Finally, the Installation Wizard is complete, and the Microsoft Windows Explorer Connector can be launched.

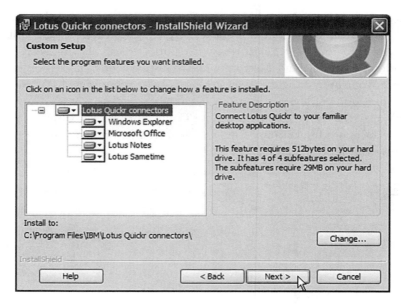

Figure 5.13   Installing Quickr connectors

After Quickr connectors are installed, you are ready to create connections to specific places. An initial connection to the Quickr server is necessary, and then the places within that server can be made available. Figure 5.14 illustrates the steps required to connect to a Quickr place.

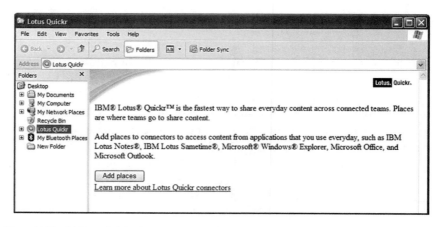

Figure 5.14   Adding a Quickr place to connectors

Note that Quickr connectors provide an additional menu item on the left side of the screen named Lotus Quickr. This menu item is where the Quickr places will be listed after they are added to your list. When you click on the button to Add Places, a series of windows will display to walk you through adding places to your list. Figure 5.15 shows Windows Explorer with a sample Quickr place added.

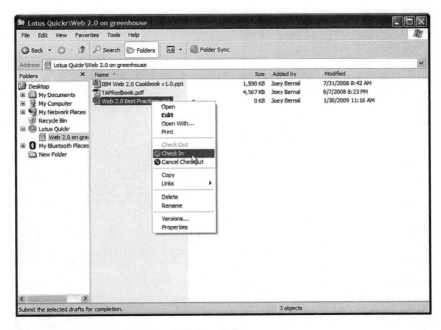

Figure 5.15 Accessing a place through Windows Explorer

The connections integration provides much of the same functionality that is available through the Quickr web interface for working with documents. Documents can be opened and edited directly through connections as necessary. In addition, the ability to check in/out a document is available when multiple team members are working on a set of documents. In addition, drag and drop functionality is now enabled so that you can drag documents from other folders into your places.

The Microsoft Office applications connector works in a similar fashion (see Figure 5.16). An additional drop-down menu with the integration options similar to that shown in Figure 5.15 is provided. New documents can be created within Word and added directly to a place for access by other team members.

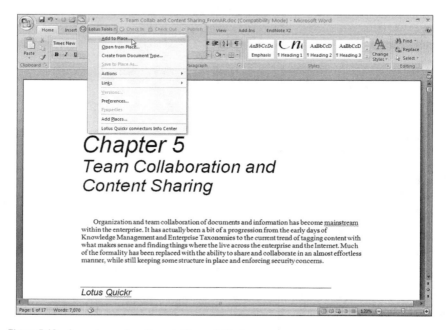

Figure 5.16   Accessing a place through Microsoft Word

It quickly becomes apparent how useful this technology is to an organization. With the installed connectors, Quickr can begin to operate seamlessly in the cloud. And although some server information is required for system connectivity, the documents themselves now live somewhere on the network. No longer are documents and information hidden away on desktops or shared folders. Information now becomes immediately shareable at almost no extra cost to user productivity. In most cases, users become more productive as discussions (or endless emails) about how to edit documents become a thing of the past. The key message with Quickr connectors is that the connectors do not interfere with the way people work.

Quickr Integration Through Feeds

As you might have noticed, Quickr is all about Atom feeds. We discussed the idea of Atom and RSS feeds in Chapter 1, "Web 2.0 and Social Networking," and why they are important in the Web 2.0 world. Quickr shows us exactly how to use those feeds for integration into everyday applications. A place can become an abstract location that is accessible not only through available connectors, but can also be integrated in meaningful ways into users' everyday applications. It is interesting to understand exactly how a data feed can be accessed through Quickr. The best place to start is with an inspection of what places and content are available on the Quickr server itself. This is done via an introspection feed that is provided through Quickr itself via the following URL:

```
https://<quickr hostname>/dm/atom/introspection
```

Replace <generic hostname> with your Quickr server hostname. Some authentication will probably need to be performed at this point to access the server. This could be done by logging in to one of your places or when you actually try to access an Atom feed from the server. Figure 5.17 illustrates how to access the introspection feed and authenticate to the server.

Figure 5.17   Accessing the main feed

Introspection feeds are not recognized immediately as a file type that can be used by a browser. This is because it returns an Atom service document that contains a list of available libraries. The result of this call should be saved to a file, or you should select the browser as an application that can handle this file type when prompted. Figure 5.18 shows the resulting file that has been loaded into a browser.

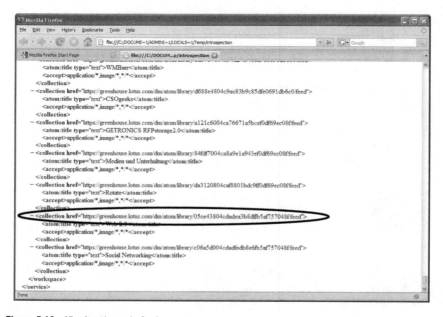

Figure 5.18   Viewing the main feed

Places are identified as a series of collections in the file, with each containing a title and a URL required for accessing that place directly. Quickr uses URLs to retrieve and work with the different types of components within Quickr. By looking through the collection list, you can determine the next URL to retrieve the feed for a specific place. The syntax for retrieving an Atom feed from a specific library is as follows:

```
https://<quickr host name>/dm/atom/library/<library uuid>/feed
```

Additional options are available for retrieving categories within a library, such as a list of folders or documents within a library:

```
https://<quickr host
name>/dm/atom//library/[libraryuuid]/feed?category_=<categories>_
```

In this case, if you just cut and paste a URL into the browser, you can quickly see how drilling down to different areas within Quickr is possible. Figure 5.19 illustrates the result of providing the URL for the Web 2.0 library.

Figure 5.19 Accessing a place through Microsoft Word

You can see how pervasive URL addressability is used within Quickr. Just about everything can be accessed directly. This is important because like using the Quickr connectors, these Atom feeds can be used to integrate Quickr into your own applications and websites. At the simplest level, specific feeds can be integrated directly to display documents from specific library or to make people aware when new documents are available. More important is the integration using custom code to provide first-class integration into Quickr libraries.

Writing Quickr Portlets Using WebSphere Portlet Factory

One of the easiest ways to integrate Quickr libraries into your portal is to create a custom portlet using WebSphere Portlet Factory (WPF). This section demonstrates how you can create a simple integration portlet in just a few minutes. Then in the following section, I point you to a more complex but very usable integration example. In Chapter 3, "Ajax, Portlets, and Patterns," we looked at building portlets using WPF in more detail. In this section, we look at a simple factory model that includes two builders. Figure 5.20 shows this initial model with a REST Service Call builder and a View and Form builder.

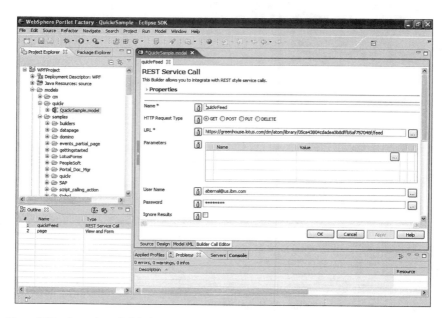

Figure 5.20 Accessing a Quickr feed using WebSphere Portlet Factory

The REST Service Call builder should look pretty familiar based on some of the URLs that were shown earlier. This builder pulls back the feed from a URL, the same feed displayed in Figure 5.19. Along with the URL, additional information is required, such as authentication information necessary to access the feed.

The second builder added to the model is the View and Form builder to display the data that has been pulled in from the REST Service Call builder (see Figure 5.21). This builder displays a generic page that displays data from the execute method of the service call.

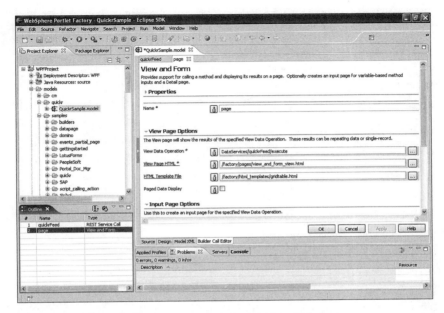

Figure 5.21 Setting up a View and Form builder in WebSphere Portlet Factory

The format for an entry type can be confusing, but it provides all the information needed to access a folder or specific document:

```
<entry xml:lang="en" xmlns:td="urn:ibm.com/td">
<id>urn:lsid:ibm.com:td:37108...</id>

<link href="document/37108.../entry" rel="self"></link>

<link
href="https://greenhouse.lotus.com/lotus/mypoc?uri=dm:37108...&verb=view"
rel="alternate"></link>

<link href="document/3710838.../entry" rel="edit"></link>
<link href="document/3710838.../media" rel="edit-media"></link>

<link href="document/3710838.../media" rel="enclosure"
type="application/vnd.ms-powerpoint" title="Web 2.0 Best Practices.ppt"
hreflang="en" length="0"></link>

<category term="document" scheme="tag:ibm.com,2006:td/type"
label="document">
</category>

<author>

    <uri>
    uid%3Djoeybernal%2Ccn%3Dtestusers%2Co%3Dtestorg%2Cdc%3Dgreenhouse%2
```

```
Cdc%3Dibm%2Cdc%3Dcom</uri>
<name>Joey Bernal</name>
<email>abernal@us.ibm.com</email>

</author>

<title type="text">Web 2.0 Best Practices.ppt</title>
<published>2009-01-30T17:16:25.219Z</published>
<updated>2009-01-30T17:27:48.484Z</updated>

<td:label>Web 2.0 Best Practices.ppt</td:label>
<td:created>2009-01-30T17:16:25.219Z</td:created>
<td:modified>2009-01-30T17:16:25.219Z</td:modified>

<td:modifier>

  <td:uri>
  uid%3Djoeybernal%2Ccn%3Dtestusers%2Co%3Dtestorg%2Cdc%3Dgreenhouse%
  2Cdc%3Dibm%2Cdc%3Dcom</td:uri>
  <td:name>Joey Bernal</td:name>
  <td:email>abernal@us.ibm.com</td:email>

</td:modifier>

<summary type="text"></summary>

<content type="application/vnd.ms-powerpoint" xml:lang="en"
src="document/37108.../media">
</content>

</entry>
```

Running the model displays the result shown in Figure 5.22. This display is really just a dump of the feed with no formatting provided, so it is not very usable in this format. You can get a good picture from this dump of how the feed is formatted with different sections to show the collection.

This page result is not very pretty. However, the ease with which the data was integrated with WPF is amazing. Add a PortletAdaptor builder, and this model becomes a portlet. Add a little formatting information and a few more builders, and this portlet becomes a usable list of documents that can be integrated into any application.

A Complete Custom Example

Several examples that provide the steps required for complete integration are available on developerWorks® (Alexander and Beauvais, June 2008). Figure 5.23 shows the result of a more full-featured WPF model that enables more user-friendly integration.

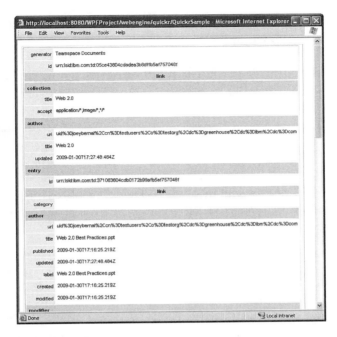

Figure 5.22   Viewing the results

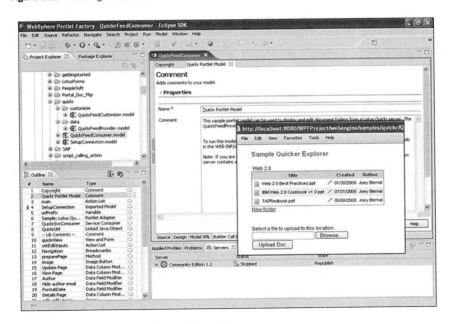

Figure 5.23   A complete integration portlet example

If you are new to WPF, these example are a good way to get started with building integration portlets.

Notes from the Field: An Interview with Richard Gorzela

Rich Gorzela is a Managing Consultant with the IBM Software Services for Lotus group. His main responsibility is to ensure IBM's customers are successful with WebSphere Portal, Lotus Web Content Management, Quickr, and related services assets such as the Web Content Integrator and the Web Content Management Multilingual Reference Implementation. He was also a key designer and developer of these assets. Previous to this assignment, Rich was a member of the product team, responsible for the design, development, and prototyping of several collaboration components.

Where are organizations struggling with content and document management?
Though some of the collaborative technologies today have been around for quite some time, web users today are now very savvy about collaboration tools and Web 2.0 capabilities such as blogs, wikis, document sharing, shared task lists and calendars, and other shared application spaces. They are using these tools not only in their private life; they are expecting them in their work environment as well. For example, some time ago, I visited a customer and they told me that their younger employees installed a wiki so that could collaborate in a manner that they were familiar with. Well, you guessed it, after some time they realized they had a lot of company-sensitive data on the wiki, with questionable security. The wiki users finally asked the IT department to help them address the problem. When the IT manager from the company told me this story, he was still in disbelief that the employees got themselves into this situation. And now it was his problem.

As this customer noted, if businesses provide these tools, then they must also meet the requirements for such considerations such as enterprise records management and security rules. Businesses should also be concerned with the scalability and reliability of their applications and infrastructure. In addition, business want to leverage the skills they have in house, and the infrastructure they have in place as much as possible in order to be cost responsible. On the other hand, businesses want to provide collaborative capabilities since they know that leads to higher innovation, and cost-effective collaboration in a global economy. As you can see, there are several tradeoffs involved in providing this technology.

Can you summarize the business value an organization might gain from using a product like Quickr?

A product such as Quickr provides many of the capabilities that businesses are looking for in collaboration tools related to content and document management. Quickr provides collaboration components such as shared tasks, custom forms/lists, blogs, wikis, discussion forums, document libraries, team calendars, and feeds. Self-service, out-of-the-box templates allow users to quickly create collaborative spaces for specific purposes such as a product launch, event planning, or executive boardroom. As mentioned earlier, these types of tools are important for innovation both inside and outside the firewall. This is particularly important now because many companies, whether small or large, have a global presence either with their customers, business partners, or both. Many companies also have offices in many locations, so collaboration tools that allow teams to share information easily are critical for them.

Good tools can help reduce travel costs, too. Sometimes there are other reasons as well that are not so obvious, at least not for me at first. Before *blog* and *wiki* were household terms, I gave a presentation to an IT department head that supported many high-end marketing folks. After the presentation, he told me that his interest in my company's products was due to the fact that the marketers found their creativity stifled when using tools that they considered antiquated. Until that time, I had thought only the technical folks were pushing for new tools, but now here were nontechnical folks who got it. It was not long after that that blogs and wikis really took off in popularity.

An enterprise-ready product like Quickr not only provides collaboration functionality, but also addresses issues important for the IT department. For example, Quickr provides integration with records management products such as FileNet®, an enterprise-ready product like Quickr also provides team spaces for collaborative components in a manner that gives teams secure places to collaborate. Finally, you have to look at integration with the applications most business users still use today. For instance, Quickr has "connectors" that provide seamless sharing of documents with applications such as email, Windows Explorer, Office applications, and instant chat. This type of integration minimizes the training required because end users can leverage the applications they are already familiar with.

On different note regarding value, you have to consider the technology platforms your IT department is familiar with. A business may need collaboration tools, but they need to do it in a cost-effective way so that the benefits outweigh the costs. For example, Quickr is supported on two different underlying technologies: J2EE™ and Domino. The choice of underlying services provides businesses the ability to leverage existing skills and in-house know-how. And finally, you have to consider maturity of technology platforms. For example, WebSphere Portal and Domino have well-known best practices to support the enterprise scalability and reliability that companies require, as well as support key features such as single sign-on.

As someone who works actively with content management and portal technology, how do you see a product like Quickr fitting into the workplace?

Early on, portals started to break down those technology silos we had for applications and data. They gave us a way to provide role-based access to content and applications in context of what the end users need to do. And of course, they provided us a way to allow users to customize their experience. Now, our expectations with Web 2.0 is that we can be content contributors just as easily as consumers, whether it's photos, videos, podcasts, profile information, documents, or content. These capabilities are so ubiquitous now, even your grandmother can talk to you like a pro about her activity on presidential campaigns, and show you photos of her grandkids on her smart phone from her Facebook profile or some similar site. You can see this concept generalized to other areas, too, such as business exchanges on a micro level for things such as person-to-person loans, concierge services, and job networking. In the enterprise, these capabilities and concepts are being adopted and adapted, in part, due to the changing business environment to be more global and responsive online both inside and outside the firewall.

I should not neglect to say that despite all the additional information we have greater demands to find what we need when we need it. That need can manifest itself in several ways: an effective search engine or tagging service; the ability to get to our important stuff on a portable device such as a smart phone; the ability to get an alert of something new happening of interest like a micro blog post; or the ability to get a consolidated, personalized view of items of interest. Another trend is the idea of end users to be readily able to mix data and services. The idea is to support the immediate need of an individual or community. This is commonly referred to as a mashup or situational application.

The way this all fits is that I think a product like Quickr provides many core collaboration capabilities everyone is looking for these days, but in conjunction with a portal it can do it in a way that does not create new silos of information and applications. We still want our important information and applications in close proximity. We want to mix our information as we need it personally or as our group needs it. Collaboration tools in context of a portal make sense; that is, I don't think of portals and collaboration as being separate concerns, or alternatives. You have to consider your business needs from different perspectives.

With WebSphere Portal, I think you will continue to see greater and easier integration of collaborative products like Quickr with other tools that bring value to collaborative work. For example, we will see greater integration of Lotus Connections components such as communities, profiles, activities with Quickr places. Taking it one step further, my opinion is that the line between our work and nonwork online environments and experiences will start to blur. Of course, the IT department will still want to be able to set and enforce policy, administer efficiently, and provide security for company resources, but even how that will be done will most likely change.

What are your comments on Quickr integration into WebSphere Portal? What are the pros and cons of available approaches?

Of course, the approaches will change over time, but there are a number of ways to consider integration with Quickr today. The first is to consider the portlets that are in the Portal Catalog. The portlets currently available include MyPlaces, Quickr Search Service, and feed readers for various sources, including Quickr. The advantage of portlets such as these is that they require no programming but can provide a lot of commonly required functionality. Another integration approach that is fairly easy is the Web Application Integrator (WAI). WAI is also in the Portal Catalog. WAI enables you to inject WebSphere Portal navigation into applications such as Quickr.

Although these approaches can be quite flexible, they might not suit a company's every need. If that is the case, you may need to consider custom portlets. Custom portlets can be built a number of ways, and great tools support their development. The first to discuss, because it minimizes the coding that needs to be done, is Portlet Factory. Portlet Factory comes with a number of builders, including one for REST application programming interfaces (APIs) that Quickr supports (more on this below). If you need a tool to support your low-level programming needs, then Rational Application Developer or RAD may be your choice. RAD tooling supports building JSF- and Struts-based portlets, both popular frameworks these days. RAD will give you the most flexibility for building custom portlets.

With some idea of the tools available to build custom portlets, we have to discuss the API options. I think the most important thing to realize is that both WebSphere Portal and Quickr provide REST service APIs. REST APIs provide an easy, technology-agnostic interface to services of all kinds these days. Most programmers are very familiar with them. REST APIs are remote APIs that are readily called from clients such as browsers and from other applications. For Quickr, you are encouraged to be both a consumer and producer of these APIs. That can be a powerful combination, allowing both custom portlets and custom content sources. Combine that with Quickr connectors for your favorite applications and you have some great possibilities for collaborative tools in portals that meet your organization's needs from top to bottom. Also note that Lotus Connections provides REST APIs. That provides even more integration possibilities for combining collaboration tools to suit your specific needs. Looking longer term, my opinion is that you will also be able to consume, create, edit, and share mashups within WebSphere Portal. On the other side of this are the WebSphere Portal REST APIs. There is too much to talk about here, but one possibility is that your organization creates a custom user experience that mixes portal navigation with Quickr and your other key corporate services.

Conclusion

This chapter has provided a tour of Lotus Quickr and some of the basic functionality. It is worth pointing out some of the key advantages to using a product like Quickr in your organization. First, the basic concepts of document and media storage and sharing are important. Providing a simple-to-use web-like interface for uploading, sharing, and browsing documents adds to the total package. Add in Quickr Connections and users can continue to work the way they normally do, while still contributing to the global community in a seamless manner.

Next, Quickr takes the idea of using Web 2.0 to the next level. Everything about Quickr is Web 2.0 enabled, with Atom feeds available for complete integration into other applications and environments. This provides the next-generation application by embedding Web 2.0 technologies as key components within the application. As more applications take advantage of this approach, integration of applications will become even easier.

Finally, there is an out-of-the-box portlet (MyPlaces portlet) available for Quickr integration with WebSphere Portal. This portlet lets you display all the places that a user is a member of or public places that are available to access, as well as favorites that have been marked by a user.

developerWorks Links

Alexander, A. and Beauvais, T. (June 28, 2008): Accessing IBM Lotus Quickr REST Services using IBM WebSphere Portlet Factory, http://www.ibm.com/developerworks/lotus/library/quickr-portlet-factory.

Lotus Quickr Wiki: http://www-10.lotus.com/ldd/lqwiki.ns.

Portlet Catalog: My Places Portlet.

http://www-01.ibm.com/software/brandcatalog/portal/portal/details?catalog.label=1WP1001GJ.

6

Mashing Up Data and Applications

It is a common joke that mashups always have to contain a map. The business question that stems from this might be this: How many maps do we really need? Surprisingly, the answer to this question can be a lot, potentially. Of course, this doesn't mean topographical maps in the Google Maps sense, but mapping data in any form is visually appealing to end users and often allows a better understanding of what might be happening within a particular dataset. Essentially, a mashup occurs when we combine data from two or more sources. As noted, there is often a visual aspect to mashups. However, data mashups can also occur and combine pure data from multiple sources that result in a combined data stream.

It's More Than Just Maps!

It is much more than just about maps, and although we often use the term *mashup*, you might be better served to think in terms of situational applications—that is, data that can be quickly integrated, mashed, folded, spindled, or mutilated in such a way to give us a better view of the data we are using. Figure 6.1 shows how mashups in situational applications can be combined on the page. One example of a situational application is when multiple components or portlets are combined on a page and work together, as shown in Figure 6.1. However, it is also the case that one of the portlets is a mashup that combines some set of data with a map to provide a visual representation of the data.

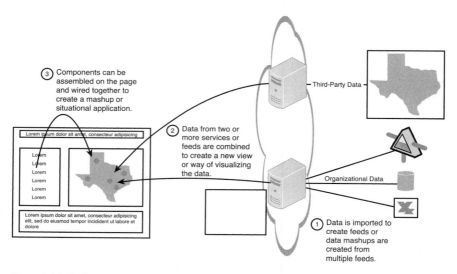

Figure 6.1   Mashup types

Maybe you need data from several sources to be combined before its display. Perhaps the data can be mashed into a feed. This combined feed can then be used to integrate or combine (mash) with other data to provide a clearer view of the requested activity. Traditionally, you might do this using SQL queries, provided all the data lives in the same database. Unfortunately, experience tells us that data rarely lives in the same database. The fact that you can take data from a traditional database and mash it with, for example, an Excel spreadsheet that you maintain on the desktop shows some of the power that mashups can provide. The ease with which that data can work together is directly proportional to productivity in today's busy workplace. When a business situation requiring fast action arises, the sooner the application is delivered to meet the needs of the specified users, the greater the impact.

Moving Technology Closer to the End User

A common goal is to enable end users to manage and mash up data on their own. In many organizations, the development team has a large backlog of requests. Requests for new projects, features, or functions have to be managed in such a way that it can sometimes take a long time for a particular request to be addressed. Wouldn't it be nice if you could do some things for yourself?

Suppose, for instance, that you have several different sources of information about your business. One is a list of customers and their locations, another is a list of employees, and a third is a list of office locations. These pieces of data might be stored in a database, in a set of spreadsheets, or perhaps in some enterprise resource planning (ERP) application. You might want to do several things with this type of data. For example, if you are working with standard mapping technology, you might want to map which offices are closest to your customers, or present a ratio of customers to offices based on different locations. Admittedly, this is just the beginning. You can also bring in sales data, lead times, seasonal data, and so on as you begin to see new trends within a customer base.

Every industry and organization has key performance indicators (KPIs) that are used to measure growth and success within the organization. But building good dashboard technology to represent organizational data in a meaningful way continues to be a challenge. Again, this stems from a sense of priority within the IT organization about where the most value is to be gained from business dollars. On the other end of the spectrum is the focus on situational applications, or more appropriately line-of-business applications, that can provide quick analysis to support decision making.

What if you could build a situational application yourself by taking data that might be hiding on your hard drive and combining it with enterprise data to reveal information in new and beneficial ways? Beyond that, what if you could share that data with your coworkers and collaborate to build new views and strategies? This is one of the key goals with defining a mashup strategy: to remove the barrier of IT wait times to deliver applications and to put the power into the hands of the business as much as possible. This approach in itself brings up several concerns, such as the following:

- The business participant must be technically savvy because any new technology or applications requires some learning.

- Performance must be managed so end users don't bring some system to its knees.

- Support from within IT should be made available to provide education and knowledge transfer to end users working to build situational applications.

- Security issues should be raised to ensure that end users are not providing confidential data to the wrong audience.

These questions are not trivial. There are infrastructure concerns, training and support questions, and much more. However, the ability to unleash mashup capability within your organization can be compelling indeed. This type of framework can help to provide new views of organization data that we cannot even imagine yet.

IBM Mashup Strategy

IBM's mashup strategy is diverse in that it meets the needs of a technology-savvy business community and a community of developers. As you might suspect, it consists of two major offerings. The first offering is a set of products called IBM Mashup Center, which consists of projects from both the Lotus and Information Management division of IBM's Software Group. The approach combines the power of managing data from across the enterprise with an easy-to-use mashup interface that enables end users to drag and drop widgets. A widget is a common name for a mashup component. Widgets can be connected to data feeds, wired together, and published for future use. These two products are joined by a catalog containing widgets, feeds, and other mashups, which can be made available to end users or combined to create new mashups or applications (see Figure 6.2).

On the other side of this strategy is WebSphere sMash, which is a lightweight REST-style product that enables developers to quickly and easily build Web 2.0 situational applications. WebSphere sMash leverages Project Zero (www.projectzero.org), which is an open community project to help drive new features and ideas into WebSphere sMash. Although not completely integrated, WebSphere sMash can be used to

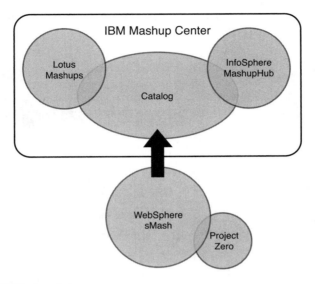

Figure 6.2   IBM Mashup strategy

create feeds that can be leveraged within IBM Mashup Center and thus enable organizations to take advantage of all the skills and technologies available to them.

Lotus Mashups

Lotus Mashups attempts to close that gap between IT and the backlog of applications that are waiting for attention and required by a small user population. Mashups enable organizations to attack the long tail of application demand within the enterprise (specifically, the unique applications that are important to a smaller set of users). Malcolm Gladwell describes the long tail as the less-popular or lower-demand items that when combined together as a whole can create a larger demand than more popular items currently available. Mashup technology is designed to provide the same effect. Use mashups to solve the one-off problems that individuals or small groups require. This will result in a reduced demand on IT services who can then continue to provide new applications for the larger business need.

Lotus Mashups is all about putting mashup technology in the hands of the people. It enables users to assemble new situational applications using existing components and data feeds, or to create their own feeds when the right data is not readily available. Figure 6.3 shows the initial

Lotus Mashups screen, filled with information and tutorials to get a user started on the right track.

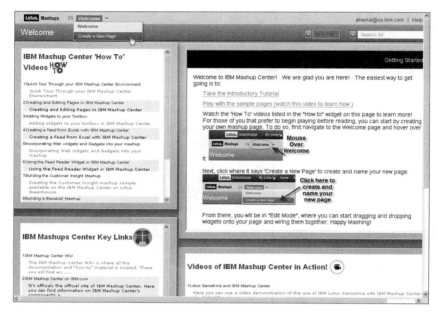

Figure 6.3   Lotus Mashups

New users definitely need to walk through some type of training. Lotus Mashups is intuitive for end users. However, many of the concepts are new to everyone, so some learning is necessary. You can start by creating a new page, as shown in Figure 6.3. This enables you to create a starting place on which to build your mashup. Figure 6.4 shows an initial empty page that has been created.

The page that was created in Figure 6.4 has a number of menu items or drawers across the top, which hold your available components or widgets that can be added to a page.

Interestingly enough, I was discussing Lotus Mashup technology with a developer at a client organization who was using IBM WebSphere Portal technology. This developer was very excited about the technology, or at least the idea, as I continued telling him about its capability. He was envisioning a way for him to deliver quicker, more-compelling applications to his end users through the portal. Where he started to struggle was with the idea of end users leveraging the technology

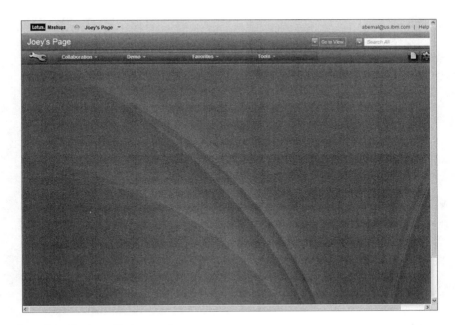

Figure 6.4   New Lotus Mashups custom page

themselves to build unique applications for their own use—the idea being that he could then focus on core applications that resulted in greater value to his business. As we talked through some of the potential issues, such as security, performance and scalability, and support, he started to "get" how this mashup technology could be introduced into the organization in a meaningful way. (I think technologists love to embrace new technology, and he was slightly disappointed when he thought he would not be able to play with this new toy. I assured him this was not the case, as he and others would probably need to be an expert in order to provide initial feeds and components for end users to work with; however, building these one-off mashups would not, I hoped, be his core responsibility.)

Figure 6.5 shows an open drawer holding several demo widgets. By right-clicking on a widget, you can open a context menu that enables you to add that widget to the page. In this simplest example, we have already added a weather component to the page and will now add a customer list widget to the same page. Lotus Mashups comes with many samples, and it is pretty easy to add new components to the catalog that is provided as one of the key components. Users can build simple mashups very easily by just pulling components or widgets from the catalog.

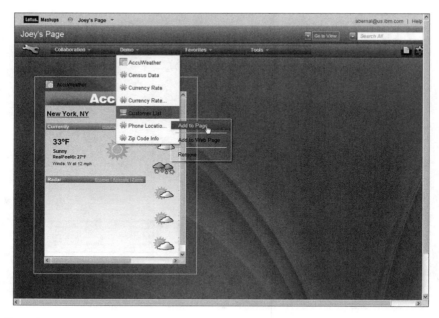

Figure 6.5   Adding widgets to a Lotus Mashups page

After you add two or more widgets to a page, the real fun can begin. Wiring the widgets together to allow them to share related data is really the basis of a mashup. Some of the original mashups were based on mapping technologies that are publicly available. Many public sources of data can be integrated into your business display. Maps, weather, city or regional information, or industry-focused data can all add value to your business process. Mashing data between these public sources and feeds, however, adds little value unless it can be integrated with data that is core to your business needs. This core data can take the form of customer data, sales information, suppliers, vendors, employees, or whatever type of information you gather on a routine basis.

Figure 6.6 illustrates wiring two widgets together on a page. By right-clicking on the widget, you can choose which information you want to send to another widget and how that data is formatted. Widgets can reformat data and supply this data as a type of feed, or more often there is a single row or column of information in a source widget that can be wired together to a target widget. In our example, this is not complicated. What we want to do is display some weather information about our customer as we select a different row in the customer table.

We can identify that the ZIP code of our customer can be wired as a text field to another widget that can accept that value.

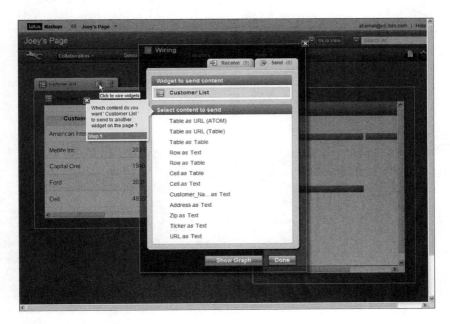

Figure 6.6 Selecting the widget source content

Identifying a target widget is shown in Figure 6.7. In this case, the AccuWeather widget is the target in the mashup with our customer data and is expecting a ZIP code.

After we complete the wiring process, this set of actions can be saved to the page. The fun part is now using the mashup that has been created to simplify the effort involved in working with your data. In Figure 6.8, the customer information has been wired to the weather widget. As a user clicks on a customer in the list, the data is updated in the AccuWeather widget to display the corresponding weather information based on that customer's ZIP code.

Because only two widgets are on the page, this example is simple, but it gives you an idea about how easy Lotus Mashups makes it for business users to drag and drop widgets to their own pages and begin to combine data in interesting ways. These pages can be published as web pages to allow others to reuse these mashups without having to go through the effort of creating their own mashup version.

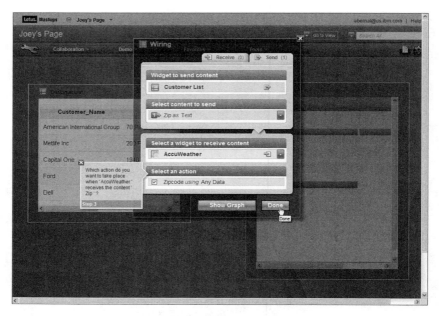

Figure 6.7   Targeting a widget to receive content

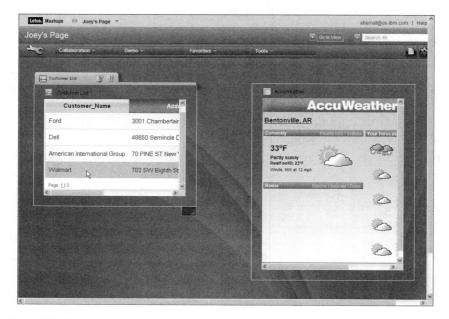

Figure 6.8   Working with your Mashup

InfoSphere MashupHub

Where Lotus Mashups is more of an assembly tool for existing widgets that enables you to combine, wire, and publish mashup pages, InfoSphere MashupHub provides more of the ability to work with the data within your organization. Figure 6.9 shows the main page and the four main components of MashupHub. As with Lotus Mashups, there are tutorials and information to teach users about MashupHub. This is important because MashupHub provides new features different from what we just covered in Lotus Mashups. MashupHub enables users to mash the data itself in new ways, combining data from several feeds or data sources and transforming that data into a new feed. MashupHub also includes a catalog where feeds, widgets, and pages can be stored and used by other tools such as Lotus Mashups.

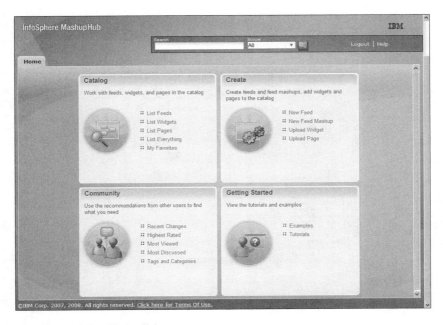

Figure 6.9   InfoSphere MashupHub

Another important part of MashupHub is the community features available to help other users understand what feeds might be most valuable. As you can imagine, over time the catalog can become filled with hundreds or even thousands of feeds, widgets, and pages. Enabling the community of users to identify the most value themselves can help others who are looking for specific and valid information. This type of identification is provided through the ability to rate, tag, and discuss components that enable others to more easily move beyond trying to wade through the noise to find what they actually can use.

Creating a new feed or feed mashup is, of course, the most powerful feature of MashupHub. MashupHub enables you to select from many different data sources to create new feeds. Figure 6.10 shows the screen options provided when selecting the option to create a new feed. MashupHub allows new feeds to be created from enterprise data sources such as system databases, web services, or a user repository such as a corporate LDAP. In addition, feeds can be created from departmental or local sources such as spreadsheets or text files that exist and are used locally within a small department. For example, if one department maintains information in spreadsheet form, that file can be lifted from the user's hard drive and transformed into a feed that can be accessible across the organization for viewing or mashing with other data feeds.

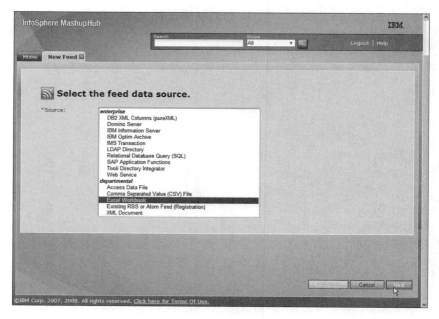

Figure 6.10   Creating a new feed from an Excel data source

As a simple example, we can select an Excel workbook as a data source. Several files are bundled as downloadable examples for this book that you can use as a data source. One of these is the CMCustomerData.xls, which contains a list of customers for the Classic Models organization.

Identifying the data within a worksheet is possible with the available input fields for this type of data source. For our example, we need to identify that row 1 of the worksheet is a header row that contains a list of headings for the dataset (see Figure 6.11). This makes formatting the data easy if the headers are something that can be leveraged in building the data feed. We can leave the range and worksheet number blank because there is only one worksheet and we want to pull in all the available data. We also want to upload the actual .xsl file to build the feed data. After filling out the necessary information for this type of data source, click the Next button.

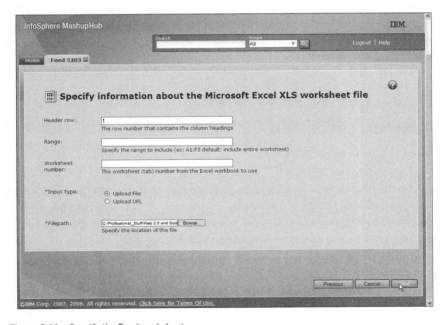

Figure 6.11   Specify the Excel worksheet

The next section is designed to enable you to provide information about the feed itself, such as the title and type of feed data that will be

made available (see Figure 6.12). Required information includes the
title, description, and version of the feed. Other information that should
be provided includes the permissions information about who will be able
to access the feed data.

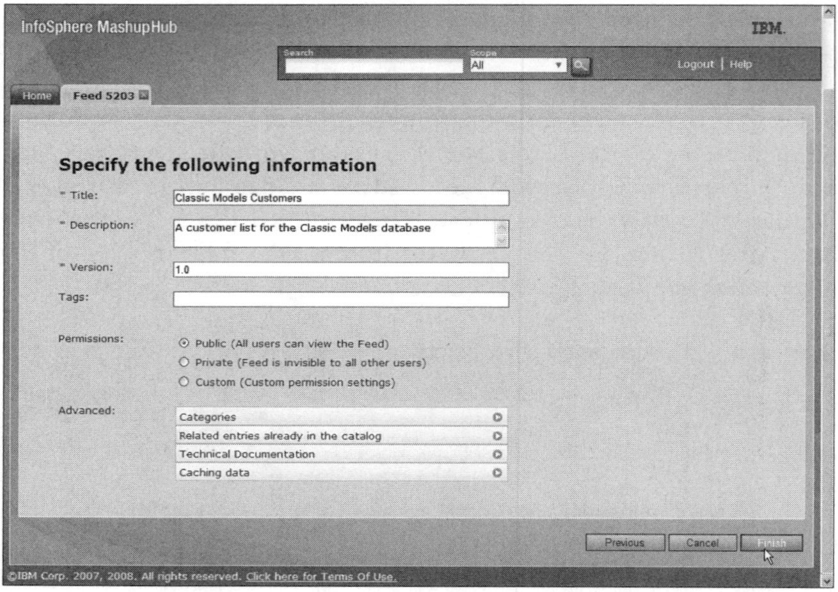

Figure 6.12   Specify the feed information

The more information you can provide, including advanced information options, the better. Users can leverage this information to understand what type of data this feed provides and how useful this feed will
be compared to the information they are looking for.

At this point, you are finished building the feed and ready to make it
available. After you click the Finish button, the feed will be saved, and a
number of options will be made available, allowing you to work with
the feed. Figure 6.13 illustrates a new feed that has been saved to the
catalog. At this point, you have two main options to consider: viewing
the feed, which is illustrated in Figure 6.14; and adding the feed to
Lotus Mashups for use in your mashup pages.

If you choose to view the feed, this will occur through a browser. In
most cases, you probably want to view the source on the resulting browser
page (see Figure 6.14). This can be accomplished by right-clicking
on the browser page and selecting to view the source. This view will

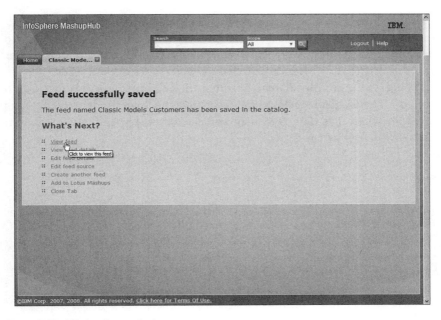

Figure 6.13   Viewing the new feed

Figure 6.14   Examine the feed details through your browser

show the detail behind the feed with the data format that has resulted. In most cases, this will be an Atom feed that can be integrated into mashups and mashup feeds. However, the feed can be consumed by other applications that can leverage Atom and RSS types of data feeds.

There are a couple of sections in this data that are interesting to review. The beginning section describes the overall data feed. This includes where the data feed originated and some specific information, such as the title of the feed:

```
<?xml version="1.0" encoding="UTF-8"?>
<feed xmlns="http://www.w3.org/2005/Atom">


<id>https://greenhouse.lotus.com/mashuphub/client/plugin/generate/entryid/52
03/pluginid/3</id>
  <title type="text">Classic Models Customers</title>
  <link
href="https://greenhouse.lotus.com/mashuphub/client/plugin/generate/entryid/
5203/pluginid/3" rel="self" type="application/atom+xml"></link>
  <updated>2009-02-27T20:42:41.534Z</updated>
  <subtitle type="text">A customer list for the Classic Models
database</subtitle>
  <generator>InfoSphere MashupHub</generator>
```

The main section, which is repeated many times within this feed, is the entry section that describes each entry in this feed. This contains the specific information to describe each customer in some detail:

```
<entry xmlns="http://www.w3.org/2005/Atom">
  <title type="text">Customers</title>
  <id>urn:uuid:2</id>
  <updated>2009-02-27T20:42:41.534Z</updated>
  <author>
    <name>abernal@us.ibm.com</name>
  </author>

  <summary type="text">Atom Feed entry 2</summary>
  <content type="application/xml">
    <row xmlns="http://www.ibm.com/xmlns/atom/content/datarow/1.0">
      <Customer_Num>103</Customer_Num>
      <Address_1>54, rue Royale</Address_1>
      <Address_2></Address_2>
      <City>Nantes</City>
      <Contact_First_Name>Carine </Contact_First_Name>
      <Contact_Last_Name>Schmitt</Contact_Last_Name>
      <State></State>
      <Postal_Code>44000</Postal_Code>
      <Country>France</Country>
      <Phone>40.32.2555</Phone>
      <Sales_Employee_Num>1370</Sales_Employee_Num>
      <Credit_Limit>21000</Credit_Limit>
    </row>
```

```
  </content>
</entry><entry xmlns="http://www.w3.org/2005/Atom">
  <title type="text">Customers</title>
  <id>urn:uuid:3</id>
  <updated>2009-02-27T20:42:41.534Z</updated>
  <author>
    <name>abernal@us.ibm.com</name>
  </author>
  <summary type="text">Atom Feed entry 3</summary>
```

In three or four short steps, we have uploaded an Excel spreadsheet and made it accessible to users and applications across the organization. As part of the mashup catalog, this feed is now part of your organization data layer. You should think about the data that is uploaded to the catalog in the form of feeds and think about what restrictions might be necessary. If other users use this data to build their own situational application, a dependency is created that necessitates the management of the feeds that other users create. Chapter 9, "Managing a Changing Social World," talks more about governance strategies that your organization might need to put into place. For now, enjoy the ease at which things can be created.

Getting a Feed from the Catalog

Just to tie up a few loose ends from this walkthrough, Figure 6.15 shows how feeds that are created within the MashupHub can be used within Lotus Mashups. Although "automatic publishing" is available in MashupHub, one of the key features is the ability to search the catalog from within Lotus Mashups. By searching the MashupHub, as shown in Figure 6.15, you can find multiple feeds or widgets that you can add directly to Lotus Mashups. Notice that the search results provide more than just the name and type of feed. Additional important information is displayed, such as the rating of the feed, author, and when this item was last updated.

It is easy to see with these last two sections how InfoSphere MashupHub and Lotus Mashups can be combined to create a powerful weapon in the unending fight toward the construction of situational applications. Mashups are only as good as the data that they use, and that data might live in many places across the enterprise, including on the user's desktop. InfoSphere MashupHub helps organizations unlock that data and make it usable to build into applications that can be created using Lotus Mashups.

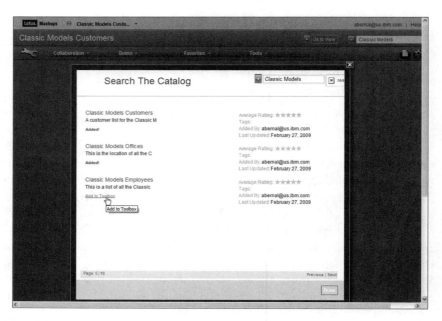

Figure 6.15   Retrieving feeds from the catalog

InfoSphere Feed Mashups

Before we finish with Mashup Center and InfoSphere MashupHub, let's look at another important feature referred to as feeds. Feeds are themselves mashed together to create a new way of looking at the data. Combining data at this level can remove unnecessary complexity from other users who are trying to unlock relevant business information. MashupHub provides a graphical interface for building mashups of feeds. Within this graphical view, you can lay out and connect various operators to provide the required result. The operators allow you to add multiple feeds or data sources to the page and then wire them together in different ways.

Figure 6.16 illustrates a simple feed mashup using the Classic Models feeds that were created earlier in this chapter. Two sources were added, CMEmp and CMOffice, and then merged using a Merge operator.

The Merge operator allows you to define the mapping that is necessary to combine the two data sources. In this case, each employee has an OFFICECODE value, which can be matched up with the CMOffice data. Other operators allow you to group, sort, and filter the data in different ways. Each operator allows you to provide comments and preview the

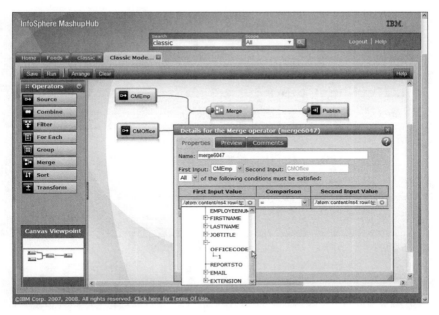

Figure 6.16 Creating a feed Mashup

data at any stage in the process. Figure 6.17 shows an overview of the data feed after you have completed and saved the feed mashup.

The term *feed mashup* is used in the context of mashing data sources and feeds to distinguish from more graphical focused mashups that were discussed with Lotus Mashups. This allows a user to understand that a specific feed is made up of multiple data sources. Although not entirely necessary, it is an easy way to allow users to track data back to the source if necessary.

Overall, Mashup Center provides a complete and robust set of tools. It is not hard to understand how the combination of Lotus Mashups and InfoSphere MashupHub provides a one-two punch that is required to knock out the technical complexity of creating situational applications. As you can see, the overall strategy is based on user-friendly tools that allow for users to get started and be productive as quickly as possible.

WebSphere sMash

Mashups can play as much of a role in the service-oriented architecture (SOA) space as they do in end-user situational applications. The idea of using feeds is important. Although feeds are seemingly a simple

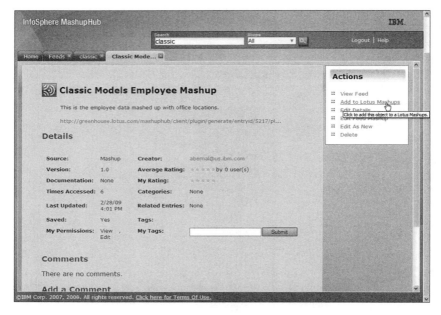

Figure 6.17   Adding feed Mashups to the catalog

idea, the point is that feeds can be pervasive throughout the enterprise. This is one of the ideas behind WebSphere sMash. WebSphere sMash is a lightweight platform designed to enable developers to quickly build Web 2.0-enabled applications, including situation applications and mashups. WebSphere sMash has a different focus on agile technologies and supports several web-based development languages, including PHP and Groovy.

A development version of WebSphere sMash is downloadable from www.projectzero.org, which is the supporting open community for sMash. This site includes all the information needed to download, unpack, and build the sMash application framework. WebSphere sMash also includes an application builder to help you create new applications to run on the framework. Figure 6.18 shows the app builder startup sequence when run from the command line of your system.

We should start with just trying to build a simple feed or service. Using JavaScript Object Notation (JSON) as the feed format, we can provide some Classic Models data to client applications very quickly using sMash. JSON was introduced in Chapter 1, "Web 2.0 and Social Networking." This approach is somewhat similar to the feed that we

Figure 6.18   Starting the App Builder application

created earlier with MashupHub, but in this case, we will connect to a database instead of using a spreadsheet to provide the data.

Figure 6.19 shows the WebSphere sMash App Builder interface. This interface is very robust and provides all that you need to build an application. From here, you can also run applications that you build with sMash.

If you click Create a New Application, it will display a dialog that allows you to provide information about the application. This includes basic description information as well as the module group that this application should belong to. There are two main module groups: stable and experimental. This identifies the state of the application or module. You would usually use experimental when you are first testing an application. Figure 6.20 shows this setup dialog window.

At this point, you can click the Create button to create the outline of a new application. WebSphere sMash actually uses Apache Ivy to manage the dependencies of your project. You can view the ivy.xml file that

Figure 6.19 App Builder welcome screen

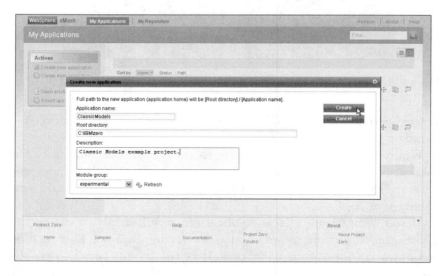

Figure 6.20 Create a new sMash application

is created to understand how the description information is used. We
will expand on this file when adding module dependencies in a few
steps:

```
<ivy-module version="1.3">
```

```
<info revision="1.0.0" module="ClassicModels" organisation="zero">
  <license url="http://license.page" name="type of license"/>
  <ivyauthor url="http://authors.home.page" name="author name"/>
  <description homepage="http://module.description.page">
    Classic Models example project.
  </description>
</info>
<publications>
  <artifact type="zip"/>
</publications>
```

You can actually run the application, although it might not do much at this point. If you click on the green arrow next to your application, you will start and run the new application (see Figure 6.21).

Figure 6.21   Starting an application

All that will really end up running is the default index page for your application. It is enough to see that you have the framework in place for a sMash application. Figure 6.22 shows that default index page for the ClassicModels application. Notice that the index page contains links to documentation and tutorials to learn more about using WebSphere sMash. It also contains a link to the Project Zero website at www.projectzero.org. Project Zero is the community-driven version of this tool. It is the place where you can help to drive the direction and function of sMash as the product evolves.

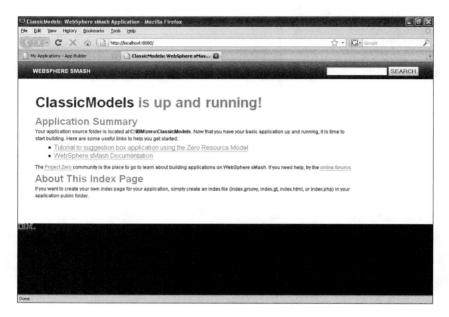

Figure 6.22   Access the application

When you are done reviewing the application as it stands, you can close that browser window and stop the application from the App Builder page. Now we can start to build out the application. Our goal is simple: Take the existing Derby database for the ClassicModels Company application and expose the customer data as a JSON feed. We will need to add a few more dependencies to the application in the form of libraries (see Figure 6.23). WebSphere sMash provides many different libraries that can be used to help build out your application and get you up and running quickly. As with any new programming language or framework, it takes some time to learn what modules to use when you are building new functionality. You can find much of the javadoc for Project Zero at www.projectzero.org/javadoc/archive/, which will be helpful as you continue to learn.

The two main modules that need to be included in this application are zero.core and zero.data, which will allow us to pull data from the

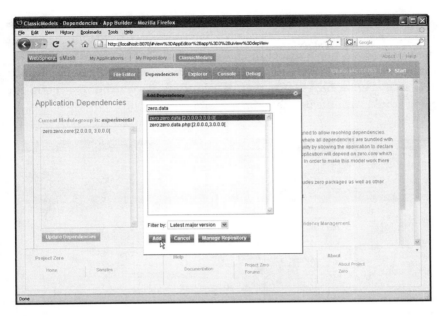

Figure 6.23   Adding application dependencies

embedded Derby database. Additional modules can be added to perform separate functions such as providing the feed in Atom format, rather than as a JSON feed. You can find information about these modules and new modules on the Project Zero website:

```
<dependencies>
  <dependency org="zero" rev="[2.0.0.0, 3.0.0.0[" name="zero.core"/>
  <dependency org="zero" rev="[2.0.0.0,3.0.0.0[" name="zero.data"/>
  <dependency org="zero" rev="[2.0.0.0,3.0.0.0[" name="zero.atom"/>
  <dependency org="org.apache.derby" rev="[10.0.0.0,11.0.0.0["
name="derby"/>
  <dependency name="zero.dojo" org="zero" rev="[1.0.0.0,1.1.0.0["/>
  </dependencies>
</ivy-module>
```

To get this to work, we need to add a data source. The Derby database is included with the downloadable samples. This database needs to be unarchived to a directory called db. This will result in a directory structure of <project root>/db/ClassicModelsDb. In this case, it is a manual step to provide this file in the correct location. In other cases, you could actually provide setup scripts to build the database if necessary.

After the database is in place, we can configure the connection information in the zero.config file. This is the main configuration file for the project and where you define much of the information that sMash needs to run your application correctly. The file zero.config is processed when your application is started. Figure 6.24 shows the file editor open with the zero.config file being edited with the database connection information.

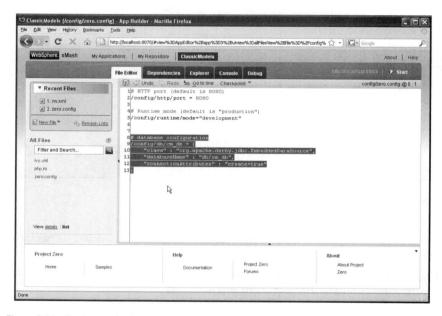

Figure 6.24   Setting up the database configuration

The following code sample shows the actual information that needs to be added to this file:

```
# HTTP port (default is 8080)
/config/http/port = 8080

# Runtime mode (default is "production")
/config/runtime/mode="development"


# database configuration
/config/db/ClassicModelsDb = {
    "class" : "org.apache.derby.jdbc.EmbeddedDataSource",
    "databaseName" : "db/ClassicModelsDb",
    "connectionAttributes" : "create=true"
}
```

Note the other information contained within this file, such as the port number that your application should use. At this point, most of the configuration is in place and we are ready to expose the data to the outside world. While this feed can be exposed to the outside world, the feed could also be readily used by other applications, or even added to the catalog included with Mashup Center. It could also be the case that this feed is used by the same application to Web 2.0 enable a user interface that is wrapped around this data. To expose the feed, a resource handler should be created using the New File option, as shown in Figure 6.25. This resource handler manages create, read, update, and delete (CRUD) events that are called by the user. These CRUD events map to REST functions that are described later.

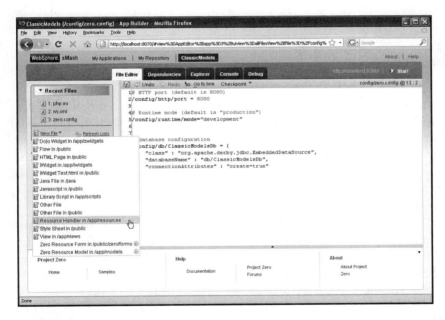

Figure 6.25   Creating a new resource

WebSphere sMash works well with both Groovy and PHP types of files. In some circles, Groovy is often described as Java on steroids, or kind of an enhanced Java. It is still Java, but new features have been added to simplify the effort needed by a developer. Figure 6.26 shows a new customers.groovy file created to provide us with a place to set up the customer data feeds. In some cases, we might add additional resources to expose employee, office, or even sales data that is contained within the database. The path and filename are important in setting up the right access URL for the resource feed.

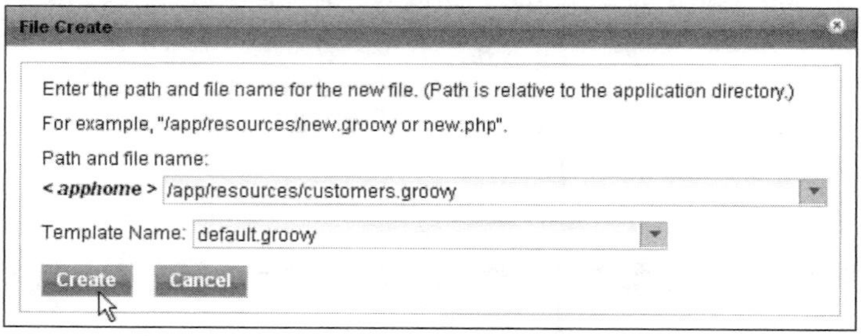

Figure 6.26   Defining a Groovy resource file

The Groovy template that is provided contains several methods (identified by the word def). These methods correspond to standard servlet methods of GET, POST, PUT, and DELETE and common REST functions. The method signatures are clearly defined for the functionality that they will provide: onList(), onRetrieve(), onCreate(), onUpdate(), and onDelete(). For this example, it is necessary to set up only the onList() method (see Figure 6.27).

The following code sample shows the actual customers.groovy file that should be created to expose the JSON customer feed. In reality, only five lines of actual code are required to create the feed. The first two lines create the database connection and perform the actual query on the CUSTOMERS table. The other three lines format and output the resulting data:

```
def onList(){
  try {
    // Get configured DataManager for data access
    def data = zero.data.groovy.Manager.create('ClassicModelsDb')

    // Retrieve records via Data Zero
    def result = data.queryArray('SELECT * FROM CUSTOMERS')

    request.view = 'JSON'
    request.json.output = result
```

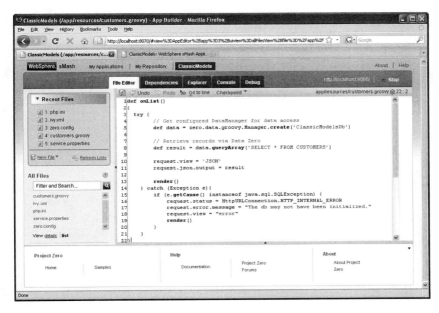

Figure 6.27 Writing the resource access code

```
    render()

} catch (Exception e){
    if (e.getCause() instanceof java.sql.SQLException) {
        request.status = HttpURLConnection.HTTP_INTERNAL_ERROR
        request.error.message = "The db may not have been initialized."
        request.view = "error"
        render()
    }
  }
}

def onRetrieve(){}

def onCreate(){}

def onUpdate(){}

def onDelete(){}
```

What did we build? In keeping things as simple as possible, we actually only created one new file. However, we edited a couple of existing
files (ivy.xml and zero.config). Figure 6.28 shows the folder structure for
the project and all the existing files.

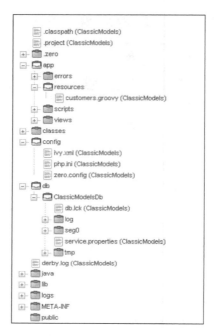

Figure 6.28 Reviewing the application

After you save the file and run the application, the feed should be accessible with the right URL. Remember, the Groovy filename and path are needed to know how the resource should be accessed. When running the application, you can use additional tools such as Firefox Poster, which is a Firefox add-on for working with web services and other web resources. The URL for the application is something like http://<mydomain>:8080/, which means that the service can be accessed by adding /resources/customers to this URL, as shown in Figure 6.29.

From here, you are ready to continue building the sample application and learning how to develop exciting Web 2.0 applications. This style of development can be accomplished quickly using the existing modules and the Groovy or PHP language to glue everything together. From this overview, you should have gathered that WebSphere sMash does not have the same focus as IBM Mashups in enabling end users to build their own situational applications. It does, however, provide a comprehensive environment for quickly building feeds and Web 2.0-style applications.

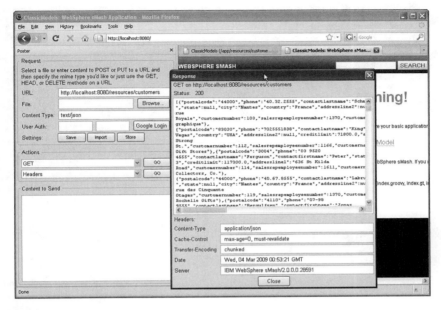

Figure 6.29   Retrieving data from the resource

Sample sMash Applications

There is some middle ground with WebSphere sMash besides build-ing an application from scratch. Predefined sMash applications can be created that allow end users to view their own data in interesting ways. Figure 6.30 shows one of the sample applications that comes with sMash.

The sample application allows end users to upload their own spread-sheet for viewing.

This is somewhat similar to what we showed with the IBM Mashups scenario. However, it is an actual sMash application and not sMash itself providing this capability.

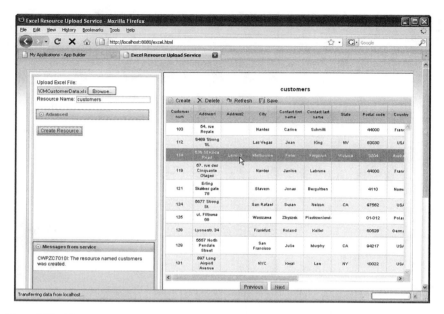

Figure 6.30   Viewing the Excel application

An Interview with IBM's Mashup Architects

Building a strategy around mashup technology can be quite difficult. Do I use a product or build from scratch? Which set of products and technologies are most useful? These and other questions are often the decisions that have to be made as you define a strategy for your organization. Talking with experts can often help in understanding viewpoints of people who help define the vision for other organizations, and also have their own vision of where things are going. The following questions were posed to two expert architects who work daily with IBM's mashup products. This session also provides an opportunity for you to compare and contrast some of the features and vision of WebSphere sMash versus Lotus Mashup Center.

Usman's Bio:

Usman Memon is the co-founder and CEO of Streebo Inc. (www. streebo.com). Headquartered in Houston, Texas, Streebo, an IBM Business Partner, specializes in building automated solutions that streamline complex business processes. Usman advises his customers on

IT strategy and enterprise architecture and remains an oft-requested technical speaker at seminars and conferences. He recently spoke at the Mashup Conference in Mountain View, California, on "Automating Your Enterprise: Applying Parametric Modeling in Mashups." He is coauthor of a book (*Programming Portlets*, IBM Press) and has contributed to several articles and white papers related to portals and SOA in leading publications. Usman holds a Bachelor's degree in engineering from National Institute of Technology, Trichy (India) and a Master's degree in mathematics and computer science from Ohio University.

Jason's Bio:

Jason McGee is a Distinguished Engineer (DE) and Chief Architect for WebSphere Extended Deployment (XD), WebSphere sMash, and the leader of Project Zero. Previously, Jason was the Chief Architect of WebSphere Application Server on distributed platforms. He is a senior architect on the WebSphere Foundation Architecture Board. Jason serves as the Director of WebSphere Advanced Technologies, responsible for productization of new technologies into the WebSphere platform. Jason joined IBM in 1997 and has been a member of the WebSphere Server team since its inception. Jason graduated with a Bachelor of Science degree in computer engineering from Virginia Tech in 1995.

How are mashups and situational applications changing the way we think about application development?

Jason:

In many ways, I do not think mashups and situational applications are changing how we think about application development at all. Rather, I think mashups and situational applications have always been with us, have always been a component of the landscape of applications we have developed. What has changed is the technology behind mashups and the ease with which these applications can be built and deployed. The combination of modern web browsers with powerful JavaScript/CSS/DHTML capabilities and lightweight dynamic scripting engines on the server side has enabled developers to build mashups and situational apps both more quickly and more compellingly. And the mass of people using the same technologies has enabled a feedback cycle to develop where my mashup can feed into your mashup and the value can start to grow exponentially.

Usman:

Traditionally, application development has always been thought of as an "IT exercise." With the evolution of Web 2.0, however, and with the advent of tooling for mashups, there is a game-changing shift happening in IT departments around the world. Finally, the business users who actual run the day-to-day operations are becoming empowered to create their own situational applications without intervention from IT. This does not mean that IT's role is undermined; instead, we (in IT) need to focus on opening up data pipes and giving controlled access to these business users and ensure that they become successful with mashup tooling. Companies that have been early adopters on mashups and situational applications are seeing different dimensions and gathering more insight into their traditional business problems.

How should organizations think about your product(s) in terms of their overall strategy?

Usman:

Lotus Mashups will be a natural extension to the product portfolio for a wide spectrum of organizations that are getting ready to evolve and start handing controlled access to silos of data that have been traditionally locked and controlled by IT. Companies that are looking for an enterprise-level platform that serves both IT and the "business developers" should look to invest in Lotus Mashups. Further, the tight coupling with WebSphere Portal and IBM Automation technology (Widget Factory) employed in creation of widgets puts Lotus Mashups in a "disruptive technology" slot and allows our customers to stretch their ROI on IBM (WebSphere App & Portal, Data Power, Process Server, etc.) investments further.

Jason:

Organizations should think of WebSphere sMash as complementary to their existing application development and deployment strategy. Often, organizations have a variety of development projects underway or waiting to commence. Some of these projects are for mission-critical or high-value systems that will support the business and last for a long period of time. For other projects, time to deployment, speed of development, and cost of operation are the primary drivers. These smaller projects might be situational in nature or simply applications that are needed to respond to short timeframe demands. WebSphere sMash is a perfect development and deployment platform for the creation of this second class of projects. It allows rapid construction, easy reuse, and mashing together of assets, and cost-effective deployment.

What concerns should people have as they bring mashups and situational applications into their organization.

Jason:

The primary concern people should have is security of information. As more and more applications are built that access and expose an organization's data, it becomes harder to ensure secure access to that data and privacy of the information that is being exposed. Mashup platforms like WebSphere sMash provide all the technical tools needed to manage this security, but it is important that organizations put practices and policies in place to help them govern and control access to information and its appropriate use. There is always a tension here between the power of exposing information in new ways and the importance of controlling and restricting access to that same information.

Usman:

When I am on the road discussing mashups with my customers, I hear IT executives getting concerned about security and scalability. What happens when thousands of business users start pounding your back-end legacy systems as you expose your services? How can you ensure that Bob in marketing does not get access to sensitive data only meant for HR? Hence, when IBM started planning Lotus Mashups, the product strategy team aligned themselves closely with the InfoSphere Hub (Information Management Brand) and WebSphere Portal team. Therefore, Lotus Mashups and InfoSphere Hub together now formulate a complete IBM Mashup portfolio and it ties very well into the WebSphere Portal, thus allowing IT to leverage the investments made in a robust platform.

How can your products close the skills gap and help organizations deliver value more quickly?

Usman:

IBM planned and built the Lotus Mashups with two distinctive user communities in mind. First was the IT developer, the widget creator. IBM ships Widget Factory, which allows wizard-based creation and modification of widgets that tie into disparate back ends. With little or no programming, developers from a wide variety of backgrounds can very rapidly start churning out widgets with rich interfaces. We have trained ASP, Domino, Java, and even RPG programmers on IBM's automation tooling, and they quickly latch on, as the widget factory abstracts the underlying gory details. The second community, the business user who would use the mashup tooling to create situational app—here the product management and engineering team emphasized and focused on usability and attempted to create a browser-based rich Internet interface that would be intuitive and easily adaptable. Customers and analysts have lauded IBM's effort to provide a platform that allows IT and business users to collaborate in a more meaningful way.

Jason:

When we developed WebSphere sMash, one key consideration was skills and how to leverage the skills people had. If you want to build something quickly, it is critical that you do not have to start with learning an entirely new set of skills from day one. To accomplish this, we used scripting languages that many developers knew already, namely Java and PHP. So, from the outset, the initial skills needed to build the application are already present for most people using sMash. Next, we removed as many concepts from the system as possible. No installation. No packaging. No complex deployment model. We did this so that developers could deliver value quickly because they did not have to understand too many concepts to be productive. Finally, we helped close the skill gap by making the system intuitive and optimizing for the common scenarios people would want to accomplish. So when developers got into uncharted waters, they could use their intuition to figure out how to proceed. The combination of these three approaches allows WebSphere sMash to be agile and productive for developers, and therefore helps organizations deliver more quickly on their goals.

What are the next steps or future direction for your product?

Jason:

The future direction of WebSphere sMash is really to evolve the platform to meet a broader set of needs more easily. Better tools, better runtimes, more capabilities. However, one of the really unique aspects of WebSphere sMash is the open development model being used to create the product. At Projectzero.org, developers and customers can collaborate with us and help to define the future direction. So in reality, the next steps are up to them. The goal of sMash is to make mashup and situational application development easier, so we will move the product in whatever direction our users dictate to achieve that goal.

Usman:

IBM's Lotus Mashup product roadmap has continual emphasis on improving the business user's experience with the tool. IBM realizes that for business users to adapt this tool and create meaningful apps it has to be intuitive and easy to use. The Widget Factory, on the other hand, seems to be adding more builders to connect to a wider spectrum of enterprise back ends and Web 2.0 (Ajax and so on) builders that enable developers to rapidly create widgets with rich interfaces. Widget Factory seems to be keeping in sync with evolving iWidget specifications, and this will allow IT to create SOA-compliant, standard-based widgets that can be deployed not only on the Lotus Mashup server but on other IBM products such as WebSphere Application Server or Portal Server, too. IBM is working to ensure that customers have to develop applications just once (using Widget Factory) and that they can then deploy them across platforms, including Lotus Mashups.

Conclusion

Strategic applications come in all shapes and sizes. It is really about making the most of your business and IT dollars. The business needs to decide what functionality, services, or capability they need, and those decisions need to be timely. While IT needs to support the business, it should also try to keep everyone honest about the effort and cost involved with providing any requested services. Heavyweight strategic applications cost time and money during the initial rollout, but also in services and support for continued operations. And let's face it, money is tight and should be controlled wisely. Because demand always outpaces the capability that IT can provide, it is necessary to find alternative ways to provide the ability to quickly release new applications and meet pent-up demand.

Situational applications can help with this effort by providing the ability to quickly deploy what are sometimes referred to as long tail mashups and situational applications. That is, applications that do not have a large enough demand for IT to make a high priority, but which can provide significant business value to some users. It is well known that the combination of all long tail activity might well provide significant value beyond the top-tier strategic applications. Figure 6.31 shows the recommended approach for using these types of tools to provide this capability.

You can see how these tools can provide the basis for your organization to start building these situational applications quickly and easily with minimal resource support. Beyond that, much of the capability we have discussed is simply cool. There is much value to be derived here in

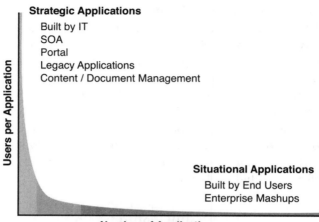

Figure 6.31   Mashups fill the long tail

quickly and easily exposing services and data that continues to remain hidden away within every organization.

References

Gladwell, Malcolm (Gladwell, 2002), *The Tipping Point.*

7

Enterprise Search Strategies

Search is one of the most important components of any site and yet many organizations struggle with providing comprehensive and intuitive ways to search for information within the enterprise. This is not a comment on the level of IT skills within the organization; instead, it refers to the complexity of the task at hand. You can prove that statement simply by asking your end users, many of whom will probably say that their current search is inadequate. Think about some of the requirements that one might put together when defining a search strategy.

- Index data from multiple data sources, including databases, file systems, and legacy applications.
- Layer a common taxonomy and a common metadata vocabulary on top of the data from multiple systems so that a single search shows a comprehensive view of what information is available for a given topic.
- Maintain all security restrictions on existing information so that the search engine does not expose data to the wrong person.

- Provide an easy to use and intuitive interface so users can find what they actually need.
- Allow users to rank and tag search items to help others understand which data could be very useful.
- Oh, and make it fast!

These are just some of the basic requirements that an organization might consider; this list could easily grow to tens of items. But you get the basic point; search can be hard. An important point to consider, as with most enterprise-wide projects, is not to bite off more than you can chew initially. This is sound advice in almost any IT area, but specifically with search it is easier to prove out a single case and then watch the effect on users and the systems as you add additional sources to your search collections.

Why Not Use Google?

More and more often, I hear the phrase "make it Google-like." This is a testament to the popularity and speed of the Google search engine. There are even appliances that people can purchase to provide Google-like capability for their own web applications. However, consider that the Google that we know and love provides us with access to a public and homogeneous Web. In other words, most websites appear to be similar, and Google has optimized the crawling and indexing of these sites and then allows you to search for them through their search engine.

But many of the factors that go into an *Internet* search are different from what would be required in an *intranet* search engine. Popularity of pages within an enterprise might not necessarily be based on the number of links to a page (although it could be). In addition, the amount of data that Google has to draw from is enormous, much larger than any internal sources you may have within your organization, so you are more likely to find something interesting within their results.

In addition, think about your organization and some of other requirements listed previously. Do you have a lot of documents and content in Lotus Notes or Domino applications? Would you like to make some applications or content stores searchable but the security risk is too high? These factors and more are what make your organization unique, and because of that, your search strategy has to be unique, also.

Introduction to IBM OmniFind

IBM's OmniFind Enterprise Edition provides enterprise search, classi-
fication, and analytics to help solve the information and search challenge
that many organizations face. Like most IBM products, the solution provides a comprehensive portfolio of functionality that organizations can
customize for their specific needs. IBM also offers OmniFind Enterprise
Starter Edition, which is a scaled-down version of the Enterprise
Version.

The goal of OmniFind is to help users become more productive by
helping them to find information and content that may be scattered
across the enterprise. At the core of OmniFind is a middleware layer that
sits between end-user web applications and content repositories within
the enterprise that are used by those applications (see Figure 7.1).

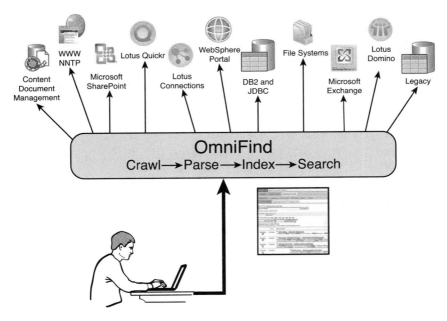

Figure 7.1   Search integration for all of the enterprise.

Note that in Figure 7.1, OmniFind provides several core functions.
They are crawling, parsing, indexing, and searching, and each of these
steps builds on the other to provide maximum value to your end users:

- **Crawling:** The crawling process is what extracts the data from the content stores within your enterprise. This is the key component in getting a comprehensive view of the information within your organization. Most search engines provide an initial set of crawlers that enable you to easily set up and crawl, say, your corporate intranet. Other prebuilt crawlers might also be available, such as database and file system crawlers. For most enterprise situations, you must have the capability to create your own crawlers (adaptors) that allow you to index the content within your specific legacy systems, or the search engine should provide an application programming interface (API) that will allow you to push data into the indexing process.

- **Parsing:** Parsing is breaking down the content into individual words or tokens. This allows the search engine to perform additional analysis on the content, such as identifying names, places, or keywords within the content.

- **Indexing:** After parsing the information, tokens can be indexed to allow for quicker searching by your users. Indexes are important because users expect searches to be fast. However, indexing is a time-consuming activity, and with search data, the indexes need to be updated often to reflect the most current data within the system.

- **Searching:** This is the actual search application that usually runs within an application server, such as IBM WebSphere Application Server (WAS). Search queries are submitted through an HTML page, and the results are displayed the same way. Additional search interfaces could be built or extended (e.g., deploying a set of search portlets to IBM WebSphere Portal).

Behind the scenes, the search itself has to be blazingly fast, even though the previous steps can sometimes take some time to run completely. The only thing the end user should see is the response time of the search request page.

Defining Collections

OmniFind uses the concept of a collection to identify and maintain a set of data sources that is searched. A collection enables for management of sets of similar data sources, or it enables you to limit the size of your search data by breaking it up into multiple collections. Conceptually therefore, a *collection* is defined as the set of data sources that can be searched in a single query. However, there are ways to federate multiple collections to get around that constraint. Actually how you are able to federate data from multiple sources within your organization resides within the search application and its ability to provide that type of functionality.

The next obvious statement is this: "Wait, I want to search everything simultaneously!" Even though you might hear this often, in reality searching all data sources simultaneously is not usually feasible or even really what you want to do. Remember, one of the biggest barriers you will face is the concept of defining a common taxonomy or set of metadata for all the different content and data sources within your company. You might want to separate your searches into different collections; for example, you might want one or more collections for informal information, such as corporate blogs, wikis, and forums, and another set of collections for more formal data, or "corporate gospel" as some customers call it. In addition, all the data sources within a collection should use the same ranking system so that the search results are consistent. For example, some sources, such as websites, use the number of links to a page to determine its rank within the results, whereas other data sources might use the document date to determine whether that document should rank higher in the results. If you use these inconsistently, the results might be somewhat inconsistent for different searches. Another way to break out your collections is by the data type itself, as shown in Figure 7.2.

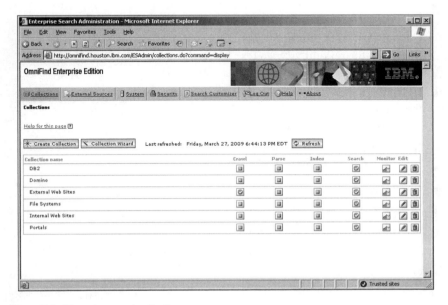

Figure 7.2 Managing search collections.

This is a more technical approach to organizing your collections and might not be the right business approach. The idea is to break down your data sources into what is relevant and should be grouped together logically to provide the most value to your search users. Currently, a collection in OmniFind is limited to 20 million documents per collection, so this fact should also weigh into your collection design and scoping effort.

Within each collection are one or more crawlers. Crawlers connect to each individual data source and pull the data within that data source to make it available within the search. OmniFind comes with many out-of-the-box crawlers, most of which are listed here:

- IBM DB2® Content Manager item types (documents, resources, and items)
- IBM DB2 databases
- IBM Domino Document Manager (formerly Domino.Doc) databases
- IBM Lotus Notes databases
- IBM Lotus QuickPlace databases
- IBM Lotus Quickr content libraries
- IBM WebSphere Information Integrator Content Edition repositories, including Documentum, FileNet Panagon Content Services, FileNet P8 Content Manager, Hummingbird Document Management (DM), Microsoft SharePoint®, OpenText Livelink Enterprise Server, and WebSphere Portal Document Manager (PDM)
- IBM WebSphere Information Integrator nickname tables for many database system types, including IBM DB2 for z/OS®, IBM Informix®, Microsoft SQL Server®, Oracle, and Sybase
- IBM WebSphere Portal sites
- IBM Workplace Web Content Management sites
- Microsoft Exchange Server public folders
- Microsoft SQL Server databases
- Microsoft Windows file systems
- Network news transfer protocol (NNTP) news groups
- Oracle databases

- UNIX® file systems
- Websites on the Internet or on your intranet

This list makes it easy to quickly add core content to your search collections and then follow up with custom solutions for other legacy applications.

You need to consider several key factors when creating and configuring a crawler for a specific data source. Aside from the typical information about the type and location of the data source, it is important to consider both the security and the ranking information around the data. Security considerations are perhaps one of the most important. Web searches, such as Google, do not care about security, which allows the query to consider all the data in a quick manner. Internal enterprise searches that display results to the end user have to be much more discriminating. You should not display search results to users that they cannot readily access. The better solution is to initially filter out non-available results. Document-level security can be applied if you have defined a collection to be secure.

The reality of security constraints is that maintaining a high level of security is sometimes easier said than done, and it requires constant effort to ensure that security constraints are applied correctly to data. In OmniFind, custom Java classes can be created to map the security tokens within the data to that of end users. This security data can then be stored with the index information for the search. In addition, OmniFind provides some identity management capability that allows you to control secure search results that are provided to end users.

Creating a Search Application

Out of the box, OmniFind comes with a pretty standard search application (see Figure 7.3). This application can serve as an example for any custom search applications you might need to build. When you allow end users to search one or more collections through the interface, your overall strategy actually comes to life.

If you have designed your approach with multiple search collections, you need to define how users might identify which collection or sets of data they are trying to search. This might be through the use of page tabs, or possibly a set of radio buttons or check boxes. For most search applications, you have several options.

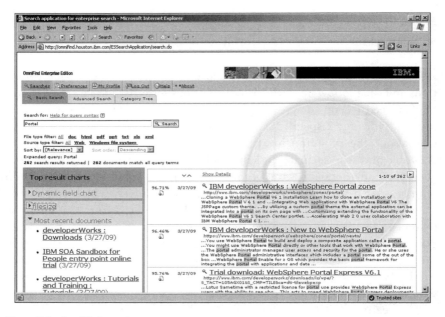

Figure 7.3   OmniFind search.

- Use the standard search interface that is supplied out of the box with OmniFind.

- Use the standard portlets that come with OmniFind to integrate your search with IBM WebSphere Portal.

- Build your own interface using the IBM Search and Index API (SIAPI).

With any approach, there is plenty of flexibility within OmniFind to design an approach that fits your specific needs.

How IBM Uses OmniFind Enterprise Edition

In Chapter 2, "Portals in the Enterprise," we talked about IBM's intranet, or w3. w3 is a comprehensive portal that provides information for employees about all aspects of the organization. Search is obviously an important part of the w3 strategy, with OmniFind being at the forefront of this approach. w3 supports hundreds of thousands of employees and gets several million hits per day. And as you can imagine, information within IBM is scattered to the four corners of the globe, in just about every type of repository you can imagine.

w3 provides searchable content from thousands of HTML and XML pages that are found within the intranet as well as Lotus Notes and IBM DB2 databases, blogs, wikis, forums, and so on (see Figure 7.4). The system supports as many as 200,000 searches per day at a rate of 14 transactions per second.

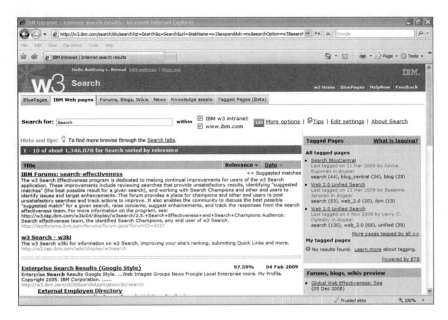

Figure 7.4   Search strategies for the enterprise.

One important takeaway shown in Figure 7.4 is that some searches are broken down by tabs across the top of the page. Note that not every collection has to flow through a single search request. Search types are often broken down into groups, allowing users to decide which repository or set of repositories they want to search. This is important for two reasons:

- Some repositories might be determined to be not as comprehensive, or the information is not as valid.

- This approach allows IT to add new search repositories in a responsive and flexible manner. New searches or collections can be added as they are developed without interfering with any current search collections.

Figure 7.5 illustrates a couple of additional areas of interest. With Web 2.0, we should think about a search strategy. It is important to categorize data as it is parsed and indexed within the search engine. This provides a starting point for the search of new data. We can use tagging and rating to provide additional input into search results, but an initial categorization mechanism is almost always necessary.

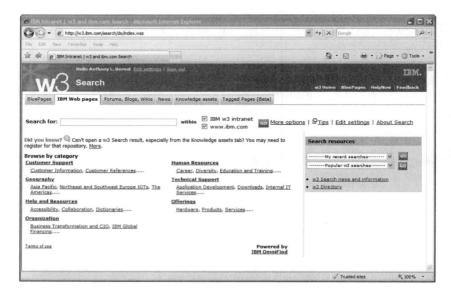

Figure 7.5   Basic categorization.

OmniFind allows for the creation of categories and rules for each category, which are then used during the document-parsing phase to identify a particular document with one or more categories. Most category rules are based on the URL for the document or the document content itself. If either of these contains one or more of the categories, they will get associated with those categories.

Using Tagging to Find Information

You can think of tagging as the new wave of categorization. Traditional knowledge management experts often think of categorization as a top-down effort, where the sum of knowledge within the corporate knowledge is divided into predefined categories (in other words, a taxonomy). This taxonomy is often domain or industry specific and is designed to allow organizations within the same or complementary industries to share this domain knowledge, or at least maintain a common understanding of how that knowledge should be defined.

With the advent of Web 2.0, something started to change. Web 2.0 is the interactive Web, where end users can help define not only what is important to them, but also how they might categorize the data. This helped facilitate a change from the traditional "taxonomy" to the more interactive "folksonomy," where common folks helped drive the categorization of information in a more meaningful manner. There is actually some debate within the community about the value of a knowledge management-driven taxonomy versus a user-driven folksonomy. The truth is that it is probably necessary to have both in some manner within your organization. Figure 7.6 shows a partial tag cloud that is driven by user tags.

Figure 7.6 Using Dogear to refine search results.

During any initial search design, some amount of organizational categorization needs to be done. At a high level, you can add a category for content items relevant to the keyword portal. However, as users continue to tag data, they can refine this content in ways that are much more relevant to end users.

Encouraging Tagging, Ranking, and Bookmarking

Sometimes the terms get mixed up, so some definitions are in order:

- **Tagging:**   Tagging is a way to mark a piece of content or even a bookmark with a relevant name or phrase. This helps others see this content in relation to other content that might be similarly tagged. For example, a piece of content that is categorized with the term *portal* might be tagged by users with keywords *process, collaboration,* or *Social Networking* to help users understand what context this piece of content has with portals.

- **Ranking:**   Ranking is a way of marking a piece of content as something valuable to you and possibly others who might be looking for similar information. You can rank via a number (1–10, for example) or maybe with stars (five-star ranking). This enables others to see the content that has been useful to others within the organization and helps weed out the less-valuable stuff.

- **Bookmarking:**   Bookmarking is the act of saving a link to a particular document for use by yourself or others within your team or organization. Often, items can be bookmarked based on a specific technology or as something that may be of interested to a specific community.

The key to making this strategy work is getting buy in from end users to participant in the experience. Encouraging participation is one way to get things started. It is often the fact that new technologies need to reach critical mass before full adoption by everyone happens. People need to understand the value of new technologies and how a new technology will help them before they are willing to expend valuable time learning a new system. Bookmarks are another way to share relevant information with coworkers and others. Figure 7.7 shows a Dogear feed with information that has been bookmarked by a user.

This type of data feed using the Atom syndication format can be easily integrated into other pages and environments using query string parameters. The Atom syndication format was discussed in Chapter 1, "Web 2.0 and

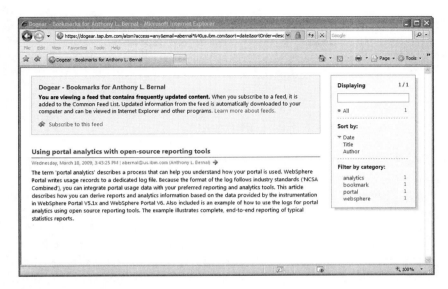

Figure 7.7   Display Dogear bookmarks.

Social Networking." For example, as a sidebar to the main search results, additional tagged content can be displayed (see Figure 7.8).

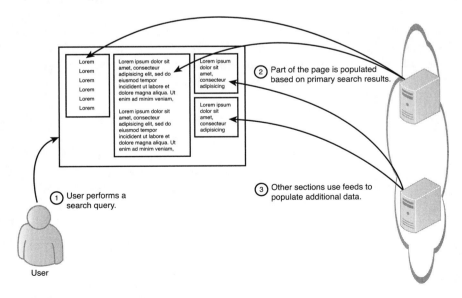

Figure 7.8   Integrating multiple sources.

This approach provides a full view of multiple data sources to the user and immediately shows the benefit of user-based tagging and bookmarking. The concept of ranking can be used across all these display areas to ensure that the more highly ranked content is displayed first in the results.

Conclusion

Much of the Social Networking strategy that you implement within your organization could be rendered useless without a well-defined search. However, you should also have noticed that there are a lot of considerations when defining a search strategy. Technology can provide a lot of the search framework that you need, but additional customization is required for it to fit well within your enterprise. Two of the key factors that we touched on in this chapter are speed and security—without either of which your search approach might be rendered useless or, worse yet, proclaimed unusable by your users. This could be a disaster for your search if users do not find it useful.

The key to implementing good search is to start small. This is an important factor for most major organizational undertakings; however, search is one enterprise project that a team needs to grow into. Trying to do too much at once usually just raises too many issues to be widely successful. After you have a proven approach with a few collections or data sources and you are sure that the right level of security and performance is being reached, you can begin to monitor your approach and add additional data sources as resources permit.

References

1. OmniFind Enterprise Edition 8.5 InfoCenter. Retrieved April 23, 2009 from http://publib.boulder.ibm.com/infocenter/discover/v8r5m0/index.jsp.

2. IBM Lotus Connections InfoCenter. Retrieved April 25, 2009 from http://publib.boulder.ibm.com/infocenter/ltscnnct/v2r0/index.jsp.

8

Web 2.0 Security and Performance

The Web 2.0 world opens up a variety of new security and performance concerns for IT organizations. On the security side, moving business logic to the browser and exposing data via client-side services should give any IT manager pause. This exposure can be managed, and tradeoffs have to be examined to understand what gains there are to be had from adopting more of a client-based platform.

On the performance side, adopting a Web 2.0 approach and using much of the technology can help reduce many of the performance problems that plague current server-side applications. Although true in theory, there are also tradeoffs, and the same amount of discipline and testing that should be performed with the current service-side model should also be applied to a new client-side model.

This chapter looks at some of these concerns and helps you learn what steps you can take to ensure success as you adopt new Web 2.0 strategies and implement the technology within your organization.

Common Attack Vectors

As with any technology, common security issues can plague an application. Web applications are no exception, and while Web 2.0 provides new flexibility and usability, it also provides new ideas for hackers and attackers to disrupt your site. As of this writing, the most common attack in the Web 2.0 world is cross-site scripting or XSS. The acronym XSS is used to avoid any confusion with CSS (Cascading Style Sheets), another issue altogether.

You need to be aware of other types of attacks, too, that are not covered in this book. The second most common attack is SQL injection attack, which was covered in detail in my last book, *Application Architecture for WebSphere* (IBM Press).

Same Origin Policy

The original inventors of the Internet saw that XSS might be a potential concern and adopted a concept called the same origin policy. This was originally targeted toward client-side programming languages such as JavaScript and is designed to ensure that all client-side code comes from the same server or domain and adheres to the same protocol. If this policy were not in place, it would be too easy for a hacker to also gain access or set up a malicious attack.

Cross-Site Scripting

As it is, hackers can still get around the same origin policy and set up an XSS attack on unprepared websites. The goal is to make the browser think that the malicious code is coming from the same domain as the rest of the site. In most cases, it is actually coming from the unsuspecting website. Figure 8.1 shows how an attacker can find a potential security issue with a site. The attacker simply enters some data into the text field to see whether that text is echoed back to the screen on the next page refresh.

You can try this on many sites and see this is the case. Of course, the data entered in Figure 8.1, text, is benign, so having this show up in the display will not cause any problems. It does, however, identify a potential hole that an attacker can exploit. What if the attacker decides to further test this site by entering some JavaScript to see whether that is

Figure 8.1   Testing for CSS vulnerability

returned and interpreted by the browser as coming from the original application (see Figure 8.2).

In this case, the attacker enters the following code in the search box:

```
<script>alert(document.cookie)</script>
```

The browser receives that code in the returning page and interprets it as if the script is coming from the original server. There is now a large window of opportunity for a potential hacker who can generate a URL similar to the one that follows:

```
http://demo.testfire.net/search.aspx?txtSearch=%3Cscript%3Ealert%28document.
cookie%29%3C%2Fscript%3E
```

This URL embeds the JavaScript into the URL parameters of the request. The "trick" at this point is to get the user to somehow click on this URL. In itself, this is not hard because the URL can be wrapped with any exciting message, but often a hacker wants, without raising suspicion, the user to want to click on a URL (for example, an email seemingly sent from the site in question asking you to check or update something on the site). Figure 8.3 illustrates this.

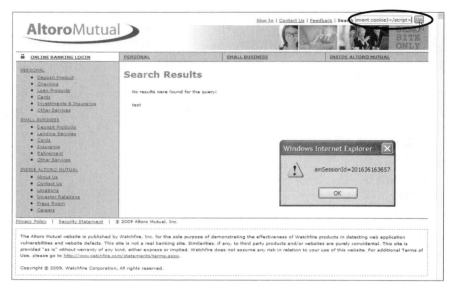

Figure 8.2   Verifying a potential security hole

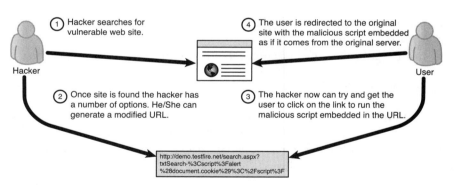

Figure 8.3   Staging an XSS attack

Admittedly, this hack is not sophisticated. After all, a pop-up would alert the user that something is amiss. However, a security hole such as the one described here provides opportunity for complex hacks that can compromise an entire site and all the supporting data, such as login and account information. By injecting the right set of JavaScript, a hacker can change information on the page, or redirect any submitted information to a completely different site (or, more important, to their hacker site).

Persistent XSS

Persistent cross-site scripting is even more insidious because the hacker does not have to trick the user into clicking on a modified link. In this case, if there is a way to embed the code into the page, it can run when an innocent user simply displays the page. Let's use the example of someone's blog or a user group forum that allows comments. If someone can upload a comment that consists of pure code that runs natively on the browser, it is even easier to hack a user's browser (see Figure 8.4).

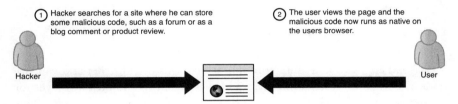

Figure 8.4   Staging a persistent XSS attack

XSS is often misunderstood, but I hope these simple examples outline the danger that they can pose to your website. Of course, there are ways to protect your website that are outlined in the rest of this chapter, but understanding the problem and the extent of the potential exposure is the first step.

Server-Side Code Is Important

Many developers who start to embrace the client-side model or Web 2.0 model might start to make a dramatic shift in their thinking. To them, everything belongs on the client, and server-side processing is dead. Those individuals should understand that server-side development is still alive and well and should play an important role in enterprise applications.

Server-side validation is still necessary to ensure that changes have not been made client side to the validation on that end. Remember that if you have a problem on the client side (for example, some type of security hole), good hackers can do pretty much whatever they want with your code. This is not to say that you have not written good code, but it is open for inspection and modification on the browser at will. You just do not have a choice. Figure 8.5 shows how important information might be validated several times to avoid issues.

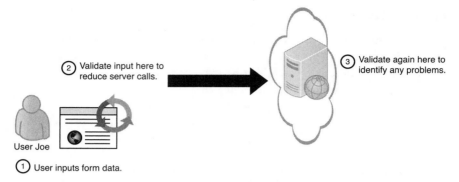

Figure 8.5   Client-side and server-side validation

A good application architecture might take this even further and validate data in both the presentation layer and then again in the business layer for deeper business functionality. You probably do not want to expose business logic on the client, but rather keep some of that on the server for processing. We can define business logic as anything that is important to the way you run your business. For example, if you use a specific formula to determine whether a user is valid, this might be better done on the server side, instead of letting potential hackers see and try to duplicate your formula. Typically, you would want to check the following in the server to determine whether the data is valid or problematic:

- Validate all required fields.
- Check the field data type or convert HTTP strings to the required data type.
- Validate the field length.
- Validate the data is within the field range.
- Ensure that field options are valid for those items that provide options.
- Check the input data pattern.
- Validate any cookie values and/or the HTTP response itself.

Adopting this approach ensures that malicious users do not gain more information about your business and business processing than they need to know.

Keeping State Information on the Client

Related but sometimes different is the idea of keeping state information on the browser to be submitted with each request. State information is data maintained between user requests. For example, if you enter data into a form that is several pages long. That data is often stored with the form until you have completed the entire workflow. This form is said to be in a specific state. Usually, this is done with the use of hidden elements in a form that are used to store information that a user has previously entered, or a calculated field. Without proper validation, keeping state information on the browser can lead to major issues.

Escaping User Input

One good way to ensure that malicious code is not injected into your site is through the use of good validation and escaping of user input. This enables you to sanitize the input before it is processed or returned to the browser, effectively filtering out the bad stuff. This is a black list type of approach in that we are removing things that we know can be bad. Table 8.1 shows some of the characters that can be validated and removed from incoming fields.

Table 8.1 Characters That Can Be Validated and Removed from Incoming Fields

Symbol	Definition
|	Pipe sign
&	Ampersand
;	Semicolon
$	Dollar sign
%	Percent sign
%	At sign
'	Single apostrophe
"	Quotation mark
\'	Backslash-escaped apostrophe
\"	Backslash-escaped quotation mark
< >	Triangular parenthesis
()	Parenthesis

Table 8.1   Characters That Can Be Validated and Removed from Incoming Fields

Symbol	Definition
+	Plus sign
CR	Carriage return, ASCII 0x0d
LF	Line feed, ASCII 0x0a
,	Comma
\	Backslash

The result of finding invalid codes can simply be an error message returned to the user explaining that the information entered cannot be processed.

Portal Proxy

The beginning of this chapter talked about the same origin policy that helps protect your web applications from rogue code, but this policy can also cause some problems when you are trying to deliver solutions to your end users. For example, perhaps you need to consume services or data from a new or existing service that might reside within a different domain. This might occur when you leverage a public service such as Amazon or Google. This could also be the case when internal services that start to arrive within the enterprise as new applications leverage this technology and attempt to share information across business domains.

WebSphere Portal tries to help with this issue by introducing an HTTP proxy that can be used as a local proxy for Ajax applications. This proxy allows the local application to access the service as if it were from the same domain or origin as other services, as shown in Figure 8.6.

What is important to realize is that this essentially bypasses the same origin policy that was put in place to protect end users. Therefore, when you proxy a service, it is important to understand what or who is behind that service and know that no malicious activities will take place from that location.

Some security measures are available with the portal proxy allowing you to define security roles and provide authentication mechanisms for proxied services. However, this does not absolve you from the main responsibility of ensuring the data is valid and secure.

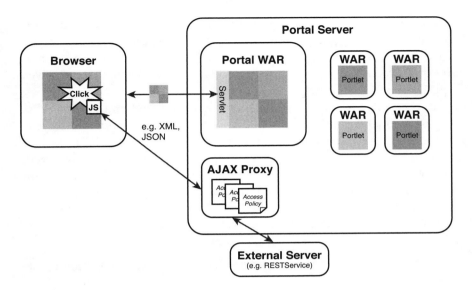

Figure 8.6   Portal proxy

REST Service Security

It is a simple thing to build a REST service that enables your application to consume data and display it to the user without a browser refresh. This is often used in the case of a partial-page refresh where one part of the page or a portlet is updated without the entire page having to make a round trip to the server. We discuss this from a performance point of view later in this chapter; but from a security viewpoint, it is important to understand that these services now exist within your application and across the enterprise, and proper security is necessary.

In most cases, this could be reviewed on a case-by-case basis, but it is important to know when these services are being used and exactly what data is exposed to the user. Through the previous discussion, you have seen that because browser is inherently unsecure, there should be no trust that what you are receiving from the browser is correct or validated.

Rational AppScan

Customers often look for tools to help identify and diagnose potential problems with their application. In my previous book, *Application*

Architecture for WebSphere, I discuss this same topic and some of the tooling available to ensure that standards put in place are used correctly within an application. In the Web 2.0 world, Rational AppScan is another product that can be used to conduct and even automate web application security testing.

Rational AppScan comes in a number of packages and editions that can be used at various places within your software development lifecycle. For example, Rational AppScan Standard Edition is an Eclipse-based version that can be used by nonsecurity professionals to identify potential security issues within a web application (see Figure 8.7). You might think of AppScan as a hacker in a box, but one under your control (of course). IBM Rational keeps tight control over the use of this product to be sure that it will not be used for nefarious purposes

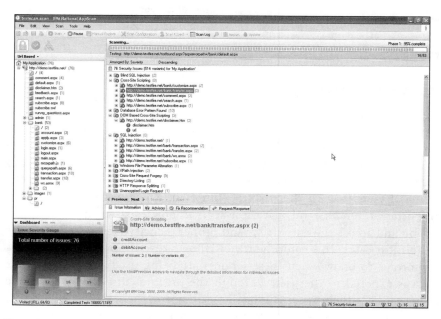

Figure 8.7   Rational AppScan

Threats to web applications such as XSS are cause for a lot of concern. If an application is public facing or contains sensitive information, there may be regulatory and business concerns to think about. AppScan can help you generate reports to help you address regulatory compliance.

AppScan identifies potential threats and then provides you with a security rating for each potential risk that is found.

The rating system that AppScan uses is based on the threat ratings provided by the Web Application Security Consortium (discussed later in this chapter). However, more than that, AppScan provides detailed recommendations to fix potential problems. Rational AppScan provides a number of out-of-the-box templates to help you define and run a scan on your application, including a template for WebSphere Portal (see Figure 8.8).

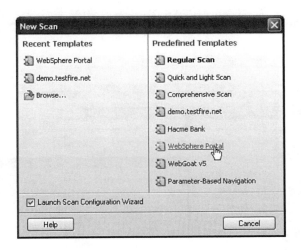

Figure 8.8 AppScan testing templates

Rational AppScan is not a lightweight tool. Rational AppScan provides comprehensive security scanning to ensure that no potential holes are uncovered in your web application.

On a side note, I will admit that I had trouble creating a portlet with an obvious XSS hole, which is why there is no portlet example in this chapter. There is a setting within WebSphere portal that provides some protection against this type of attack. Also, the fact that portals use highly complex URLs that contain navigation and state information means that it is more difficult to compromise a specific portlet using URL hijacking. This certainly does not mean you won't have any security issues, but portals provide some additional security by default. Just remember that the more custom your application is, the more security risk you may incur.

Web Application Security Consortium

So where can you go to learn more about web application security? The Web Application Security Consortium (webappsec) is a group of international security experts and practitioners who make standards and best practices related to security issues available. WebAppSec also publishes a set of threat classifications on security issues, as shown in Figure 8.9. This is a comprehensive set of security concerns, and WebAppSec shows how big of a threat they may be to your application. Rational AppScan makes use of the webappsec provided references in helping you to identify how serious a threat may be to your system.

Figure 8.9   Web Application Security Consortium

Webappsec also provides papers and studies on web application security and statistics; these can help you identify the prevalence and potential of different attacks.

Public Sites Security Issues

This chapter would not be complete without a discussion of public Social Networking site security. Sites such as MySpace, Facebook, and LinkedIn are becoming more popular with the business community, and corporate members are joining in increasing ranks. The corporate concern is more about employees wasting their time visiting them rather than about security issues. This is a valid concern in some organizations. However, in many organizations where the employee base is composed of mostly knowledge workers, this is less of a concern. Employees might visit these sites, but it rarely becomes so distracting that work suffers, and in some cases the benefits of being better connected can help productivity. From a security perspective, however, there are major areas of concern. These should be identified so that users are aware of potential risks to both individual employees and the overall corporation.

Am I Really a Friend?

One of the latest scams taking place within public networking sites is fake users who pretend to be someone you might know. If a user logs on as a fake user and you then friend that person, they gain insight into your friends list and can continue to integrate themselves into your community. Often there is an immediate high level of trust because you think this other person is someone you know. This can open up a large security risk in the community. Imagine if you disclose information to someone you think is a friend or coworker, or even your boss? Proprietary information might not be at risk because most people are very careful about that type of data, but you might disclose enough to allow some type of social engineering attack within your organization.

Privacy Policies on Public Social Networking Sites

By their very nature, Social Networking sites thrive on their openness and community interaction. Corporations can leverage this by allowing knowledge workers to collaborate in ways as never before. However, guidelines need to be put in place to remind corporate users that some information should not be shared in the public domain.

From a standard security practice, it is important to see how public any information that a user contributes can be. Applications designed for these Social Networking sites usually can access any user information that they need to properly function. After this information is shared, it becomes part of the public domain.

Performance Is Never Free

If you want something to be fast, you have to pay for it in some way. Your options may be to add more hardware or make some additional effort in the design and development of the application.

The idea that performance is always a compromise is true, and rarely does a web application run too fast. I have been lucky enough in my career to see a couple of portal sites fast enough that we could not really expect better performance. A fast site is one that can return a page in less than one second (fast enough that you cannot really measure it with the human eye). However, for all the other (slower) sites, it is mostly a matter of determining when performance is "good enough." One of the first things that a technical team tries to do is get the business owner to identify some nonfunctional requirements, such as response time, number of concurrent users, and so on. This is exactly what should happen. However, the effort should not stop there (as it often does). Instead, those numbers should be used to guide the rest of the design to ensure those benchmarks are met, and if not, that the decisions around the design have been fully documented.

Consider the example that a standard portal page within the application can be returned to the user in under two seconds. However, some back-end systems take four to five seconds to return data that is needed on some pages. In most cases, not a lot can be done here. It is important that service level agreements be put in place for all applications so that interactions do not adversely affect or slow down any new or existing applications. Keep in mind that the portal is always blamed for problems with back-end systems! This is not fair, but a sad truth of end-user perception.

From a business owner standpoint, a decision to be made when adverse interaction occurs between two systems. Either modify the back-end system, remove it from the portal, or relax the page load time requirements for any page that interacts with a slow system.

Heavy Personalization

In some cases, the decision on how much personalization to use is much more complex. There are areas of functionality that are not as clearly defined. Personalization is one area where the impact is not as well known. Personalization is often so specific to the organization and the application that is it almost impossible to measure the impact of the effort without doing ongoing analysis with a live production system. This is the basis for the common recommendation that a team starts slowly with building a heavily personalized system, rather than trying to personalize everything for everyone all at once. Before we get too far on this topic, let's define a few terms:

- *Customization* is what users can do for themselves on a site. The user can add or remove portlets from the page, or define the categories of information they want to see.
- *Personalization* is what you define that a user can see. This is often a direct targeting of content to specific users or sets of users.

A good example is where you as an end user decide to customize the news portlet to show, say, the specific financial news about a company. However, the set that is shown to you may be filtered or personalized to show only the news about your division or not show you sensitive information that you are not allowed to see. This information is often filtered based on attributes about the user. Figure 8.10 illustrates the two different yet complementary areas.

So why are these concepts a big deal? Mostly it is because too much personalization can be a huge performance drain on your application. There are several steps or layers of granularity where personalization can be performed. The more granular you define your personalization rules, the more effort it is to retrieve the right content for a user. Here are some examples:

- **Company level:**   Everyone who works for the company will see some content. This is pretty broad and gives us a lot of room to tune performance. In a large organization, you might define this as the division level, where everyone from the same division sees the same set of content items.
- **Department level:**   This is still fine depending on how your departments are set up. You might think of this as HR, IT, Operations,

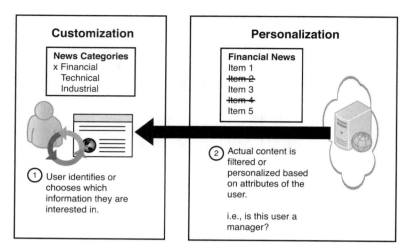

Figure 8.10   Customization versus personalization

Support, or Logistics. In most companies, large and small, this ratio is well defined.

- **Location level:**   This level of granularity is defined based on the physical location that a user works from. At a high level, if there are fewer locations, this is a good approach for some content. If you have lots of small offices, however, this can become a problem

- **User attribute level:**   This can be one of the most problematic ways to break down your personalization rules. If you are defining rules based on specific elements of a user, the engine has to work that much harder to identify the right content for each individual user.

This is only a subset of the types of personalization that can be performed. At the very granular level, you can define content for each individual user. Besides making the system work hard, we lose a lot of benefit from caching, which we discuss later in this chapter.

Using personalization features can greatly benefit your application and your end users. Because of the custom nature of how it can be used, however, it is very difficult to benchmark how it will affect performance. The best advice is to completely understand your usage patterns and perform a lot of testing.

Using Ajax for Performance

As you have seen throughout this book, JavaScript is making a rebound within web applications in the form of Ajax and interactive applications. This is actually exciting stuff, but it does change the paradigm we have been using over the past few years to build web applications.

Partial-page refresh can provide an enormous benefit in terms of performance and an enhanced user experience, but even this approach entails tradeoffs. In the portal space, partial-page refresh at the portlet level can have a tremendous benefit. The tradeoff comes with the application itself and its intended function. Can the page be designed to take full advantage of Ajax technology, or does the user need to switch pages often (and by so doing lose some of the benefit of using the technology)?

Another point to consider is slow performing back ends or services. Web 2.0 applications that perform a partial-page refresh with slow back-end services can end up frustrating the use as much as a traditional page refresh.

For pages that are heavily loaded with JavaScript, the initial load is the biggest consideration for the application. After the application is loaded on the browser and the embedded script is cached, the application tends to respond quickly to user interaction. However, this initial page load can take many seconds for large pages. This is especially true for those outlying communities that might not have as high speed of an access as corporate headquarters does.

Load testing a new system is where many of the performance problems begin. This is especially true when you cannot realistically predict the runtime usage of the system. Individual page load times should be measured with a browser plug-in tool to understand which page elements are causing the slowdown. Obviously, those slower script files have to be loaded before any real interaction can occur on the page. This may be reflected during a load test as a large performance issue that you actually may not see in a real life scenario with a predictable set of users. After your employees have loaded the page and scripts are cached, they will probably not incur that delay when they come back to your site over and over. This is a different characteristic than for a public site, where a long load time would possibly hurt your application's image.

Consider Caching

Just considering caching is not enough—you have to actually use caching at all levels within your application to stay competitive. Caching is all about moving the data and information as close to your users as possible to reduce the time needed to retrieve or calculate the data. Consider a list of news items that are displayed on the home page. It would be nice if you could cache that list of news items for an hour or two instead of having to retrieve it from the database every time a user hits the home page. Better yet would be to cache the already formatted HTML that displays the news to a user.

On an interesting side note, I once had a conversation with a customer who was wondering why he needed to worry about all this stuff. Shouldn't products just work fast and scale as needed? I have to admit this took me by surprise, but really showed me that this situation called for some additional education. No application, either custom or off the shelf, will scale independently of a good architecture and design. Even in the best case, you will probably overwhelm your back-end system or database at some point. Experience is the key to understanding system limitations and to making the design decisions that help your system perform at its best.

However, what if the news items that are displayed are different for some users? Now it depends on the number of variations that are needed. If you have, for example, a different set of news items for each corporate location, this might be a reasonable number of items in the cache. However, if you have a different set of news items for each individual user, another strategy might be necessary because the cache would be larger than the set of users on the site at any given time.

Where Caching Takes Place

Caching is normally an in-memory activity. There is, of course, the ability to cache to more permanent stores such as to disk, but generally there are specific circumstances for doing that, such as keeping cached data between system restarts. Figure 8.11 illustrates the types of caches generally available with most systems.

In general, caching can take place in several places. These are designed to provide some flexibility in how a cache is implemented within your applications. Let's take each location in turn:

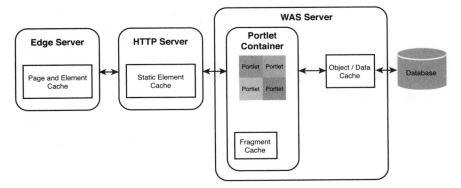

Figure 8.11   Caching points to consider

- **Object or data cache:**   This is truly a developer cache that enables you to reduce the load on a back-end system or database. Generally, if you know that multiple calls will be made to a system, you can store the results of that call to reduce that load. Another use is when you have data that needs to be filtered based on the user. Rather than call the database with a SQL call, you can retrieve the cached data and filter it in memory to reduce time.

- **Fragment cache:**   The fragment cache is often used in a portal situation where the output from a particular portlet is cached. In a portal environment, the output from different portlets are combined or aggregated to create the resulting page. If some portlets can be cached, it will reduce overall aggregation and load time of the page. In WebSphere, this is often called JSP/servlet caching.

- **Static element cache:**   Static elements such as images and JavaScript files can sometimes take a long time to load, but more than that, they can cause additional load on the server from which they are loaded. Moving or offloading those files closer to the end user can help reduce the load on the server and the time they take to get downstream to the end user.

- **Page cache:**   In some cases, an entire page can be cached, which can result in fast-loading applications. This is especially true for initial landing pages, which are very generic for every user, or public pages, which are not or cannot be customized. Another side effect of this cache is that static elements can also be moved here to be even closer to the user. Edge caching can be used in a corporate environment very effectively by placing edge servers at outlying corporate locations to improve overall efficiency of many applications.

It is important to understand the pros and cons of each of these caching locations and where they fit into your overall strategy. Caching needs to be considered at the beginning of your design cycle to be sure you can take advantage of it wherever possible.

Distributed Map Caching

WebSphere Application Server (WAS) has a number of caching services that coincide with the description provided in the last section. For your data or object cache needs, WAS provides a distributed map (dMap) service that can be used to store objects in memory. You can set up any number of these caches as needed, as shown in Figure 8.12. A number of dMap caches already exist for many portal and content management applications.

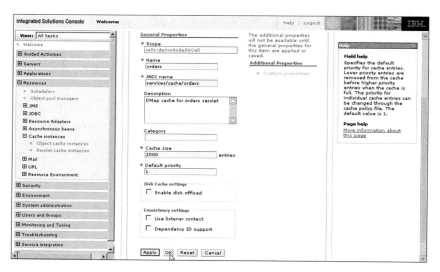

Figure 8.12   Setting up a dMap in WebSphere Application Server

Note the JNDI name of the map in Figure 8.12. This is used to access and use the map within the application code. To create a handle to the map, you can do a lookup as follows:

```
InitialContext ic = new InitialContext();
dMap =(DistributedMap)ic.lookup("services/cache/orders");
```

After you have access to the map, you can make use of it as necessary. A distributed map is similar to a HashMap in Java, so it can be used the same way. That is by using the standard put() and get() methods as used in a HashMap. One of the obvious benefits is that a dMap can be distributed or shared across server instances in a cluster, so there is some benefit for scaling your cache if necessary.

Rational Performance Tester

IBM Rational Performance Tester (RPT) is a performance testing tool for web applications. It is one of a number of tools in the Rational testing suite that help you understand the performance, functional, and security characteristics of your application. RPT is an interface-driven application that enables you to use the interface to build your test scenarios. Other testing tools in this area use specific scripting languages that can be difficult to learn or become an expert in. Figure 8.13 illustrates a test that has been created in RPT.

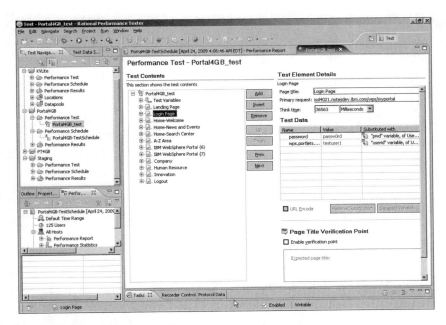

Figure 8.13   Rational Performance Tester

After you have a set of tests created that you can run, you can combine those tests into a single test schedule. The test schedule enables you to run a specific test using a virtual user. Each test simulates a single user's path through the application. You might, over time, create different tests to simulate your user base. For example, in an ecommerce test, some users might be browsing through the site, whereas others are purchasing items, searching for specific items, or interacting with the site in different ways.

A schedule also enables you to spread the actual test across multiple test servers. RPT allows you to set up a number of servers that can generate the load that a test is designed to simulate. The flexibility of a test schedule enables you to simulate complex test scenarios that can truly stress your application (see Figure 8.14).

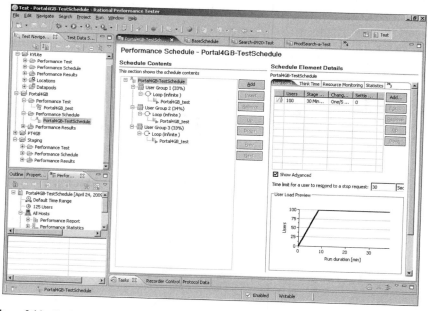

Figure 8.14   Designing a test schedule

The schedule is also where you define the virtual users who will interpret each test. Defining how each test is performed can be a time consuming process. Virtual users can iterate through the test or make decisions based on the weight of different tests in the system.

Analysis of your test and the response time characteristics of your system is the one of the more important features that a test generator can provide. Of course, everyone wants to know how many users the system can handle. It is important to be clear with your analysis and the discussion with other participants in the project. The use of virtual users can be confusing because virtual users are often equated with real users. This might actually be the case, but there is rarely a direct correlation between virtual users and real users. It is easy to overpower an application through a small number of virtual users. It is important to create a clear definition of the success criteria of your application in terms of a throughput rate, such as the number of pages per second. This is a much better defined metric that reduces the confusion that many may encounter during the testing analysis. Figure 8.15 shows the response time for each page, along with the attempt rate per second for those pages.

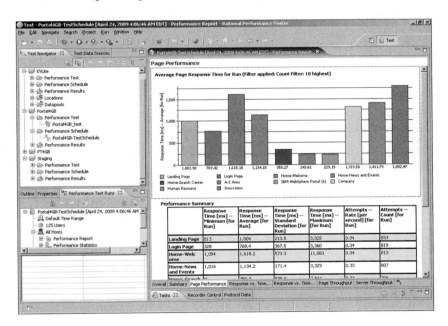

Figure 8.15 Analyzing test results

Testing has to be a large part of your performance analysis for the application. I say this repeatedly to customers who do not understand the importance of testing in enterprise applications. Again, experience shows us that proper testing can reduce production problems once your system is live. In addition, with testing you will have more information about the growth of your application and where additional scaling options will be necessary over time.

Conclusion

We have covered some of the basics on web application security, some potential threats, and some recommendations to address your security concerns. I recommend making security the number one priority within your project or application. Few things can cause greater harm than having a security breach on your site. The risk of not keeping security in mind is just too great.

When thinking about performance issues, keep in mind good application architecture techniques. Standard design patterns and practices are not ignored simply because the technology is evolving; rather, the design approaches need to evolve with them to ensure that applications are both secure and performing. From a global application architecture standpoint, what are we trying to achieve, anyway? We have discussed several items in addition to security and performance here. These additional elements require focus throughout the entire project lifecycle:

- **Portability:** WebSphere focuses on using industry standards to help with this, but there are specific WebSphere competitive advantages that you don't want to ignore.

- **Security:** A primary focus in this chapter. We need to ensure that information and data is kept private, and that users are who they say they are when posting to a site.

- **Scalability:** We want to be able to scale as needed and take advantage of our hardware as much as possible.

- **Stability:** A layered approach with enforced standards can help achieve this goal.

- **Expandability:** Agile methods promote the idea of YAGNI (you aren't going to need it) within development cycles. This means that designing for future requirements that don't exist yet, or may never exist, may not be a good use of business dollars.

This chapter has given you a lot to think about and helps you ask the right questions about your own enterprise web applications.

References

Revisiting Performance Fundamentals. Bernal J. (August 2007). WebSphere Developers Technical Journal. Comment Lines: taken July 5, 2009 from http://www.ibm.com/developerworks/websphere/techjournal/0708_col_bernal/0708_col_bernal.html.

9

Managing a Changing Social World

I don't think we can deny the impact that Social Networking is having on the world around us. From our personal lives to our professional relationships, Social Networking has become integrated into every part of our daily routine. Initial analysis from Web 2.0 and social pundits put Social Networking activities squarely in the lap of younger generations who are growing up with this technology and embrace the idea of technology continuing to change and evolve. Although this might be true, the more experienced workforce is not blind to the advantages new technology provides, although they may be more hesitant to adopt these ideas until the true value is proven. Many workers just don't have the luxury to *play* with every passing fad as it comes along. And that mindset is exactly what allows an organization to focus on their core business and find the integration points and value proposition for new technology adoption.

The New "Virtual" Water Cooler

From an organizational perspective, Social Networking has changed and continues to change the way that I work every day. As a consultant, my job is to travel to customers and help them build solutions and solve problems within their organization. In this role, I do not work in the traditional office settings of days past. Thousands of others work in this same manner. My manager lives on the other side of the country, and my immediate team are often spread across the globe. Yet I consider them my teammates just as if they were sitting in the cubical next to me.

Even traditional office settings are being disrupted in a similar manner. Outsourcing of routine tasks, allowing employees to work from home, and distributed teams offer the same challenges as the lone consultant. Social Networking has opened up our ability to communicate and collaborate in ways that we probably would not have imagined.

Reaching Out to Experts and Coworkers

My colleague Julia considers her social network to be broad enough that she can elicit information using Social Networking sites such as Facebook. Reaching out directly to her base of known experts is definitely the first option, but in some cases Julia might not be sure who has the exact information she needs. Rather than try to chase down someone who might or might not know where to find the information, she can broadcast a request knowing that someone with the right expertise will emerge to help if they can. In addition, Julia understands that her coworkers have their day job, too, and are not always readily available to answer her questions. Of course, some give and take is necessary, but being mindful of other people's schedules can go a long way toward maintaining lasting relationships.

Blocking External Social Networking

Many organizations block sites that they believe may distract their employees. These blocks include sites that have questionable content, but also those sites that do not have apparent business value (at least initially). Often, the mindset is "we do not want our employees messing around on the Internet all day." This is valid, but it does echo early thinking that the Internet itself was a distraction. Of course, we know now that most people could not function effectively without it.

With the advent of mobile phones allowing access to the most popular sites, and even full access to the Web, this is mostly becoming a moot point anyway, but we will discuss a few cases where some decision points can be made.

Knowledge Workers

More and more teams are working in a distributed manner where Social Networking can provide new productivity gains as these teams struggle with time zones and cultural issues. External Social Networking sites can provide some of this capability if you have not yet implemented your own approach. Of course, security and privacy issues need to be understood, but there can be some productivity gains in these situations.

In addition, knowledge workers are often salaried employees who work long hours and mix their personal and professional lives. IBM, for example, actually encourages employees to understand and use new tools and collaboration technologies. Doing so often enhances productivity (and is not a distraction). If a worker is not getting his job done, there are usually other reasons rather than someone playing on the Internet.

For noninformation workers, a decision must be made as to whether access to Social Networking sites is needed or allowed. Blocking access will probably not affect these workers either way.

Nonknowledge Workers

I lump a lot of roles into this category. This consists of people who work in a shop, on an assembly line, in a factory, or perhaps in a warehouse of some type. The point being that they would not generally have access to a computer when performing assigned tasks. If a computer is involved, as is becoming more often the case, this system would generally be a custom application that provides specific information or input needed to perform the task.

For these workers, access to Social Networking sites, or even the Internet as a whole, is probably not an option. It is obvious that this would be a distraction and even harmful if access were allowed because often the computers used in these roles are designed for a specific purpose.

Special Cases

In some cases, allowing full access is warranted for some employees. For example, sales and marketing people who are interested in reaching customers in new ways should be allowed to fully explore these opportunities as needed. People who are customer facing should be looking at new ways to interact with their customers. My personal Facebook profile has friends, family, coworkers, and customers with whom I have developed good relationships that extend beyond just the customer/consultant relationship to real friendship.

Obviously, we have to be careful in these situations to understand who is asking questions and why. A long, drawn-out conversation in a semipublic venue is probably not the right approach to helping customers be successful with our products. However, informal situations, where a question can be raised and answered quickly, especially to a broader audience, benefit from Social Networking.

Strategies for External Social Networking

Social Networks are generally more informal than traditional marketing approaches. If you are going to allow Social Networking to exist for your employees, setting expectations correctly is important. Like all standards or expectations, guidelines have to be put in place before you unleash your organization to the unsuspecting Social Networks of the world. Blogs and wikis enable you to communicate information to customers as never before, but there is also a loss of control as to what information is provided. After something is unleashed, it is difficult to reel it back in. Communicators (perhaps bloggers) in your company can have a wide reach, so it is important that they represent the company honestly and openly. However, they may not speak for the entire organization and strategy. It can be the case where blog entries that are posted do not necessarily speak for the organizational strategy.

This is actually a common problem as thought leaders within an organization flesh out new ideas and concepts in a public way. However, it should be made clear that ideas and strategies can change over time in every organization and comments made are not commitments. Bloggers get questioned and criticized about topics that sometimes find their way into their blogs. This interaction of different viewpoints is one of the benefits of working for a large organization where there are many competing ideas and directions. Figure 9.1 provides some guidelines for external bloggers and others who speak publically about your organization, either directly or indirectly.

Figure 9.1   Some important external Social Networking guidelines

This list shows employees that certain guidelines and expectations apply to their behaviors. This list is not comprehensive and should be customized to your organization, but it's a good starting point.

Where Do You Start?

From an enterprise standpoint, many projects are justified based on business need. However, with Social Networking, this is much more difficult because the return on investment (ROI) is particularly hard to calculate. Recent studies have helped to identify and calculate that value, but it is still a moving target and will continue to be so for some time.

Every organization's Social Networking needs and strategy is different, and no one roadmap can provide a "one size fits all" approach. Undoubtedly, as you have read through this book, you have seen some areas that you intuitively know can bring tremendous value to your business, but determining benefit in terms of real numbers is difficult.

Initially, take a close look at your organization to see what factors exist that can help or hinder your overall strategy. Figure 9.2 provides an overview of the types of factors that should be considered.

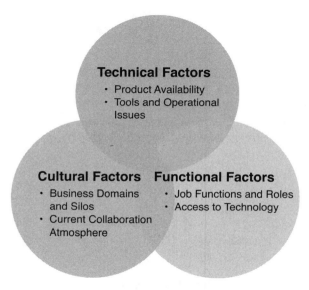

Figure 9.2   Initial considerations for a Social Networking strategy

Three main types of factors have been identified to help you understand what barriers may exist to a successful implementation:

■ **Technical:**   Consider product availability and tools and operations issues.

■ **Cultural:**   Consider business domains and silos and the collaboration atmosphere.

■ **Functional:**   Consider job functions and roles and access to technology.

These are discussed in the following sections.

Technical Factors

Technical factors are generally the easiest to overcome as you move forward on the path toward a Social Networking implementation within your organization. This is a matter of determining what products exist within your organization or what solutions can be purchased, leveraged, or built to provide new capability to different teams. Generally, any roadblocks can be overcome with some funding and executive sponsorship from high up within the organization. What should not be understated is there will probably be a need for new processes and skills within the IT community that might not be well understood at first. Two competing factors will work against you in this endeavor. First is the need to start small and build up capability as you go. In direct competition to that approach, however, is *if* adoption really starts to take off on the new tools, you might not be able to step back and see what is needed to continue to scale. The point here is that even as you start small, keep in mind a strategy to grow capability as needed and do not think that you can scrap your proof of concept and rebuild a more scalable and robust environment after everyone is hooked.

Functional Factors

Functional factors are important to your strategy. We talked about this a little at the beginning of this chapter. Primarily, this is looking at job function and role with the business. For example, a small shop where a large percentage of the workers provide manufacturing or manual labor might not be a good fit for large-scale implementation of Social Networking tools. However, those organizations might implement some collaboration capability on a smaller scale for managers situated at different locations to share trends and ideas. Even something as simple as forums will allow best practices to be shared and discussed with a very small investment.

The other obvious factor here is the availability of technology to large groups of employees. Many manufacturing organizations provide some kiosk capability to their employees, in common areas where an employee can access the machine during nonworking hours or breaks, to find information and sign up for services. These types of interactions with a shared platform do not usually lend themselves well to Social Networking because only intermittent interaction with the system occurs. However, who knows what ideas might lurk in the heads of thought leaders within your organization?

Knowledge workers (white-collar workers) provide much more opportunity for immediate and measureable success with Social Networking and collaboration tools. Most people in this category have access to computers and technology and can receive almost immediate benefit when adopting new approaches and tools.

Cultural Factors

Cultural factors are probably the most important in determining a strategy. We need to ask the questions about how well your organization will function and grow with collaboration and networking capability. Most small teams probably already have good communication processes and collaboration techniques, but the interaction between these teams and members of different teams is the real goal. Silo-ed organizations will have further to go to recognize the same benefits as more collaborative teams.

The idea is that Social Networking and collaboration capability will help to start breaking down those silos and increase teaming in a broad way within the company. However, investment and effort are different depending on where you are starting from within your organization. Cultural factors could also arise from different geographical locations, language barriers, or competing factions within the organization.

A Three-Stage Roadmap

If you are getting started with a Social Networking strategy from scratch, iteration is the key to success. Many of the patterns shown in this section have been described in detail throughout this book, starting with Chapter 1, "Web 2.0 and Social Networking." There are a lot of Social Networking patterns to understand, and too many to try to do them all at once. A recommended three-phase strategy is as follows:

1. Communicate
2. Collaborate
3. Innovate

Communicate, collaborate, and innovate—doing so will enable you to know where you are on your roadmap and what the next step is in your evolution.

Communicate

Phase 1 for a Social Networking strategy is illustrated in Figure 9.3, which shows the basic patterns that can be implemented fairly easily using commercial or custom products or tools. The focus is really on increasing communication, but in new forms. People are used to official communication coming in a one-way manner from within an organization. However, opening up new channels and enabling two-way discussion loosens up communication and shows participants that you care about them and their concerns.

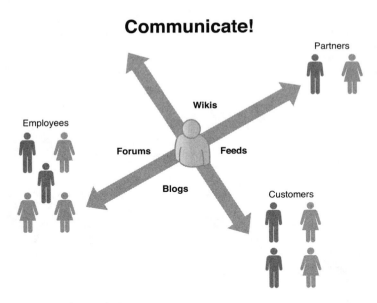

Figure 9.3 Phase 1: Communicate

Information becomes more fluid and easily digestible as wikis and blogs start to form within the organization and provide ideas to both internal users, and externally to the organization. Additional new information about the enterprise becomes available as thought leaders and others in the company talk more about what they do and how they do it. This is the unknown component that can often surprise everyone because much of this information is not always readily available in more traditional ways. A common approach is to try to seed some of this new communication by encouraging experts and leaders to publish early and often.

Collaborate

Phase 2 of your strategy provides for collaboration and integrates new features and functions into the environment, such as networking discovery, expert location, communities, and activities. The focus here is on two-way collaboration between the organization and targeted participants, and there is also a focus on communication between participants. This is where the true interaction starts to occur—adding value that can best be measured as it affects your organizational processes and efficiency. Figure 9.4 shows how some of those patterns can start to take effect within the community.

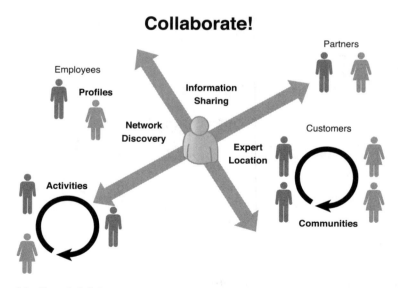

Figure 9.4   Phase 2: Collaborate

None of these existing patterns are bound to a particular area or set of users. Figure 9.4 simply shows where patterns might emerge. Communities can happen both internally and externally. In fact, the idea of a community is such a broad concept that it can occur anywhere and everywhere at once.

Innovate

You might imagine that there are several months between phase 1 and the release of phase 3's functionality. In addition, it would probably be several months or years for full adoption of Social Networking tools. After you are beyond the first two phases, however, real innovation can transform the way you do business. Adopting and embracing a full innovative Web 2.0 and Social Networking strategy enables you to implement many of the patterns that have been discussed throughout this book. Figure 9.5 shows the next generation of patterns that can be adopted through phase 3 of a Social Networking adoption strategy.

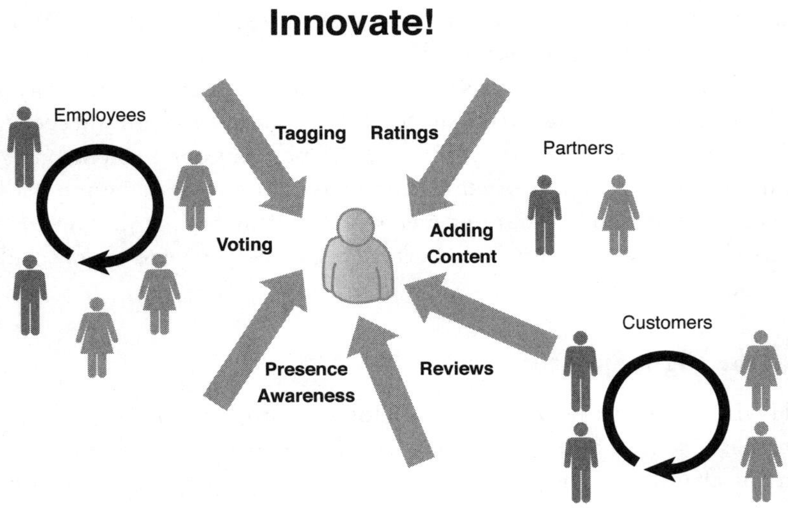

Figure 9.5   Phase 3: Innovate

Phase 1 or 2 might actually be enough for some organizations depending on some of the factors that we discussed previously. The key here is that implementing ideas and products should be iterative, in the sense that you do not try to do too much at once. Because of the nature of what we are doing and the somewhat cloudy measurements of success, you might not even know if you are headed in the right direction with some components.

There is also a bit of a mix-and-match capability here as you define the right approach for your organization. For example, presence awareness (finding others online) might be integrated into applications in phase 1, enabling instant communication with subject matter experts and thought leaders across multiple teams.

Defining Goals and Business Requirements

It has been said that implementing a Social Networking strategy in an organization that does not value collaboration will fail. That failure will result because Social Networking is fundamentally based on collaboration and knowledge sharing. This type of statement could be considered a scare tactic to help ensure that leadership at the highest levels of the organization provides support for Social Networking efforts. I doubt too many C-level executives would admit that they do not value collaboration in their companies, even if it is the truth. That being said, there is something to the fact that if a company is not well versed in collaboration techniques, your Social Networking and collaboration strategy will need more investment to be successful. So how can you succeed? By making smart decisions along the way. Remaining open to change. And asking others within our organization to remain open to change. Failure in these circumstances does not mean you are finished; it just means you need to change your strategy to better encourage your end users to adopt the tools you are providing.

Find the Right Sponsor

Having a good executive sponsor for any project is a great thing. In fact, it is essential for success. An executive sponsor is someone who supports or champions the effort, and who can break down social or organizational barriers when the team encounters them. Social Networking projects have additional requirements, including having a sponsor that is higher than your targeted audience. If you are running a pilot for folks within IT, then having the CIO is probably a good start. However, if you are releasing functions across lines of business or departments, you have to go a little higher. People within an organization respect their own chain of command more than someone from another division.

To ensure that when adoption is not immediate there is no waffling on funds or support for the project, it is important that the sponsor be truly sold on the value of the project. Be sure that it is understood that this is a long-term project that will help change the way the organization works, rather than something that will bring an immediate ROI. The end game here is increased communication, knowledge sharing, and collaboration, with all the good things that they can bring. This means increasing communication and sharing with customers, partners, departments, and in small teams. In addition to understanding where expertise and knowledge resides in the organization, specific patterns enable informal information to emerge in the form of blogs, wikis, and forums. It is sometimes mentioned in technical circles that "you don't know what you don't know." Social Networking provides an avenue for information, that you "didn't know" existed to emerge.

Provide the Right Value

Besides having the right sponsor, it is equally important to implement the patterns that you think your organization will use. You might want to talk to people in the organization to find out what is important to them. People always have ideas about how to make things work better, and they love to share these ideas. Blogs might provide an outlet to creative individuals within the organization who want to do that sharing. Teams might be looking for a way to share or collaborate on documents or other files. Expert location and finding someone with the right skills might be more important than other patterns that are suggested.

Even if you do purchase a Social Networking product such as Lotus Connections, you might not want to implement all the provided features immediately. Determine what is important and decide what you can support initially, because the initial tasks will help define your goals. Remember that technical decisions should be considered when it comes to robust and responsive services you can provide.

Target the Right Audience

Finally, you have to target the right audience for your initial launch, which might be nothing more than a small proof of concept. I will warn you, however, that for some patterns, small might not be the right approach. That is because for widespread adoption, you need a much larger audience than those you actually hope will use the tools you are providing. Adoption is slow, and if your target audience is small, your effort may never gain enough critical mass to be of value to an organization. Consider a pilot of 100 people. If only 10 percent try the tool, they might find little value with only nine other people working with them. If you target a pilot toward several thousand people, however, you have a much better chance of gaining critical mass with that proposed 10 percent adoption rate.

Also consider the technical depth and breadth of your audience. Targeting toward a very technically savvy audience will probably result in better adoption as these types of users understand how technology is changing and are more willing to try to improve the way they get things done. After you have some tools running successfully with this audience, it becomes easier to increase the user base and allow for incremental adoption of what are now common patterns within the enterprise.

Getting Acceptance and Adoption

Without some type of mandate, adoption of new Social Networking applications can be a slow process. However, mandating usage can trigger some resistance from those who do not want to be forced to collaborate. It is often a matter of "what was wrong with the old way" in the minds of some potential participants. Forced adoption is no way to gain acceptance of a new system; people have to see the value beyond the initial novelty of a new system.

As someone who works with development teams, I see this reaction to new systems often. Applications are put into place that cause team members more work. Developers are generally smart people and technically savvy. They will learn how to bypass a cumbersome process or system quicker than it can be fully released to the community.

It is important that people see the value of Social Networking to the organization. Many employees have a strong enough bond with the company to want to see it succeed. In come cases, if a user knows that by contributing to the effort, they can help the system grow and be useful, then this may override any personal discomfort of having to learn a new system. However, if you can also illustrate the benefits to the individual, users may be even more willing to contribute for the overall good. For example, some people are clamoring to gain more visibility within their own organization or to outside customers. Blogs are a perfect way for people to showcase their expertise and gain that much-sought-after visibility. Others are looking for new ways to find other coworkers within the company who hold the information they seek. In this case, something like expert location is another function that can provide tremendous value within a very short time.

Start and Stop Syndrome

We have all done it at one time or another, gotten excited about an application that does not pan out to be as interesting or helpful as we originally thought. This is actually common in the IT world and somewhat expected. Sometimes we go back to that system again and again, eventually finding some comfort and familiarity with the way things work enough to become a regular user. This will be the same with many of your users, who will try out the new and exciting features and then go back to their old way of doing things.

Your challenge is to entice them to stick around long enough to gain that familiarity with the new way of doing things. This is not an easy challenge, so everything we have discussed in this book needs to come into play. Getting feedback from your user base about why someone has stopped using the system can be helpful, and learning what issues users might have with new functionality can help you make adjustments over time. The best advice for avoiding this possibility is to keep things as simple and easy to use as possible. Complex systems are never fun to learn, especially when there are still concerns about the value.

Seed the Environment Correctly

For successful adoption, your environment needs to be seeded with the right information and support. This will help you jump start your community adoption. No one wants to be involved with Social Networking features by themselves. Adoption requires collaboration and interaction in the environment. Ways to initially seed your environment and speed adoption include the following:

- Blogs can be seeded by asking well-known individuals within your organization to start blogging.
- Expert location and people finders can be seeded by migrating or linking into the existing user repository.
- Communities can be preestablished and seeded with existing information.
- Mashups can be predefined and created for some common cases to showcase how the technology can solve business problems.
- Activities can be seeded by asking key project managers to try using an activity for their next project.

Of course, you don't want to take things too far until you are sure that adoption is going well. Making a huge effort to seed applications that are rarely used is a waste of business value (exactly the opposite of what we are trying to achieve). It is often helpful to showcase new applications by seeding them with beneficial components that offer immediate and real value to some users.

Communication Is Key

You have released your Social Networking masterpiece to the community at large, seeded the environment with thought leaders and important content, and now you can sit back and wait for your users to come to you. Sorry, you just lost the project. The most important step in all of this is communicating to your user base what you are doing. Communication of all types should occur to build some excitement around the release. For example:

- Your sponsor should provide regular communications well before and during the release to help users understand that the company is looking for participation.
- Marketing your site can help users understand what is going to be available and how it will help them and the organization.
- Use regular communications to seek out early adopters or participants to beta test or become moderators or community leaders.

In addition, you might implement training or mentoring strategies to help new users grow with you. For example, mentoring future leaders in how to blog correctly and helping them formulate your message helps everyone grow.

Assessing Your Strategy

Measuring success should be a major goal for your project. However, unlike other types of IT projects where there are very concrete metrics, Social Networking metrics can be somewhat fuzzy. One obvious place to start is with the usage of the applications that you put in place. This should be way beyond the usual web-based analytics common with most websites. Web analytics are part of the solution, as seen in the following list, but these do not answer many of the business questions. These standard metrics are still necessary. However, Social Networking sites also require a detailed analysis of what people are actually doing on the site. These additional business value types of metrics can be divided into a number of categories:

- **General web metrics:**   Information that includes user visits, duration, and activity. This answers the question: Where are users coming from, and when?

- **Blogs:**   Information that includes how many people have blogs, how many are active, and how many people are reading those blogs. This answers the question: What type of content do people seem to have the most interest?

- **Communities and activities:**   Generally, you can measure the number of these items and activity.

- **Search:**   This answers the question: What information are people looking for? Searches generally have their own metrics, such as the number of searches and the top search strings. You can also collect information about searches for profiles or communities.

- **Tags, ratings, and bookmarks:**   Direct measurement of the number and types of these items can show trends in growth or if there might be a problem with the way they are implemented. This answers the question: How can I help others know which information is good and what is not useful?

So why is this information important to you? Because it provides the initial framework for information that you can use to show that people are using the tools you have provided. In addition, from a technical point of view, knowing the true activity on your site can help you plan for additional features or services. This will help you know whether you are outgrowing your initial investment or underutilizing existing capability.

Understanding True Business Value

While the metrics will give you the information you need to report adoption to the appropriate management, measuring the business value that is gained is much more difficult. There are no metrics to tell you whether John in Operations was more productive because he was able to connect with Susan in Accounting. Intuitively, we know this is what happens because we experience it as users of the system ourselves, but measuring that as a productivity improvement and then multiplying it by the number of occurrences within the company is seemingly impossible. Figure 9.6 provides the key areas where Social Networking can assist and add business value—that being the three pillars of creativity, productivity, and collaboration.

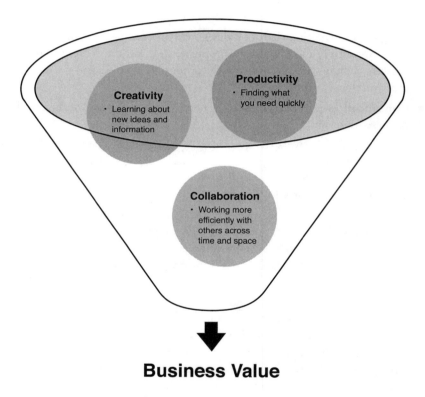

Figure 9.6 Measuring business value

Business value stems from all of these areas:

- *Creativity* often comes to light as a side effect of collaboration and information sharing. Building on the ideas of others, it is easier to take the next step and come up with new product ideas, services, or products that can add value to the bottom line of a business.

- *Productivity* is a somewhat easier metric to understand because anyone can spend a lot of time struggling to find the right information or subject matter expert that they need to answer a question. Improving that end-to-end time of getting information to people faster and easier reduces waste and allows your users to get on with their other work.

- *Collaboration* can be a friend or foe with some teams and organizations. Being able to initiate and drive collaboration quickly and easily can save time and money. The ability to share documents and ideas in a medium other than email helps to maintain version control over documents, and reduces overhead and disk space on the network.

Applying these ideas in the context of your environment will help you set up some guidelines for measuring success and help you make decisions for advancing forward.

Governance for Social Networking

One area that is always important is the concept of governance. Governance is not the same as managing a project or program. Instead, it is maintaining control of a system that influences your organization and other systems. Many organizations already have some governance framework in place, such as COBIT or CMMI.

Depending on how you look at it, governance is about keeping track of your IT projects and making sure they align with business goals. This occurs at a much higher level than standard project management practices. A traditional project focuses on releasing a new piece of technology into the organization, whereas the governance committee focuses on whether this technology should be released and what affect it will have on the organization and existing systems.

An Interview with Prabu Ayyagari

Prabu Ayyagari is an Executive Project Manager with IBM Software Group, Software Services for Lotus. As someone who deals with many projects and many organizations, he understands the value of governance in a well-run project.

What is governance?
Governance is the framework within which a team accomplishes mutually agreed on goals.

One way of looking at governance is akin to the rulebook that defines how a game is played. These rules are agreed to by all the players and are not changed during the game to suit the convenience of any particular player. That way, everyone knows what acceptable behavior is and how to go about reaching the goal. With governance in place, a team (of 2 or 2,000) is enabled to work toward its goals without resorting to power struggles to make their point.

In the Web 2.0 and IT world, governance is sometimes codified into a set of best practices, such as COBIT or ITIL or CMM.

Is governance really that important?

What differentiates the Facebooks of this world from the millions of other initiatives that bite the dust before they are out of beta is that the successful projects have governance in place (whether they use that word or not). That said, governance is in the eye of the beholder. What may appear to be good governance for one may seem like stifling bureaucracy to the next person.

We have to remember that the Web 2.0 world is populated with free souls that shrug at any constraints that they see as shackling them from becoming the next Facebook. It may take the form of written and constantly updated business plans, seasoned advisors that come on as angel investors, or a real playbook that is written down—but governance is the secret sauce that gets an interesting hack to a sustainable business.

Does Web 2.0 and Social Networking governance differ from other IT governance?

Absolutely! The fabric of Web 2.0 is a nonhierarchical collaboration of equals. So, a traditional top-down command-and-control approach to governance does not work well for these projects. Gaining mindshare early is key to successful governance on Web 2.0 and Social Networking projects.

Flexibility is another key differentiator in the governance of these projects. "Fail early and learn fast" are contributors to success—so the organization should be willing to go with processes that are not fully baked and be willing to iterate. Having feedback mechanisms in place is also important. If you are in the Web 2.0 space, it goes without saying that the wisdom of crowds is an idea that you subscribe to. Whether it be wikis, or something like IdeaJam that is discussed in Chapter 10, "IBM Case Studies," you need a mechanism to vote on ideas contributed by the team, so that you can be seen as responsive to input from your stakeholders.

How does an organization get started with IT or Web 2.0 governance?

Start by defining the stakeholders for the project. Cast your net wide and recognize that the ecosystem that interacts with your system is much broader than the day-to-day cast of actors.

In the first iteration, invite only the small set that can immediately influence the product to start collaborating. This group is empowered to reach out to whomever they think appropriate. Be sure to include those with a vested interest in the current way of doing things—owners of the legacy applications that will be replaced by the envisioned product. With their buy in, you increase your chances for success. Identify three to five areas that would benefit from clear definition. Tackle the hard questions first, such as agreement on a business owner for the product, how decisions will be made, and who will serve as the tiebreaker.

Quickly expand from these guidelines to include the next group of stakeholders and start going "public" (within the organization) with decisions and discussion points. The real art of governance starts now: With some ground rules in place, let your community loose on coming up with what they think needs to be done; all you need now is an enthusiastic and fair facilitator.

To reiterate: Think about governance 2.0 for your Web 2.0 project!

Additional thoughts?

There is a misconception that being "nimble" and "agile" is stifled by the "bureaucracy" of governance. Nothing could be further from the truth. Having methodology and processes in place, if anything, helps ease an organization's way to being more flexible and able to respond to the market. That way, you do not have to rethink the way you do something each time and can instead focus on just doing it. This is true for a one-person garage operation as it is for a small start-up or a global enterprise.

In most organizations, most meaningful initiatives span multiple areas of responsibility. Governance avoids turf wars and the resultant drain in productivity. Accomplished artists acknowledge that they are at their most creative when they stay within their self-defined constraints. Instead of being stifling of creativity, governance (in the right doses for the right things) enhances innovation.

Web 2.0 and Agile Development

Web 2.0 and agile development aspirations often go hand in hand. The idea of quickly and iteratively releasing new features and functions to the Social Networking community is appealing to almost everyone. The point is to try to bypass traditional and often slow methodologies where new features can takes weeks and months to flow through requirements, design, development, testing, and finally release. In my experience, many teams like to adopt the term *agile* without adding in all the fuss (that is, the discipline required to do agile development correctly). Without this added effort, however, most agile efforts are doomed to fail. I do not say this lightly, but the process simply cannot support the improved speed and quality that agile can provide without the additional structure that needs to be put into place.

The suggestion here is not to avoid an agile process. In fact, it is quite the opposite. However, make sure that you are putting all the right tools in place for an agile approach to be successful. This includes the right management and governance structure to be sure that the team is working on the right features with the right priority. In addition, many agile methods do not take into account some of the processes required to deploy new functionality into an enterprise environment. This will often lead to shortcuts as the team tries to live up to the agile premise and deploy code that is not fully tested within the hardened production environments. Make sure that your process includes the effort required to deploy, after the code is delivered from the development iteration.

Conclusion

There are many decisions here. For example, should an organization embrace public Social Networking sites, or should it set up its own internal sites? Openness and flexibility are key factors to implementing a good strategy. It is important to evaluate your strategy often to ensure that you are leveraging new technologies and tools, but also to be sure you are not opening your organization to more risk than is necessary by trying to do too much all at once.

This chapter is designed to give you a feel for the important factors involved in initiating and maintaining a Social Networking effort.

However, it in no way covers all the processes that need to be followed. Keep the simple things in mind as you move forward:

- Start simple and build iteratively.
- Focus on patterns that you know will add the most value.
- Continually measure and monitor usage and user reaction.
- Fix those areas that are seen as problematic while slowing adding new features and functions.

Follow these guidelines, and your success is almost guaranteed.

References

Institute, S. E. (2009). CMMI, from http://www.sei.cmu.edu/cmmi/.

ISACA (2009). COBIT, from http://www.isaca.org/Template.cfm?Section= COBIT6&Template=/TaggedPage/TaggedPageDisplay.cfm&TPLID=55& ContentID=7981.

ITIL (2009). IT Service Management (ITSM), from http://www.itil-officialsite.com/ home/home.asp.

IO

IBM Case Studies

As of this writing, we are just at the beginning of the adventure of using Social Networking in the enterprise. IBM has evolved along this path for several years, but even so, there is still much to learn and a lot of evolution to come until everything becomes second nature. Many tools and solutions are available to help deploy Social Networking and collaboration tools within organizations. This chapter outlines some of the readily available solutions and ideas that can help you get started.

Lotus Greenhouse

"Where ideas come to grow" is an appropriate tag line for Lotus Greenhouse. Greenhouse, available at http://greenhouse.lotus.com, is by nature designed to allow IBM and its partners and customers to come together to use and evolve the technology that IBM provides. If you have been looking closely, you might have noticed that many of the screen shots from this book have been taken from Lotus Greenhouse applications that are available online.

Greenhouse is designed as a living platform where Lotus collaboration products and tools can be used to help innovate and grow available product features. Products that are hosted in Lotus Greenhouse include the following:

- **IBM Lotus Forms Turbo,** which is a form of software designed to help nontechnical users create and distribute electronic forms to end users.
- **IBM Mashup Center** provides an easy-to-use business mashup solution. Mashup Center is discussed in Chapter 6, "Mashing Up Data and Applications."
- **IBM WebSphere Portal** is capable of delivering portal-based applications in a common framework as discussed in Chapter 2, "Portals in the Enterprise," and Chapter 3, "Ajax, Portlets, and Patterns."
- **IBM Lotus iNotes**® is a reliable web-based email system.
- **IBM Lotus Quickr** provides reliable team collaboration and content sharing.
- **IBM Lotus Sametime** is often referred to as Unified Collaboration software and provides real-time instant messaging.
- **IBM Lotus Sametime Advanced** allows for persistent group chat and provides SME broadcast tools.
- **IBM Lotus Connections** delivers social software for business, which is discussed in Chapter 4, "Social Software for the Enterprise."

I fully expect this list to grow. The ability to showcase Lotus products in a live environment enables IBM to demonstrate the products and to prove the value to customer solutions. However, there are additional benefits as well to both IBM and the community as a whole:

- Opens a social network from Lotus for social interaction about Lotus products and technology in general.
- Provides free use of a number of IBM Lotus collaboration solutions.
- Enables collaboration between customers, business partners, and IBM.
- Serves as an avenue for Lotus to provide thought and technical leadership in the collaborative space.

The community is driven primarily by Lotus products, with Lotus Connections at the core of the Social Networking functionality.

Helping Customers Grow and Learn

From a customer point of view, Greenhouse can provide tremendous benefit as organizations look to adopt new technologies and grow their capabilities. First, Greenhouse enables you to try out available products and features in a live environment, and second, users can invite colleagues to collaborate and see what works for their business needs. This type of trial can rarely be accomplished easily with most enterprise software, because infrastructure and setup costs can be prohibitive for even a trial run. More than that, however, customers can be exposed to the latest Lotus technologies and products and get hands-on experience and learning.

This is more than just a one-way experience; customers can provide feedback through Greenhouse to Lotus product development and help drive desired product features. Because much of this technology is in the early phases, there is still much to be learned by everyone, and IBM wants to listen to anyone who can make things work better. Lotus Greenhouse partners closely with the development teams to help make these suggestions a reality. Figure 10.1 shows the main Lotus Greenhouse landing page.

Of course, IBM is fully engaged in this environment and is able to learn and grow the technology stack that is provided. Through the online collaboration with customers, new information about interaction, features, and opportunities is learned. Heavy-use customers provide opportunity for sales of specific software, services engagements, or perhaps hosted services of specific products for that customer directly. Sales teams can use Lotus Greenhouse to engage directly with customers and invite them to participate in an activity or a community to help provide an integrated selling experience.

Having customers see, test, and comment on the latest technologies and products before general release into the market provides a built-in test environment for Lotus products. This is not a beta environment; all new product versions have been through IBM QA already. Pre-GA (General Availability) products are deployed to allow the latest features to be showcased. In addition, Greenhouse provides a built-in platform for cross-product integration that can provide linked value opportunities as cooperating features are tied together in a single environment.

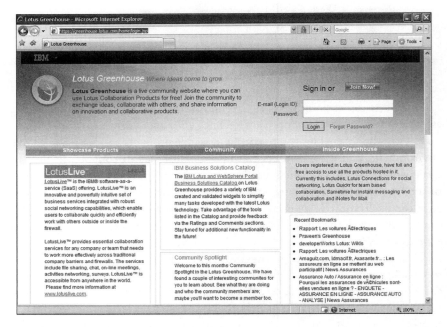

Figure 10.1 Lotus Greenhouse

Another area where everyone benefits is through the best practices learned from hosting this environment. Customers are always interested in the best way to set up and deploy IBM products. This environment, hosted and managed by IBM itself, provides the perfect environment in which IBM can understand and document what works and what doesn't when architecting a customer solution.

Figure 10.2 shows Greenhouse after the user has logged on to the system. From this home page, the available products are shown on the right side of the screen.

As mentioned, the opportunities are varied with Lotus Greenhouse. There are several use cases in which benefits can be gained from the solution. Sales and marketing teams can invite potential clients to Greenhouse to experience social software in action. These teams can collaborate with potential clients using Lotus Communities, taking part in activities to help the client understand and experience the various products. In addition, the team can chat with clients using IM, create Sametime e-meetings for demoing software, or create personalized Quickr places for clients from the company to send marketing, sales, and product information or to store information related to the sales process.

Figure 10.2 Inside the Greenhouse

Potential customers can join and visit Greenhouse to learn about the latest Lotus technologies by reading blogs, visiting interesting Dogear links to gain knowledge, or participating in social communities. Participants can also contribute new information and knowledge to the community through their interactions with various Greenhouse components. Developers can use Greenhouse to create new assets or to build custom templates for Quickr places, activity templates, or third-party widgets that access Greenhouse services. This is built on the concept that the Greenhouse is a live application programming interface (API) factory allowing access to the provided APIs in a stable environment.

So, how does all this work? A defined process outlines the steps that Lotus Greenhouse uses to determine what products and features are released and how information is collected on what works and what doesn't (see Figure 10.3).

This community-driven approach to new product development is exactly what Social Networking is about, leveraging the community and participants to help drive the immediate needs and the most requested customer features. So can this work? Well, it is working, and the numbers show that

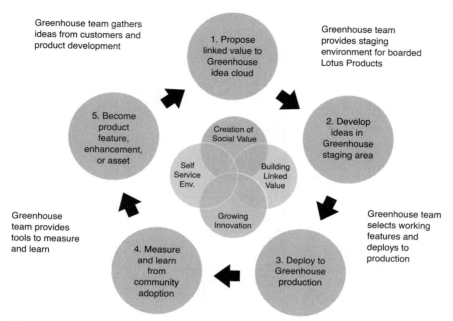

Figure 10.3   Community enhanced development focus

participation is happening in a big way. At the time of this writing, high-level metrics that have been gathered include the following:

- Almost 30,000 registered users
- More than 3,000 average visitors per day
- More than 1,000 blogs with 20,000 customers participating through comments and tagging
- Nearly 1,000 communities
- More than 10,000 Quickr places with 30,000 documents

Participation continues to grow as new product versions are released and compelling features are added. If you are interested in the products and features that have been discussed in this book, Lotus Greenhouse is where you can get some hands-on experience in what they can do.

IBM in the Cloud

One new area that has garnered recent interest is the concept of cloud computing. If you ask different people what *cloud computing* means to them, you will probably get several different answers. This section provides some definition that cuts through the myth and confusion so you can understand what constitutes a cloud and some of the apparent advantages. The most common images of cloud computing are based on the idea of systems or services on demand. Software that lives in the cloud is a common example. This concept of virtual hosting software applications has actually been around for awhile, such as with the site Salesforce.com. However, the idea of quickly deploying new applications in a virtualized environment has expanded the value of this concept to many businesses. Most organizations want to understand how to leverage cloud computing either to save money by focusing on utility computing or to make money to provide services to other organizations and end users.

For our purposes, cloud computing is the combination of virtualization, standardization, and automation to provide on-demand systems and applications to quickly meet business needs.

One of the main ideas behind a cloud approach is that it can provide services in a fairly abstract manner; the idea being that as users or consumers of the service, we do not have a strong need to know what technologies are being used to provide any particular service or application.

As an example of how cloud computing is being used to reduce costs and increase speed to market, IBM has partnered with Amazon Web Services to provide a number of IBM products to customers from within the Amazon cloud. These products include IBM WebSphere Portal and Lotus Mashup Center, both of which can provide great benefit to customers who want steady-state usage or on-demand capability to ramp up with more capacity as needed. In addition, customers can leverage the Amazon cloud for fully functional environments for development or proof-of-concept efforts. IBM business partners such as Ixion (www. ixiononline.com/) who work closely with the SMB market are seeing some initial benefit and tremendous potential from this Amazon cloud partnership and the ability to provide quick on-demand solutions to many customers, whether it be to set up a quick demo or build a full production environment. Figure 10.4 shows the developerWorks Cloud Computing space available at www.ibm.com/developerworks/spaces/cloud.

Figure 10.4   Clouding Computing with IBM Software

The Cloud Computing space on developerWorks can not only get you up to speed with the Amazon partnership, but also provide ongoing information about education and activities from IBM.

Private Versus Public Clouds

As a cloud consumer, there is a great benefit to be gained from being able to request and make use of computing resources. Anything from a base OS to full portal applications can be requested and scaled based on user demand. However, a public cloud, such as that offered by Amazon, might not be the right approach for everyone. Doing business in the public cloud can open up your organization to risks that you might not be ready to accept, or you might have information and services already existing within your organization that need to be tied into whatever services you are trying to provide to your end users.

This opens the door to establishing a private cloud for your organiza-tion. Private clouds can be serviced by your existing IT organization, or can be provided to you by a cloud vendor or service provider. Using a cloud vendor can greatly shortcut your time to establishing a cloud that can live within the firewall and work with your existing applications. Often, this vendor-provided cloud can be specialized to provide specific services or applications in an on-demand manner. We often talk about clouds as if they are just there, but the reality is a lot of discipline and maturity is necessary to be successful with hosting or managing your own cloud environment (see Figure 10.5).

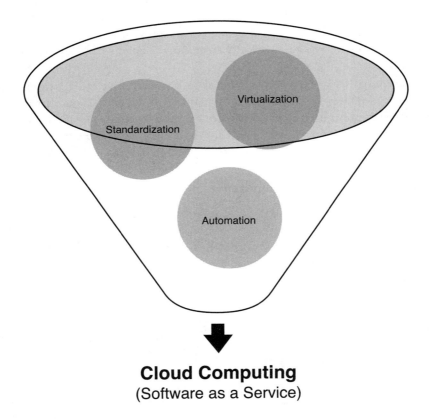

Cloud Computing
(Software as a Service)

Figure 10.5   Contributing factors for Cloud Computing

Think about what makes up cloud technology and makes it successful:

- **Virtualization:**   The ability to create new servers or services on demand. Hosted environments are more than ever becoming dependent on the idea of virtualization to quickly build new server instances for end-user consumption.

- **Standardization:** Clouds have to focus on specific services or applications that they can provide quickly and easily. The list should be well defined and preconfigured for a virtualized environment. For example, the IBM and Amazon relationship defined a set number of products that are available. Although this initial number is expected to grow, this has to be done on a case-by-case basis in a standardized manner.

- **Automation:** After the first two factors are considered, the package can be automated to provide cloud services quickly and easily. One might say at the push of a button a new virtualized server with a standard application package can be automatically created and shared with the consumer.

Putting this in perspective, it helps to be aware that some strategy is necessary before you start to embark on your own cloud project. Proliferation of multiple projects that might eventually break corporate policy is not going to be an easy thing to fix once users are dependent on those applications and environments.

WebSphere CloudBurst Appliance

Supporting a cloud-based environment can be a challenge, but there are ways to ease the maintenance and support effort. IBM's WebSphere CloudBurst™ Appliance is designed to make setting up and using a private cloud environment easier (see Figure 10.6).

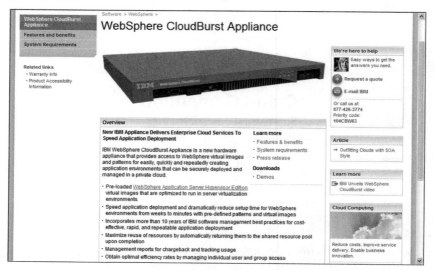

Figure 10.6 WebSphere CloudBurst Appliance

The appliance is preloaded with WebSphere Application Server Hypervisor Edition and can speed the deployment of preconfigured virtual servers as they are needed. Eventually, the CloudBurst family of products will bundle everything you need for configuring your computing resources for a cloud environment. This includes software, hardware, storage, and networking configuration, along with automation templates to manage the environment.

Lotus Live

Software as a service is one aspect of cloud computing that has actually been around for awhile. Several popular applications are available online on a subscription basis that can service an individual or an entire organization. With the advent of Social Networking technology, this approach has taken on some new meaning. Collaboration and Social Networking applications are a perfect fit for partnering with cloud computing to deliver always-on, scalable, and robust functionality. LotusLive has taken some of the best software available from IBM Lotus and can provide it to users and organizations as needed. Figure 10.7 shows the LotusLive home page, where users can demo or purchase services.

The focus of LotusLive is in three main areas, each based on one or more products within the Lotus brand:

- **Networking and collaboration:**   Also known as LotusLive Engage, it provides online collaboration tools needed to enhance your meeting and collaboration experience. Provided are tools for file sharing, instant messaging, and online community capability.

- **Web conferencing:**   LotusLive Meetings is a full-featured online meeting service formally known as Lotus Sametime Unyte®. LotusLive Meetings allows you to provide desktop sharing with hundreds of users quickly and easily from anywhere in the world.

- **Email:**   LotusLive Notes provides email capability to users and organizations as an online service, removing the need for an internal infrastructure or support staff.

Cloud computing is still evolving for most organizations. IBM is helping customers understand and take advantage of that evolution by driving business value from the cloud wherever possible.

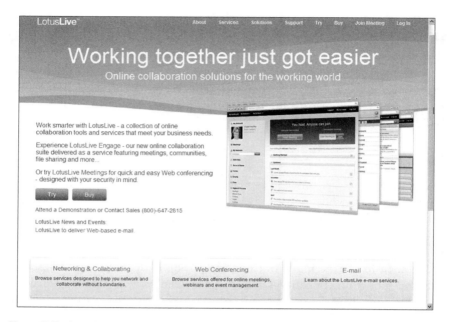

Figure 10.7 Lotus Live (www.lotuslive.com)

Cloud Computing Interview

It is always good to hear from people who have hands-on experience with any new technology. Marshall Lamb and Adam Ginsburg from the IBM Software Group are at the forefront of IBM software in the Amazon cloud. Included here are some of their comments about this technology and the advantages it can bring to an organization.

Marshall Lamb's Bio:
Marshall Lamb is a Senior Technical Staff Member and Architect with IBM WebSpherePortal development. His primary areas of focus are large-scale deployments, operations, high availability and scalability, and virtualization. He has served as the Chief Programmer on WebSphere Portal V5.0 and V5.1 and has led development teams on several other IBM software products, including WebSphere Transcoding Publisher, WebSphere Host Publisher, and Communications Server. Marshall has been with IBM since 1991 after graduating from Vanderbilt University with computer science and mathematics degrees.

Adam Ginsburg's Bio:
Adam Ginsburg is a Product Manager who has been working in the Portal and Mashups group at Lotus/IBM for the past few years. Recently, Adam has been responsible for products such as WebSphere Portal Express, which bundled a number of IBM products together and aimed at making them more usable by IBM's small business customers. Adam joined IBM as part of the Aptrix acquisition, where he was co-founder and held various roles, including VP of Technology. When he's not working, he's a husband, father of three, and a surfer. Check out his latest social experiment on http://twitter.com/aginsburg.

What are some of the advantages you see for customers and partners with the recent release of IBM products in the Amazon Elastic Compute Cloud (EC2)?

Marshall:
It can take a while for customers to realize a return on their portal investment with the time it takes to set up the deployment and wire the various pieces together. The vast majority of issues we help customers through are initial installation and configuration related. If you take that away, and provide a substantial server farm with seemingly limitless resources, then you nearly eliminate the startup costs and get down to business so much faster. This means you spend more time realizing the potential of the product and less time learning how to manage the product itself.

Second, as a developer, I can't tell you how many times I've said to myself, "If I only had a portal lying around to test this on," which is what most of the half million or so developers using Amazon Web Services today probably say to themselves as well. Most of the instances I've created for myself are used for development and test purposes. Issues with connecting to corporate LDAPs and intranet data sources are typically not inhibitors for most application development and test purposes.

Third, EC2 is a great place to prototype solutions. Whether for external demonstration purposes or internal rapid prototyping, AMI rebundling provides a useful tool of capturing work and reusing it as a template for future instances and development iterations.

Lastly, EC2 is perfect for temporary solutions. There are many useful examples of limited-use web solutions, where like renting a car instead of buying, it makes more sense to lease space on the cloud than to purchase the in-house product licenses to cover the extra capacity. Imagine being able to set up ad hoc information kiosks or "brochure-ware" sites based on WebSphere Portal and Lotus Web Content Management that have a definite lifespan, and are better served with the effort being spent in producing the content instead of setting up the infrastructure.

Adam:

The partnership with Amazon Web Services (AWS) is interesting from a number of aspects (for example, the speed of deployment and time to market for new applications). Taking 15 to 20 minutes to set up a live portal instance on the Internet is amazing. Wow! I do not think I have seen so many partner and customer deployments of portals within such a short time frame. No hardware, you just get to AWS console and you're off. Other solutions, like IBM Mashup Center and Lotus Forms Turbo can be set up in a matter of minutes, which blows me away.

The pay-as-you-go pricing is a game changer, too. The offering provides a stepping stone that allows customers to get started really quickly. They can always purchase licenses down the road if it makes more commercial sense. For customers that have a large difference between their average load and expected peak loads, the pay-as-you-go pricing can make a lot of sense. In the past, peak load usage may have made an IBM solution unaffordable, but now folks can afford it because they pay peak costs only when they need to; therefore, overall cost is significantly reduced. So you should see IBM back in the game for these types of projects.

Awesome partner opportunity—from the no-cost development Amazon Machine Images from IBM, through to the ability to rebundle and sell your solution in a community of 500,000+ developers the opportunity is *huge!* AWS has a cost-effective hosting option using a bring-your-own-license model. These factors really bring something new to IBM's well-established portfolio of software. See http://aws.amazon.com/ibm/ for more info.

What are some areas that customers should be concerned about, or that might introduce new problems?

Adam:

The cloud is just one implementation option. It's not for everybody all the time. There's a time when it will make sense and a time it won't. For example, see our FAQ we provide for WebSphere Portal,

Lotus Web Content Management, IBM Mashup Center, and Lotus Forms Turbo. We explain when it makes sense to use the cloud and when it does not. Here are some links to that information:

www.ibm.com/developerworks/downloads/ls/wps-wcmse/faq-ec2-wps.html

www.ibm.com/developerworks/downloads/ls/lsforms/faq-ec2-lsforms.html

www.ibm.com/developerworks/downloads/ls/lsmashupcenter/faq-ec2-lsmashupcenter.html

Marshall:

Adam's links provide broad coverage of many of the generic cloud concerns in the marketplace, as well as product-specific concerns, but one in particular that I've spent some time on is access to internal data. WebSphere Portal and Lotus Web Content Management got their birth in intranet website implementations, so naturally customers want to know how to best integrate internal information, such as the corporate LDAP or database, or other business data sources. I've experimented with using a Linux® private VPN client in one of my instances to tunnel into the IBM intranet, which then allowed my portal instance to integrate Lotus Connections and Lotus Mashups applications and their data into the cloud. So, it does work, and the VPN tunnel would make it secure. The reliability and performance of such a solution will depend on the VPN software, I think. Other data integration ideas include the following:

- Replicating internal data out to the cloud, such as user profile information and application data or feeds. There are ways to secure this data even in the cloud to help minimize concerns in this area.

- Client-side data integration. Leverage your users' browsers to integrate internal data with cloud data using Ajax, reverse proxies, and other Web 2.0-style application models.

- Single sign-on with internal servers can probably be worked through DNS registration of cloud instances such that they appear within the same SSO domain as internal servers. More investigation is needed in this area.

How might you recommend a customer get started with cloud computing?

Adam:

Just sign up and try it for a few hours. You'll see the power the cloud can provide. If you're a partner and are interested in building

a solution based on our AWS offerings, use the no-charge development AMIs available at http://aws.amazon.com/solutions/featured-partners/
ibm/. You can use these AMIs at no charge for the IBM software to
build, test, demo, and POC your solution. If you're a customer, you
can start to use one of the "production-ready" AMIs (see http://aws.
amazon.com/ibm/) for development, test, or production use. You
can also ask to leverage a partner's solution and try it out on AWS at
potentially no cost (e.g., POC). Even with the AMIs you pay for,
you get charged by the hour, so you really can keep the costs down
to a minimum.

Marshall:

I recommend reading through our *Getting Started Guide*, available at
http://download.boulder.ibm.com/ibmdl/pub/software/dw/cloud/
wps-wcme/Get_Started_Lotus_AMI.pdf.

   You can also find on our catalog page some really good YouTube
videos that help orient you (http://developer.amazonwebservices.com/
connect/entry.jspa?externalID=2048&categoryID=229).

   But Adam's right, you just need to sign up and start playing.

Any predictions on where this all might be headed?

Adam:

It is still too early to tell, but there seem to be some key patterns
that make sense:

- Stepping stone. Use AWS and IBM "production ready" to try out
  your solution.

- Fluctuating capacity. Do a TCO analysis and work out if it makes
  sense to stick with the pay-as-you-go variable pricing.

- For longer-term, well-defined projects, look to the Bring Your Own
  License mode.

Longer term, as the link between the cloud and the internal organization strengthens, I think it will increase the depth and breadth of
solutions that are "cloud applicable," and it may be questionable
why you'd want to have any systems in house.

Marshall:

Besides making enterprises rethink their infrastructure and deployment strategies, I think cloud computing will force enterprise software product developers to rethink how they build their products.
Cloud computing is all about simplicity at the expense of ultimate

flexibility. This has me continuously thinking about how we can simplify our products to work best in the cloud, and guess what, if we get that right, it will also work more simply outside the cloud. Some aspects of our product architecture provide a great amount of functional value to a very small set of our customers. What if we didn't include that function, especially if it helps simplify the deployment? Who loses out, and what steps up to replace it? EC2 gives us a great incubator for such ideas. Stay tuned.

IdeaJam

For Domino-based environments, there are also some opportunities for introducing some of the Social Networking patterns into your organization, or exposing Social Networking to your customer/user base. Many of the solutions and products discussed in this book have been focused on WebSphere Portal-based solutions. However, IdeaJam from elguji Software introduces a Domino-based solution that is both easy to implement and use, and that provides some compelling functionality for your end users (see Figure 10.8).

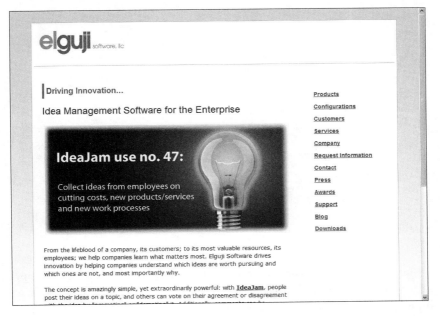

Figure 10.8   elguji Software (www.elguji.com)

One way to think about IdeaJam is as an online suggestion box where users can post ideas and suggestions to share with other users. However, there is much more to it. With IdeaJam, customers can solicit ideas and feedback from both internal and external users on just about any topic. Figure 10.8 shows idea number 47 as a suggestion for using IdeaJam within your employee base. However, for external use, you can also gather customer suggestions on products and services, or use IdeaJam in a more formalized manner within a Social Networking atmosphere.

As ideas are gathered, other users can rank ideas. This system is based on the approach of "crowd sourcing," which allows your user base to help decide which ideas are the good ones. Ideas can be separated into IdeaSpaces to allow for organization around different topics. Figure 10.9 shows IdeaJam in action allowing a user to post a new idea or review and rank ideas that already exist within the system. A significant amount of capability is provided around filtering ideas based on a particular IdeaSpace, the ideas status, ranking, or how an idea has been tagged by other users.

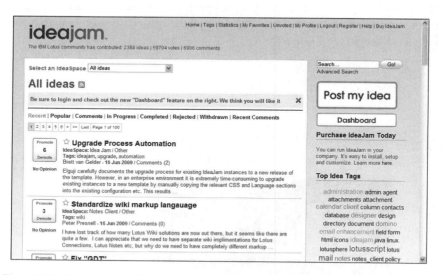

Figure 10.9   IdeaJam community demo

IdeaJam is fully customizable to ensure the look and feel of the application fits in with your existing branded websites. There is also multi-lingual support for several major countries.

IdeaJam is only one of several products available from elguji Software. Also available is their product LinkJam, which is a social bookmarking tool that allows teams to save, organize, and share bookmarks more easily.

Technology Adoption Program

Integrating new technology into your organization is always a risky venture. What works and what doesn't work? How do you go about encouraging adoption of the new technology with your end users? These are questions that can never be answered in a "one size fits all" manner. Every corporate culture is different, and so the approach has to be modified to fit each organization. IBM struggles with this same set of problems, not only internally, but also in trying to find innovations that work for our customers and provide the ongoing value that customers expect from IBM products and services.

One approach that has proven successful is IBM's Technology Adoption Program (TAP). This innovative program allows IBMers to share their ideas and projects within the organization. Employees register with TAP as early adopters of new technology and then can download and use recent innovations and provide feedback to product owners. Figure 10.10 shows the Welcome screen for TAP within IBM.

Currently, about 125,000 users are registered as early adopters who can use these tools and provide direct feedback on their use and value. These users are from all across IBM, with different job roles and from different countries, and many users are using more than one product within the TAP community. TAP identifies several types of users within the overall community:

- *Innovators* are those people who contribute to TAP with new ideas and projects.
- *First Adopters* are those who are interested in being the first to test new technology and innovations. They have the drive to provide direct feedback and participate in discussion forums about these innovations.
- *Early Adopters* also participate in the evaluation process, but this usually happens after the innovation is scaled sufficiently to handle a larger load of users beyond the First Adopters.

All the members of the TAP community contribute to the success of the system regardless of their actual role or activity level. Some users are

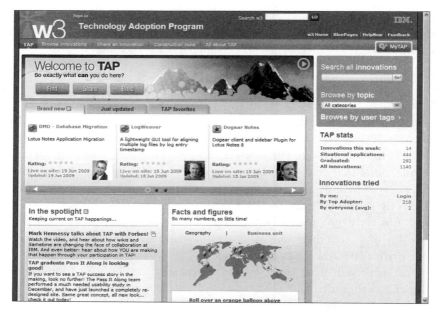

Figure 10.10   Technology Adoption Program

more able to participate based on their job role or personal interest in new technology.

The Innovation Lifecycle

Innovation does not come easy or cheap. IBM provides a tremendous investment in the support of new innovation to help transform its own enterprise and find new ways to transform its customers. Most of this process is provided through the Innovation Adoption Lifecycle, as shown in Figure 10.11.

Of course, everything starts with a new project being implemented on the private cloud that supports TAP projects. Often, this project goes through some evaluation process to determine the initial value and investment required. Measuring usage and value through a series of metrics and direct feedback from adopters allows the team to decide how to grow the pilot or perhaps eventually graduate the project to different areas. Graduated projects might move to their own production environment, or move back into development to be built in to new or existing products that will eventually be available to IBM customers.

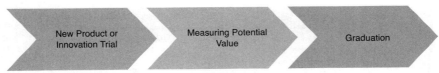

New Product or Innovation Trial	Measuring Potential Value	Graduation
• Proposal or Pilot program for testing new technology	• Measuring usage patterns and potential value of the technology	• Move the technology to a full production environment or into an advanced pilot for additional study • If it is determined that there is not enough potential value then the trial can be canceled

Figure 10.11   Innovation Adoption Lifecycle

TAP works well within IBM because of the corporate culture and business drivers that provide an atmosphere of creation and collaboration. The same is not true of many of our customers, so this exact approach might not be as successful in those environments. Many organizations could learn from this approach and adapt it to fit their needs. Although not every company is looking to build new products, most companies are looking to improve productivity and reduce overall cost using technology. What is important are the key aspects of the program that allow a new product to be piloted and measured before a large investment is made in infrastructure or customization that would not bring the right level of value to the organization. Thinking about the approach a slightly different way: This is a true example of the use of crowd sourcing to let the masses decide winners and losers in new technology.

My developerWorks

developerWorks is IBM's premier technical resource that brings together IBM technology and solutions into a fully integrated portal. Here customers can find information about IBM products and how to better use these products in their own environment. Within developerWorks is a wide range of information, everything from product documentation to articles and blogs from IBM development and services showing the usage of new features and customization of products in compelling new ways. Figure 10.12 shows the main page of developerWorks, available at www.ibm.com/developerworks.

The interesting thing about developerWorks is that it is powered by the readers of the site itself. This has always been one of the major

Figure 10.12   IBM developerWorks

draws; most of the content and how-to articles are written by the same people who go to developerWorks to learn new ideas and features. Mostly broken down by technology or brand, the content is easily findable, and an integrated full-featured search enables you to quickly narrow down to the content you are looking for to be successful in your project.

developerWorks has been continually evolving to include more Social Networking capability. The author of this book has had an externally facing blog hosted via developerWorks since 2004 that he uses to communicate with customers and other portal users. A concept called Spaces is also available within the developerWorks community. You can see an example of Spaces back in Figure 10.4. More recently, developerWorks has provided some additional functionality to create professional networking capability called My developerWorks. This greatly enhanced functionality enables users to create new networks and connections with others who share a common interest. Figure 10.13 shows some of the capability available within My developerWorks.

My developerWorks provides many of the same Social Networking patterns we discussed in Chapter 1, "Web 2.0 and Social Networking." Available are the following features:

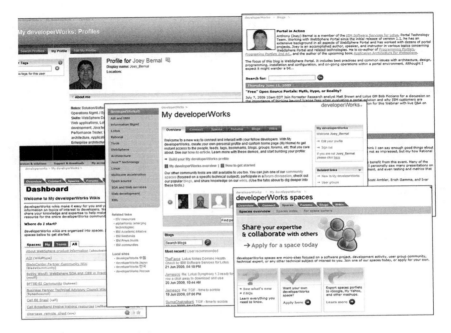

Figure 10.13 My developerWorks

- Blogs
- Spaces
- Wikis
- Profiles
- Connections
- Tagging
- Forums
- Customizable home page

All of this is based on the concept of connecting and sharing knowledge about IBM technology and services. The advantages are many with this type of environment. Some users will be able to promote their own knowledge and expertise in specific technology areas, whereas others will be able to locate and connect with subject matter experts and gain the insight they need to succeed with their projects.

Conclusion

This has been a bit of a whirlwind tour of some of the different products and ways that IBM is using Social Networking patterns to improve the capability of IBM products and extend the value to IBM customers. There is no magic here; each approach simply leverages the patterns and products that have been discussed within different chapters in this book.

My hope is that you get a feel for what is possible within your own organization, and that you proceed with some cautious optimism as you begin to put together a Web 2.0 strategy for your company. As a final bit of advice, I suggest that you start somewhat slowly, learning to crawl before you walk or run. As with any new IT project, that is one of the biggest risks: trying to do too much at once. I hope that as you have read each chapter, you were able to better understand the capabilities available and the various approaches available to leverage Web 2.0 technology within your own organization.

References

Lotus Greenhouse. 2009. Available from: http://greenhouse.lotus.com.

Ixion. 2009. Available from: http://www.ixiononline.com.

Lotus Live. 2009. Available from: http://www.lotuslive.com.

IdeaJam. 2009.

developerWorks. 2009.

Index

Q-R

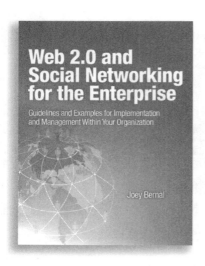

FREE Online Edition

Your purchase of *Web 2.0 and Social Networking for the Enterprise* includes access to a free online edition for 45 days through the Safari Books Online subscription service. Nearly every IBM Press book is available online through Safari Books Online, along with more than 5,000 other technical books and videos from publishers such as Addison-Wesley Professional, Cisco Press, Exam Cram, O'Reilly, Prentice Hall, Que, and Sams.

SAFARI BOOKS ONLINE allows you to search for a specific answer, cut and paste code, download chapters, and stay current with emerging technologies.

Activate your FREE Online Edition at www.informit.com/safarifree

> **STEP 1:** Enter the coupon code: LSEFREH.

> **STEP 2:** New Safari users, complete the brief registration form. Safari subscribers, just log in.

If you have difficulty registering on Safari or accessing the online edition, please e-mail customer-service@safaribooksonline.com